A GUIDE TO AMERICA'S INDIANS

Arnold Marquis

A GUIDE TO AMERICA'S INDIANS

Ceremonials Reservations and Museums

University of Oklahoma Press: Norman and London

Library of Congress Cataloging-in-Publication Data
Marquis, Arnold.
    A guide to America's Indians.
    Bibliography: p. 257
    1. Indians of North America. 2. United States—Description and travel—1960–   —Guide books.
I. Title.   74–5315
ISBN: 0–8061–1133–X (hard-cover), 0–8061–1148–8 (pb.)

9   10   11   12   13   14   15   16   17   18   19   20   21   22   23   24   25   26   27   28   29

TO

Ruby Marquis

AND

Lisbeth Eubank

with special thanks for their dedication and
devotion, their cooperation and counsel
in making this book a reality

A WORD TO THE READER

It came down to one thing: *land*. The Indians had it. The whites wanted it. The whites took it. The repercussions of that protracted and bloody transaction have become known as "the Indian problem." The "problem" has been with us since Columbus. The roots of the problem extend back thousands of years before Columbus.

To most whites the Indians are an interesting incident, vexing and perplexing, yes, but just one of those things. They see the Indians as vestiges of a situation that, at some distant time, was serious but that has little relevance today.

Most of us are scarcely aware who the Indians are. We tend to think of them as wild and savage people who were roaming the continents of the New World when the whites showed up. The significance of the presence of the many tribes escapes us.

To most whites an Indian is an Indian. Much of the mischief of this misconception lies in the erroneous term "Indian" itself. The term implies homogeneity. It implies the mistaken notion that the natives encountered in the New World were one people.

The Indians are not one people. They are many peoples, as different from each other as, say, Latins from Slavs. Many of the groups are ethnically different. Some belong to the same linguistic families, but many groups speak mutually unintelligible tongues. Many groups are strangers, if not foreigners, to each other. In the past many were blood enemies.

Today there are about 263 tribes, bands, and groups of Indians in the continental United States. Their aspirations are similar, but their tribal differences and their tribal loyalties are still barriers among them. This is one of the tragedies of the "problem." Tribalism is fading, but it is still a strong factor in intertribal relationships. What all Indians share is the circumstance of being defeated enemies of the whites. They have been striving against this circumstance for more than a century, but as autonomous groups they are still strangers to each other and certainly to the whites.

Who, then, are these strangers among us, where did they come from, and what is their status today? The "problem" has spawned many myths, many distortions, many misconceptions, and countless outrages. What most of us know about Indians is hearsay, including the way they have been depicted in the media. We have been bombarded by nonsense. This is almost a paradox, for there is a vast body of excellent literature about Indians. In fact, the literature is so formidable as to be almost overwhelming. There are many museums with fine Indian collections, and thousands of good books about Indians. But many of us are put off by the prospect of delving into such momentous studies.

This book is intended to be a guide into the world of the Indians. It is not intended to be a definitive study, and certainly not to be encyclopedic. It is my hope that it will be an easy and accurate reference and that it will motivate the reader to venture further into the world of the Indians. There he may learn something about the major tribes, what kind of people they are, where they live, what they believe, and how to visit them.

For those who wish to visit the Indians, the following pages contain calendars of Indian events, lists of reservations, and directories of campgrounds on Indian lands, grouped by region. For those who wish to learn still more about the Indians, I have included a list of Indian museums, a directory of Indian associations, a list of Indian-oriented publications, and a list of suggested readings.

It is my hope that this book, the outgrowth of more than thirty years of research, visits to reservations, and attendance at ceremonials, will provide a panoramic view of the Indians of the United States. From there the reader may choose his own direction and in that venture discover the momentous influence the Indians have had and continue to have on life in America.

ARNOLD MARQUIS

Studio City, California

CONTENTS

MAPS

Invocation, a mural painted in 1934 by Cherokee artist Joe Waano-Gano.

PART ONE

AMERICA'S INDIANS

Who Are the Indians?

The American Indians are not one people. The Indians are many peoples. In their veins run Mongolian blood, European blood, blood of the eastern Mediterranean races, even some African strains. Many of these strains were mingled in Asia thousands of years before the ancestors of the modern American Indians reached the New World.

Before they came, there was not one human being in the entire Western Hemisphere. The first came across the Bering land bridge (now the Bering Strait) from Asia to the North American continent at least thirty-five thousand years ago, possibly earlier.

Why did they come? They were seeking food. The ancestors of the American Indians were mainly hunters. They followed the animals they depended on for food. When the Pleistocene ice age moved down over northern Europe, the animals retreated southward and eastward. The hunters followed.

When the ice age ended, the animals moved eastward and northward, toward central Asia in the direction of Siberia. Ultimately they reached the Bering land bridge, the isthmus linking Asia with North America. The isthmus was a wide land bridge—possibly a number of bridges—and it was so for many years. Today the isthmus is gone, displaced by the shallow Bering Strait and the Diomede Islands, and the strait is only fifty-six miles across. Even after the bridge had disappeared, it was easily navigable in small boats.

A Florida Seminole girl sitting on a partly completed dugout canoe, hand-chiseled from a cypress log. *Seminole Tribe of Florida.*

The aboriginals came in small groups of families and possibly in bands, but not in large contingents. They could not pursue and hunt the game together in large numbers. They filtered across the land bridge, drifted through the wilderness in their never-ending search for food and furs. They followed the natural corridors, the valleys, the rivers, the canyons. Wherever the animals went, they followed, constantly seeking more plentiful hunting grounds.

They moved southward through what is now Alaska and eastward through Canada. They fanned out through what is now the United States, southward into Mexico, through Central America, and across the Isthmus of Panama. In South America they skirted the cordilleras and plunged through the jungles. At last they reached the southernmost tip, Cape Horn. They had but one objective, but one purpose—to live, to find food. Their trek had taken tens of thousands of years. In the slow process the descendants of the migrating aboriginals evolved into a number of different peoples in the New World.

Who were these remarkable aboriginals that were to become the ancestors of the modern American Indians? They were a composite of nomads from Asia and Europe, from the Near East, even from Africa. Basically they were Mongolian, with infusions of Caucasian and some other strains. They came from many different areas, different climates. They had different physical characteristics: some were very tall, some short. In skin color they ranged from dark brown and red to pale yellow. They brought many cultures, many different religions. They spoke different tongues, different dialects, even different languages.

In the New World their ceaseless quest for food drove them on, still itinerant hunters and food gatherers. They drew together in groups. They learned to eat wild vegetable foods. Some of them learned to cultivate these foods—corn, beans, and squash—and settled down to become farmers. Others remained hunters, and some continued to be hunters and raiders until only about two centuries ago.

By the time Columbus arrived, hundreds of languages were being spoken by diverse groups all over the Western Hemisphere. Today Indians are grouped or identified either by the way they gathered their food (hunters, seed gatherers, or farmers) or by the languages they spoke. Indians have been categorized in various linguistic family groups, or stocks. There is no hard-and-fast agreement on these classifications. And they do not begin to convey the many differences among the many groups of American Indians.

Today there is no clear-cut definition of the "Indian." At best his identity is blurred. In the eyes of the American government Indians are identified by their own declaration. If an Indian says he is an Indian and can "prove" it, he is an Indian.

Some who obviously *are* Indians decline to identify themselves as such. Some who obviously are *not* Indians try to pass themselves off as Indians in order to be eligible for the services of the Bureau of Indian Affairs. To be counted as an Indian, a person must prove that he is an enrolled member of a tribe, band, or group recognized by the federal government. Obviously it is easier for an Indian living among his people on or near a reservation to prove his Indian blood than it is for one whose family has left the reservation or who has lived among whites in the cities or, as in Oklahoma, is a member of the general population.

In the millenniums since the people we call Indians came over the land bridge from the Old World, many Indian groups have simply vanished —victims of wars, disease, displacement, or assimilation. Too, many persons today recognized as Indians have only fractions of Indian blood.

Who are the Indians? They are many peoples. In our complex society this fact is one of their heaviest burdens.

The Many Tribes

When Columbus "discovered" America, about 840,000 "Indians" were living in what is now the continental United States. These original Americans spoke about three hundred different languages and tongues. Four hundred years later, after the Indians finally had been subjugated, only about 243,000 remained. Today there are about 900,000 Indians in the United States. Some 440,000 of these live on Indian lands. The rest are part of the general population. There are 263 distinct tribes or bands in the country. Most of them live on 282 parcels of land—on reservations, in pueblos, in rancherias, or in colonies.

Over the years Indians have made many efforts to unite, but formidable barriers among the Indians themselves have so far thwarted those efforts. Many of the Indian groups are strangers to each other. The Indians of the southwestern deserts have little in common with the Indians of the forests of the Great Lakes or with those of the marshes of Florida. They have different customs, different traditions, different languages.

Today possibly fifty to one hundred Indian languages survive in the United States. Many of these languages are as different from each other as English is from Tibetan. The Papagos can no more understand the Iroquois than the Swedish people can understand the Ceylonese. Only a few of the Indian languages are recorded, and even the written languages cannot be compared with, say, European languages. The most complex of the languages can scarcely be translated literally into English.

Some of the Indian reservations are huge. The Navajo Reservation of northern Arizona extends into New Mexico and Utah. It is larger than Connecticut, Rhode Island, Massachusetts, and New Jersey. Some reservations in California consist of only a few acres. Ten reservations each have more than a million acres. Four of these are in Arizona. Two are in the state of Washington, two in South Dakota, one in Wyoming, and one in Montana.

Wisconsin has seven Indian reservations and four Indian communities, but none of them is as large as the major ones in the West.

The reservation policy was established in 1787, although the American government had prohibited white settlement on Indian lands as early as 1783. In theory certain lands were reserved exclusively for Indians. Today Indians are free to leave their reservations whenever they choose. Many prefer to stay. Depending upon the region, they farm, raise stock, or engage in timber production. Some earn their livings with their arts and crafts. Some get jobs off the reservations but continue to live on them. Others move away from the reservations. About one-half of all the Indians in the United States live off the reservations, many of them in urban centers and in other predominantly white regions.

After 1887 a great number of reservations were phased out, and a few others were "terminated" during the 1950's, in an effort to integrate Indian and white populations. The Indians resisted this action. They felt—and still feel—that their reservations are a priceless resource, *their* land, to be saved and protected.

Throughout the nation Indians are striving to rescue their traditions, their culture, their languages. But since their languages are often unwritten and known to only a few, the attrition of time is obliterating them. When the elderly die, what they know of the language dies with them.

Because traditional Indian life is fading, today everything that represents the Indian has become precious. His ancient arts, crafts, tools, garments, weapons are treasured, and his life style attracts national interest.

The Many Tongues

As mentioned earlier, there are today fifty to one hundred surviving Indian languages in North America north of Mexico. When the white man arrived on these shores, there were about three hundred. Since Indian languages were not written, many of them simply vanished with the passing of those who spoke them. Today only two Indian languages are still widely spoken—Navajo (Athapascan) and Siouan. Other Indian tongues are spoken, but to a much lesser extent.

Phonetically the Indian languages vary so widely that many Indian groups cannot understand each other. The differences are so pronounced that sometimes Indians speaking dialects of the same language are unable to understand each other. Yet the languages are a key to the Indians' origins many thousands of years ago. There are linguistic similarities between the Athapascans (the Navajos and the Apaches) and the Tlingits of Alaska. There are similarities between Tanoan, spoken in the pueblos of New Mexico, and the Aztecan languages of Old Mexico. And Tewa, a Tanoan tongue, is spoken at Hano in the Hopi country, where the Hopis generally speak Shoshonean.

Few Indian languages have been translated phonetically and recorded. For the most part the languages have been handed down orally from generation to generation. Indian writing was limited to pictographs, some on skins, some on birchbark, some carved on wood or stone, some painted in sand.

Sequoyah, a half-blood Cherokee who had never gone to the white man's school and could neither read nor write English, worked out a Cherokee alphabet and in 1821 gave the Cherokees a system of writing their language. In 1824 parts of the Bible were printed in the Cherokee language, and in 1828 the tribe began publishing a bilingual weekly newspaper, the *Cherokee Phoenix*, in their capital city, New Echota, Georgia. In subsequent years linguists became intensely interested in the Indian languages and worked out some Indian dictionaries and grammars. Efforts have also been made to teach the Indian languages to non-Indians, and today there are courses in Indian languages in several American and even European universities.

Several classifications have been made of Indian languages. Among the most important linguistic families are the Algonquian, the Athapascan, the Siouan, the Tanoan, the Muskhogean, the Caddoan, and the Shoshonean.

The Algonquian tribes, among them the Cheyennes, once inhabited much of what is now the United States. They extended from Quebec Province to North Carolina and west to the Mississippi River—and beyond. At one time they represented about one-fifth of the total Indian population of North America. Today there are about forty thousand in the United States and about the same number or more in Canada. Some of the Delawares and the Chippewas of this stock developed picture writing, but never a true alphabet.

The Athapascan tribes were scattered from central Alaska and northwestern Canada to Mexico and from the Pacific Ocean to Hudson Bay. There were three main groups of Athapascans: the Northern, from the valleys of the Mackenzie River and the Yukon and eastward; the Pacific, in southwestern Oregon and northwestern California; and the Southern—the division we know best—in Arizona, New Mexico, Utah, and parts of Colorado, Texas, and Mexico.

The Siouan tribes were distributed from the Mississippi River to the Rocky Mountains. One group lived in Virginia, and North and South

Carolina, and a splinter group lived in southern Mississippi. The main group of Sioux lived in the valley of the Missouri River. Another group lived in eastern Montana and in scattered regions from Saskatchewan southeast into Arkansas. Another group was situated in Wisconsin, around Winnebago and Green Bay. As a result of wide distribution three basic Sioux dialects evolved. Santee-Yankton was spoken by the Eastern Dakota bands. Teton was the dialect of the western Sioux, the Oglalas and the Hunkpapas. The Assiniboins in the Northwest developed their own dialect.

The parent stock of the Pueblos of New Mexico is Tanoan. There are three Tanoan tongues: Tiwa, Tewa, and Towa. Tiwa is spoken at Taos, Isleta, Sandía, and Picurís pueblos. Tewa is spoken in San Juan, San Ildefonso, Santa Clara, Nambé, Pojoaque, and Tesuque. Towa is spoken in only one pueblo, Jémez.

Even among the Pueblos there are two other languages. One of these is Keresan. The Keresan-speaking groups may be the oldest established groups among the Pueblos. Among them are two different tongues, Eastern and Western Keresan. Eastern Keresan is spoken in Santo Domingo, Santa Ana, San Felipe, Cochití and in Zía. Western Keresan is spoken in Laguna and Acoma. The third language of the Pueblos is Zuñian, the language spoken at Zuñi Pueblo. Zuñian seems to be a linguistic family all its own, but some experts believe that it may be related to Tanoan.

Another of the more important linguistic groups is Muskhogean, to which belong the Choctaws, Chickasaws, Creeks, and Seminoles—the Indians who lived in the Gulf Coast and southern Appalachian regions from the mouth of the Mississippi into Florida and Georgia and north to Tennessee and Kentucky.

Farther west, Caddoan was the language of the Indians of the Southern Plains, from Nebraska south to Texas and Louisiana and all the way north to the Missouri River in the Dakotas.

In the Great Basin and on the Lower Plateau (Nevada, Utah, and Colorado) the language was Shoshonean. Tribes of this group extended to southern California and eastward to Texas and included the Shoshones, the Comanches, the Paiutes, the Utes, the Bannocks, and the Hopis of the mesas of northern Arizona.

Other lesser languages, perhaps fifty of them, were scattered all over the country.

The wide distribution of the Indian languages suggests two major points: first, that the Indians of all the linguistic families once roamed over wide areas and, second, that by the time the white man arrived most Indians had established the territories they laid claim to. What they could not imagine then was that in time many of them would be relocated on reservations far, far from where they first encountered the white men.

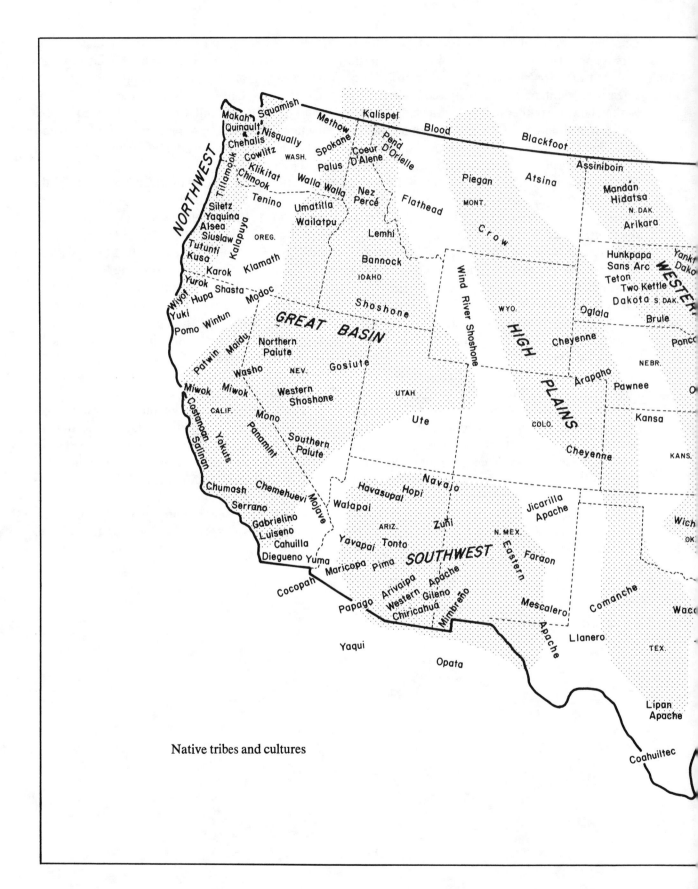

Native tribes and cultures

Ojibwa

MINN.

Santee
Dakota

Sauk

IOWA

Fox

FARMERS

Missouri

MO.

Osage

Quapaw

Caddo

chai

Tunica

Natchez

Houma

LA.

Atakapa

awa

Chitimacha

Washa

Chawasha

Lake Superior

Cree

Menomini

WIS.

Kickapoo

Winnebago

Lake Michigan

MICH.

Potawatomi

Lake Huron

Huron

Lake Ontario

Lake Erie

ILL.

Kaskaskia

IND.

Illinois

Miami

Moingwena

Wea

Peoria

Tamaroa

Piankashaw

Cahokia

KY.

Shawnee

TENN.

Chickasaw

Cherokee

ARK.

Upper Creek

SOUTHEAST

Choctaw

MISS.

ALA.

Lower
Creek

Mobile

Pensacola

Biloxi

Sawokli

Chatot

Apalachee

Timucua

FLA.

Ais

Guacata

Jeaga

Tekesta

Erie

Susquehanna

NORTHEAST

W. VA.

Mohawk

Oneida

Onondaga

Cayuga

Seneca

Iroquois

VT

N.H.

Penobscot

Pennacook

Nipmuc

Massachuset

Mahican

N.Y.

Munsee

Delaware

Unalachtigo

MD.

Nanticoke

N.J.

DEL.

Powhatan

VA.

Monacan

Nottoway

Weapemeoc

Secotan

Tutelo

Tuscarora

Pamlico

Saponi

N.C.

Coree

Catawba

Cape Fear

Yuchi

S.C.

Sewee

Stono

GA.

Edisto

Cusabo

Guale

Apola

PENN.

OHIO

MAINE

Micmac

Abnaki

Malecite

Passamaquoddy

Wappinger

Montauk

Pequot

Narraganset

Wampanoag

Nauset

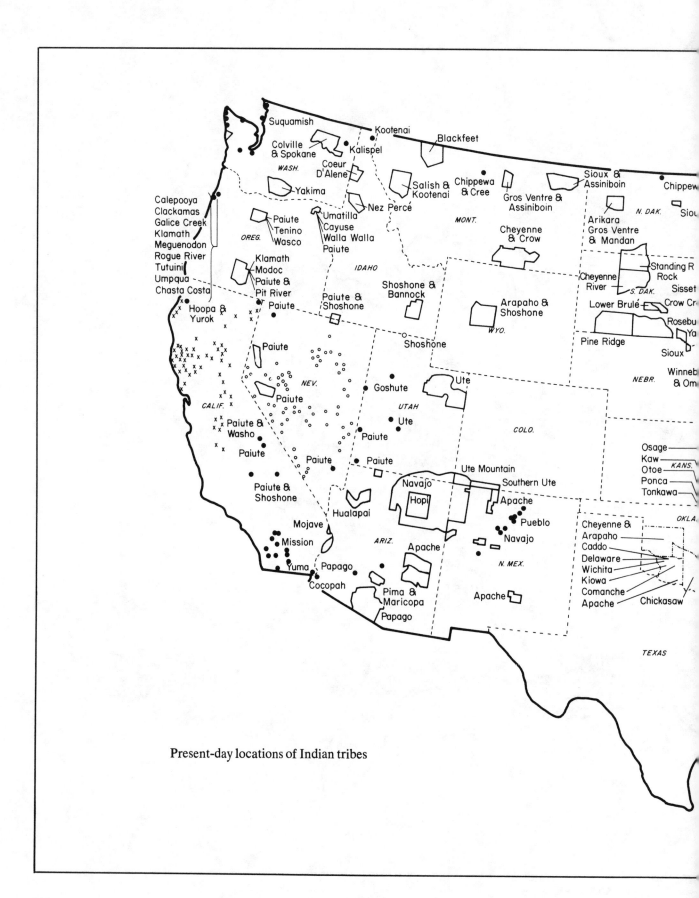

Present-day locations of Indian tribes

The Indians,
America's Displaced Persons

Today all but a few American Indians live far from their original locations. The Navajos and the Apaches came from Canada and Alaska. The Sioux came from the eastern seaboard.

At least sixty tribes from almost every quarter of the country are settled in Oklahoma, formerly Indian Territory. Others are scattered on reservations in many states, many of them half a continent from their original homes.

The Pawnees once lived in the Southwest. They were a distinguished people, numerous and strong. They lived in communities, tilled the soil, raised beans, pumpkins, squash, and corn. They developed a high order of arts and crafts, made notable progress in medicine, created music, were celebrated for their ceremonials, and were deeply religious. They migrated slowly to what is now Nebraska. There they found themselves among hostile strangers, the Osages and the Kansas. They became enemies and fought for years.

This was the situation when the white men, pushing westward, encountered them. The Pawnees were friendly to the whites, but they caught the white man's diseases. In 1831 smallpox killed half of the tribe. Eighteen years later cholera killed twelve hundred more. By 1859 the tribe had been almost decimated. The survivors, weak, sick, and fragmented, were placed on a reservation in Nebraska. There more ill fortune struck them. The Sioux raided, robbed, and killed many of them. Grasshoppers plagued their crops, and droughts almost destroyed them. Enemy Indians killed the buffaloes, cruelly reducing their food supply, and later the whites agitated for their removal from the area altogether.

Indian wars were raging in many parts of the West, and in 1875 and 1876 the Pawnees found a refuge in Indian Territory. They ceded all their lands in Nebraska and moved to the Territory. And there what is left of the once-strong tribe remains today.

Over the centuries many Indian tribes were almost constantly on the move. Though some stayed in certain regions for long periods, others were constantly roaming. Some Indians were sedentary —farmers like the Zuñis and the Pueblos of the Río Grande. Some were nomads—the Navajos, Apaches, Cheyennes, Arapahoes, and Comanches —hunting and raiding and warring. Some, like the Kansas, the Omahas, Kiowas, Poncas, and Pawnees, were migrants, moving slowly from area to area. Others were driven out of their regions by more powerful tribes and were obliged to find other places to live. But most were displaced by the pressure of the white man.

The Navajos and the Apaches, formidable nomads, hunters, and raiders, drifted down from the North (members of their linguistic family, the Athapascans, still live in Canada and Alaska). The Navajos roved over a good portion of the Southwest before they were rounded up and for four years detained at the Bosque Redondo, a forty-square-mile tract of land in New Mexico. Later they were permitted to return to a portion of the land they had occupied, the area now the Navajo Reservation. The Apaches, also raiders and warriors, terrorized Arizona and New Mexico until they were rounded up and placed on reservations there. One band, the Chiricahuas and some related tribes, were sent as prisoners of war to Florida, then to Alabama, and finally to Oklahoma. Later they were released and allowed to settle in New Mexico and Oklahoma.

The Delawares, Sacs, Foxes, Potawatomis, and several other tribes of America's northeastern woodlands suffered a fate similar to that of the

Pawnees. The pressure of white colonists forced them westward. They drifted to the Great Lakes and settled in what are now Wisconsin, Illinois, and Indiana. But ultimately the white men came there, too, and the Indians were forced to cede their lands and move to Indian Territory. The land hunger of the white men was relentless. The Indians were forced to move, only to be forced to move again and again.

The Cherokees, Choctaws, Chickasaws, Creeks, and Seminoles came to be called the Five Civilized Tribes because of their remarkable attainments, their intelligence, their industry, their advanced tribal governments, and their adaptability to the white man's ways. But none of that mattered. They were obliged to move from their lands in the East and Southeast to Indian Territory. As an inducement they were given title to all of Indian Territory except the northeast corner, which was to be occupied by the Senecas, Shawnees, Quapaws, and some other eastern tribes. In 1830, Congress passed the Indian Removal Act, which provided for "voluntary" exchange of their eastern lands for acreage in the West. The new land they were to be given was to be "held by the tribes under perpetual guaranty by the Government of the United States."

Accordingly, if reluctantly, most of the Indians acquiesced—but not all—not the Eastern Band of Cherokees of North Carolina and not all the Seminoles. Some of the Seminoles retreated, hid in the Everglades of Florida and were never caught, and the Eastern Band of Cherokees took refuge in the mountains and escaped. In 1835 the rest of the Cherokees signed an agreement to move, and the United States Army rounded up fourteen thousand of them and escorted them, under guard, on the eight-hundred-mile "Trail of Tears" to Indian Territory, where they finally prospered again.

When the Civil War broke out, they supported the South. Entire contingents of Indians were raised to fight the Union. One Indian, Cherokee Stand Watie, rose to the rank of brigadier general in the Confederate Army. When the South was defeated, the Five Civilized Tribes were punished. The western part of Indian Territory was taken from them and was assigned to Indians transferred from other states.

The Eastern Band of Cherokees who had escaped to the mountains stayed there, and their descendants are still there today, on the Cherokee Indian Reservation of western North Carolina.

Captain Jack, a chief of the Modocs of northern California, resisted when the Modocs were ordered to Klamath, Oregon. The Modoc War followed.

The Kansas, Omahas, and Poncas came from Virginia and the Carolinas, migrating slowly westward. When they reached the Mississippi River, they separated. The Kansa Indians moved into the area that is now Kansas. The Omahas went farther north, into the Nebraska area. The Poncas also went to Nebraska. All three tribes eventually were resettled in Indian Territory.

In 1833 some of the Oneidas were moved from New York to a reservation near Green Bay, Wisconsin. Two other eastern Indian tribes, the Munsees and the Stockbridges, also were moved to Wisconsin about the same time. Only a handful of Winnebagos still live in Wisconsin, their home. The main body of Winnebagos were moved to Iowa and then to Minnesota. After the Minnesota Uprising by the Sioux, in which the Winnebagos took no part, the Winnebagos were forced to move to the Crow Creek Reservation in South Dakota. This proved a disaster, for they were relocated next to their blood enemies, the Sioux. In the winter of 1863–64 they were forced to move again. Of the two thousand who started the bitter and heartbreaking trek through storm and snow, eight hundred died. The remnants at last settled in Nebraska.

By 1887 most American Indians had been settled on reservations. That year Congress passed the General Allotment Act (the Dawes Act). It provided for Indian lands to pass from tribal ownership to individual Indian ownership. About thirty million acres were allotted to individual Indians. The land remaining after the allotments were made was opened to white settlement. Today little more than one million acres remains in the hands of individual Indians.

The Basketmakers

When the southwestern Indians learned how to plant corn (maize) and cultivate and harvest it, the course of their life changed. Once they could raise corn, they could settle down. Until then they had roamed the Southwest for centuries, hunting, trapping, gathering seeds, living off the land. To grow food they had to stay in one place. They devised tools to till and cultivate the soil, containers to carry water, and methods to harvest their crops. They ceased to be nomads, settled in communities, and became farmers.

Their first corn, cultivated from wild plants, was hard, almost flintlike. The cob was only the size of a finger. Patiently they improved the grain and developed several varieties of corn. They used the same methods to cultivate beans and squash and found ways to utilize feathers, making robes and headdresses and later on using them for decoration. They cultivated cotton and learned to weave it into cloth.

At first they lived in caves. Then they learned to fashion mud into shelters. Eventually they learned to build huts, then clusters of huts, and finally "apartment buildings," the massive pueblos. Within these shelters they devised means to store their grain.

First they dug pits within their dwellings. They learned to line the pits with stones and brush and to build covers of poles, branches, and leaves. These became their storage bins. To gather and carry the grain they experimented in fabricating many kinds of containers and receptacles. They used reeds, grasses, and vines, interweaving and coiling them into various pocketlike utensils. Gradually they evolved the craft of basketmaking. They learned to vary the sizes and the shapes, to make them light or strong according to their use and to make them watertight.

In time they applied the craft to other facets of their lives. They fabricated woven bags and pouches of all kinds, wove sashes and belts and headbands, and began weaving garments and rugs.

Baskets became the pots, pans, and panniers for food gathering and burden carrying. Into watertight baskets they put water, heated it with hot rocks, added ground corn and seeds, and made mush. They used the same process to boil and stew meat, replacing the cooling rocks with hot ones as required.

They learned to shape their baskets for special needs. Baskets for carrying water, conical in shape, were slung over the shoulders, making it possible for water bearers to descend to a stream or climb up to a reservoir, using both hands.

Nearly all the tribes made baskets. They used them for carrying, for storage, for sorting, for holding water and other liquids, for cooking, for drinking. At first the baskets were solely utilitarian. Then the Indians began decorating them, simply at first, then with complex designs and in colors, adding tassels, fringes, and even tiny, tinkling devices to produce soft, musical tones as the baskets were carried. Each band developed its own style of basketry, its own sizes and shapes, ranging from miniatures, one-half inch in diameter, to massive containers too large for one person to carry.

The Apaches made small, light baskets and bowls that were unbreakable and easy to carry. Now their skill in this craft is almost lost. They produce only a fraction of the number they once made, and the quality cannot compare with those of the nomadic period. Today only two western groups approximate what they once created, the Hopis and the Papagos. The Hopis make both coiled and wicker baskets—good work, but not

An Apache basket, coiled construction: devil's-claw (black) and willow sewed over a three-rod (twigs) bundle. *Heard Museum Collection, Phoenix, Arizona.*

A Navajo wedding basket made from sumac. *Heard Museum Collection.*

A Pima olla. *Heard Museum Collection.*

comparable to that of years ago. The Papagos have done well in commercializing their basketry. They make many different kinds of baskets—covered baskets, dishlike baskets, plaques, and trays. They also make small toys and women's handbags in basketry. The Papagos use both the coiled and the open-stitch styles, decorating their work in natural colors and in black, red, and shades of green. Ironically, the Pimas, from whom the Papagos learned much of their basketry, have almost forgotten how to make fine baskets. Once they made beautiful close-coiled decorated baskets of willow and devil's-claw. No more. They have virtually lost the art. Although the Pimas live cheek by jowl with the Papagos in Arizona on the Mexican border, their basketmaking art is dying.

Almost the same thing has happened to other southwestern Indians. The Mescalero Apaches have been trying hard to restore their basketry art. From split yucca they make coiled bowls and some other styles, but they have lost their earlier excellence in the craft. The Jicarilla Apaches, who got their name from making "small baskets" for drinking cups, and the western Apaches of Arizona are doing little in basketry.

Today the Navajos make only a few baskets for their own use. Like many other Indian tribes of the Southwest, they have for years been buying commercially manufactured containers to use in place of baskets and have virtually stopped making baskets because the length of time it takes to make baskets is not economically feasible. Blanket and rug weaving is far more profitable.

With a few exceptions basketmaking among the Indians of the Southwest has become a token art.

Few craftsmen still make baskets. The Yavapais make coiled baskets similar to those of the western Apaches, and the Hualapais continue to make their diagonally twined baskets with geometric designs and aniline-dyed colors, but these are largely individual efforts. As groups they are producing very little.

Thus genuine basketry of an early period is extremely valuable and irreplaceable. Fine old Indian baskets are treasures indeed.

The Pottery Makers

Somewhere between A.D. 400 and 700 the Indians of the Southwest began making pottery. The craft evolved naturally from their basketmaking. They used open baskets as molds. They lined the baskets with clay or mud, fashioned the pottery, and then simply permitted it to dry. In time they found that they could make pottery without the basket molds. They developed the coil method, building up the walls of the pottery with successive coils of rolled clay. This they smoothed evenly with a gourd tool or a smoothing stone. Through experimentation they learned to increase the strength and utility of the pottery by firing it. This made it possible to evolve many different shapes and sizes to be used for cooking, storage, mixing, and carrying.

In the ensuing centuries pottery making became a sophisticated craft. Each tribe developed its own designs, which still distinguish the pottery of one group from that of others. Familiar pottery designs are the symbols of the serpent, the firebird, the rainbird, the rain, and the sun. The pottery of Zía Pueblo has its sky symbols and cloud motifs. That of Santo Domingo has vigorous geometric designs. The pottery of San Ildefonso is characterized by intricate yet dynamic angles and curves. Santa Clara and San Juan are famous for their black-burnished and matte pottery.

Excellent-quality Indian pottery can still be found in the Southwest. The Pueblo Indians of Acoma, San Ildefonso, Santa Clara, and Zía produce good work, as do the Hopis on their three mesas. On other reservations the craft is dying. Only the inspired interest of talented individuals is keeping it alive. Yet some of the most noteworthy advances in form and design have come in recent years, some as recently as the World War II period and even in the 1950's.

Most Indians have found it necessary to turn to other ways of earning a living. They simply cannot afford to make pottery. As with other Indian handiwork, the scarcity of authentic pottery increases its value. If it is good, whether it is old or new, it is expensive. Good old pieces are rare; most of them are collectors' items or museum pieces. It is now possible to see the beginnings of pottery making—and tragically the end of the craft.

The remnants of early-day pottery are among the archaeologists' most valuable keys to the study of ancient civilizations. When items were broken, the Indians threw them onto refuse heaps, and in time these heaps became historical chronicles. Modern archaeologists read them like books. Potsherds (fragments of broken pottery) tell the story. Carefully excavating them, layer by layer, the scientists read the sequences. The potsherds on top are the most recent; those on the bottom, the oldest. From these bits of evidence, noting the changes and modifications of the pottery, they can trace the evolution of tribes and even determine the patterns of trade with other Indians.

In 1908 archaeologists found a form of pottery clay that had not been used by the ancient potmakers. They turned it over to María Martínez and her husband, Julián, of San Ildefonso Pueblo. From the clay they made pottery that turned out so well that they started a new epoch of pottery making. María became widely known, and a resurgent interest in pottery making followed.

Among the Indians of the Southwest most pottery is made by the women. They use the coil method—never a potter's wheel. Coils of soft clay are wound around and around and fashioned into form and shape. Then the clay is smoothed inside and out, polished, and decorated. The classic designs are used: the stylized serpent, the tri-

A Zuñi olla maidens parade, Gallup, New Mexico. *Mullarky Studio.*

angular rainbird, and representations of clouds, rain, sun, and wind. These designs have been elaborated in geometric patterns of flowers, fauna, and scrolls.

The character of the pottery is determined as much by the materials used as by the potter. Each pueblo uses the clays available. The pots may be brown, yellow, buff, gray, black, or combinations of colors. The pottery reveals the character of the Indian groups that make it. The Navajos, nomads and late-comers to the Southwest, learned pottery making from the Indians who had been settled in the region for a long time. Genuine Navajo pottery is often unsymmetrical and bulky and sometimes clumsy. The color is usually buff or black with no decoration. The Indians of Acoma Pueblo produce thin-walled, fragile, beautifully designed pottery. Some of it is incised in a gray-white, with bases and interiors of a rust color.

San Ildefonso, the home of the famed María, has become noted for its "black-on-black" pottery. The Pueblos of the village also produce pottery with free designs, and some pottery almost the color of bronze. Santa Clara has also produced excellent black-burnished pottery (some of it very expensive). Zía's pottery is characterized by designs with clouds, birds, and the ancient sun symbol, which has been adopted as the design on the flag of the state of New Mexico.

The Hopis' penchant for masks is reflected in their pottery. In their patterns they use stylized bird symbols, usually in yellow-orange or in red with black figures. Among the Hopis, as among most other tribes, the pottery is made by women. The women of San Juan Pueblo make good polished red-and-black ware, some with incised designs. The pottery of Santo Domingo Pueblo is less original: the forms and designs are borrowed from other groups. These Indians use strong geometric designs and bold patterns. Some of their pottery is good; some inferior.

The Zuñis have all but ceased making pottery. Now they concentrate on ceramic owls and jewelry. The people of Jémez and Tesuque make pottery almost entirely for the tourist trade. The Apaches have not made pottery for years. The people of Cochití make some pottery, usually decorated with floral designs and fauna, and some pottery of white and reddish-brown, decorated with black designs.

The Maricopa Indians, whose reservation lies south of Phoenix, produce good-quality polished red pottery, bowls, and jugs. The Papagos produce heavy pottery, usually decorated in black.

Some fine pottery is still to be found, but the day of Indian pottery is ending. The art has about run its course. The key to identifying good Indian pottery lies in the established museums listed in Appendix A of this book. There the best of Indian pottery may be seen and studied, and there information is available on the true standards of quality.

Julián and María Martínez. *Photograph by Wyatt Davis. Collections in the Museum of New Mexico.*

María Martínez, the famed potter of San Ildefonso, at work on her black pottery. Note her squash-blossom necklace. *Chapman Collection in the Museum of New Mexico.*

19

A Chippewa potter. *Bureau of Indian Affairs.*

The Gifts of the Indians

Before the Renaissance, before the Dark Ages, before the Christian era, before the Golden Age of Greece, and ten thousand years and more before that, the Indians of the New World were domesticating wild food plants that today yield two-fifths of the world's agricultural products. Corn, cotton (also cultivated and woven in Asia), tobacco, potatoes, peanuts—all were gifts of the Indians. So were scores of other plants that have become staples of modern civilization.

When the colonists from the Old World arrived in America, the Indians had already established trails marking the easiest ways through the wilderness, over the mountains, across the rivers. They had established portages—the overland ways between rivers—to facilitate travel by water. They had discovered the places where gold and silver were to be found, where springs flowed, and where useful plants grew. They were already cultivating more than forty plants unknown in the Old World.

They had been cultivating corn for tens of thousands of years. Long-fiber cotton was already developed. Tobacco was being cultivated in the West Indies and in North and South America. Potatoes had been domesticated in Bolivia and Peru, tomatoes in Central America, and peanuts in South America. By the time Columbus arrived, the cultivation of many of these plants had spread throughout the Western Hemisphere from the northern reaches of Canada to Cape Horn.

The Indians of the Northeast showed the colonists how to grow corn in that forbidding wilderness along the Atlantic Coast. By that time the Indians had already developed corn to an advanced stage. Today it is cultivated around the world. Corn is more widely used than any other grain—food for man and beast. It is also the source of countless by-products. It has become an economic bonanza. The annual yield of corn in the United States alone is between four and five billion bushels.

The explorers of the New World found the Indians wearing cotton in the islands of the Caribbean and in the pueblos of the Southwest. Hernando Cortes sent gifts of Indian cotton back to Charles V of Spain. Today the uses of cotton are almost endless, from clothing and explosives to brake linings and cosmetics. Some sixteen million bales of cotton are grown annually in the United States, and American long-fiber cotton is now raised in Egypt, India, and other countries. Though cotton was grown from ancient times in the Eastern hemisphere, the Indians' contribution to the industry is immeasurable.

Two billion pounds of tobacco are grown annually in the United States, and it is also produced in China, the Soviet Union, Turkey, Egypt, Japan, Canada, India, and Bulgaria. Potatoes have become the world's most valued and widely grown staple. Some thirty-two billion pounds are grown annually in the United States alone. Millions of tons of tomatoes are grown throughout the world. They are the leading canning crop in the United States. About three billion pounds of peanuts are harvested each year in the United States.

All these are gifts of the Indians. And there are more. The Indians also discovered and cultivated sweet potatoes, pumpkins, squash, beans, artichokes, sunflower seeds, cranberries, and manioc (the tuberous cassava). They learned to make acorn meal, maple sirup, chocolate from cacao beans, hominy with the use of lye, persimmon bread, and pemmican. They concocted succotash, a mixture of corn and lima beans, and gave it its name. They devised the technique of clambakes, baking the clams on hot rocks.

When the whites came, they found indigenous food plants already adapted to the soil and climatic conditions, ready for their use. They found foods they had never heard of already developed to a point of yield sufficient to support them. With this advantage they were able to survive in the wilderness of the alien New World—and in time to pull the continent out from under the Indians. The Indians' gifts were not limited to food plants. They also discovered and cultivated some sixty wild plants for medicinal purposes. They had learned to use, and passed on to the whites, quinine, cocaine, cascara, witch hazel, oil of wintergreen, curare, ephedra, all used in modern pharmacology.

At the same time the Indians were making imperishable contributions to the white-man's language. Indian phrases, words, names, and expressions have become an integral part of the American scene—expressions like "speak with a forked tongue," "on the warpath," "bury the hatchet," "making good (or bad) medicine," and "bites the dust."

Hundreds of Indian words and phrases have become part of the American vernacular: wampum, wigwam, papoose, moccasin, tipi, toboggan, tomahawk, sachem, sagamore, tobacco, wickiup, hominy, tumpline, powwow, Manito (nature god), tuckahoe, caucus. Other words and terms have been inspired by contact with the Indians: firewater, peace pipe, blood brother, war party, brave, bucks, Great Spirit, Indian sign, Indian file, Indian summer, medicine man, happy hunting ground, and many others.

Many states have Indian names, among them Illinois, the Dakotas, Kansas, Ohio, Massachusetts, Missouri, Iowa, and Oklahoma. So do a thousand or more cities and towns, such as Chicago, Omaha, Manitowoc, Topeka, Wichita, Miami, Seattle, Chehalis, Snohomish, Seneca, Shawnee, Arikara, Sheboygan, Cheraw. And lakes, such as Michigan, Ossipee, Oneida, Winnebago, Shishibagama, Okeechobee. And rivers, such as Mississippi, Kickapoo, Potomac, Chippewa, Apalachicola, Savannah, Chattahoochee. And bays, such as Narragansett, Chesapeake,

Pascagoula, Choctawhatchie. Indian names are part of the charisma of the New World.

While the Indians were bequeathing this legacy to the newcomers, the whites were learning wilderness skills from the Indians. They learned to build canoes and to hunt and trap Indian style. They learned how to survive by adjusting to nature, using Indian techniques. They learned fire striking and new methods of fishing. They learned how to make laced snowshoes to facilitate travel in the dead of winter. And several centuries later the whites took their main inspiration for the Boy Scouts and similar organizations for the young from the ways of the Indians.

At the same time, while the Indians were resisting the encroachment of the whites, struggling against displacement, striving for survival, they were mastering their own domestic crafts. They evolved new techniques in basketry. They perfected the coil method (unknown in the Old World) in pottery making. They devised ways to spin with spindles, to weave with bar looms, to chip and polish stone. They worked out ways to treat and utilize animal skins and to make feather cloaks. They mastered techniques of beadwork and created a craft of porcupine quillwork.

All these crafts they gave to the white man. And they gave more. Indians have fought in every one of the white Americans' wars. They fought for the white man's causes even though in the United States they were not given blanket citizenship until 1924. They fought on both sides in the Civil War and suffered grievous casualties. They fought in the Spanish-American War. Some were members of Teddy Roosevelt's Rough Riders in the charge at San Juan Hill. In World War I they served in all branches of the services. About 25,000 Indians served in World War II. Of these nearly 22,000 were in the army, 2,000 were in the navy, about 800 were in the marines, and the balance were enlisted in other services.

Of the 3,600 Navajos in the army in World War II more than half were in the Signal Corps. They made history in communications, transmitting messages in the Navajo language, a code the enemy never broke. They served in the air force, many as pilots. The casualty rates among the Indians were appalling, more than three times the rates suffered by the whites. The death rate among whites in combat was 3 per cent. Among Indians it was 10 per cent.

Among the Sioux Indians who served in World War II, not one was a draftee. All were volunteers.

Indian givers? Ironically, that is a white man's term.

Symbols

What do Indian symbols mean? The thunderbird, the rain, the sun, the animal tracks, the geometric designs, the world of Indian art—do they all have hidden meanings?

Most of them do, but hidden meanings are attributed to some figures and designs for romantic or commercial purposes. The Indian lives in a world of symbolism. It extends into every aspect of his life. Pictorial symbolism is only part of it. He sees symbolism in color, in sounds, in rhythms, in artifacts, in myths, in actions. The dance is symbolic. Smoking the peace pipe is symbolic. To

Southwest Indian symbols.

some Indians shooting an arrow into the air is symbolic of sending a prayer to the Great Spirit.

Some Indian groups use more symbols than others. Symbolism is especially important to the Arapahoes. They apply it even to the most commonplace routines of their lives. They use it in their designs, their beadwork, and particularly their ceremonies. Their Sun Dance is a symbolic ritual. Nearly all Indians employ symbolism in their religion.

A symbol is more than an emblem. It is almost anything that conveys a meaning beyond its literal meaning—a color, an action, a sound. Each Indian tribe has its own symbols. Indeed, each nation or clan of a tribe has its own symbols. While some Indian symbols are similar in design, they have different meanings from group to group. A form that means rain clouds and rainfall to one tribe can mean mountains and running water to another. The symbols reflect the kind of life a tribe leads, and often its location.

The Tewa Pueblo Indians ascribe a different color to each of the six cardinal points. North is symbolized by blue or green, west is yellow, south is red, east is white. Above (the zenith) is represented by all the colors of a rainbow. Below (the nadir) is represented by black.

The Tewas' neighbors, the Keresan Pueblos, symbolize the directions with different colors. To them yellow symbolizes north, blue the west. In Acoma Pueblo the zenith is symbolized as black, the nadir as gray. In yet another pueblo, Laguna, the zenith is symbolized as brown, the nadir as green.

The range of symbolism among the Indians is wide. Interestingly, those who use it most are the most numerous today—the Indians of the Southwest, the Northwest, and the Plains. They use it to portray the seasons, the flora and fauna around them, their hunting and trapping, their enemies, and the sun, moon, stars, clouds, rain, sunshine. Lacking a written language, they have employed symbols as a way of communicating, of conveying ideas and concepts.

The early Indians incised symbols on the rocks of caves or on canyon walls. They recorded not only their battles, their hunts, and their relation-

Indian designs and symbols.

Sioux designs.

ship to their deities but also what they hoped to accomplish. Their symbols reflected their beliefs. In these pictographs and petroglyphs they developed a sort of "shorthand" of symbolism. They conveyed a whole idea by illustrating part of it— a bear track, a deer track, a tooth, a claw, a quill, a buffalo horn, a walrus tusk, an eagle's talon.

25

They placed symbolic decorations on their weapons, their spears, arrows, war clubs, tomahawks, lances, and shields. So firm was their belief in symbols that they believed that, while their shields might not stop an enemy's thrust, the symbolic design on it certainly would.

They applied symbolic designs to their horses and to themselves. They painted vivid circles around the horses' eyes and symbolic figures on the flanks. Many tribes decorated themselves with warpaint. Some even tattooed themselves. In every way they sought to express their feelings, their hopes and prayers, their visions of good times to come, their courage and compassion, their battle exploits and victories, their coups, their scalpings.

In their arts and crafts they reflected the world around them. They represented the animals and the birds in simplified symbolic forms and the mountains, the clouds, and the sun in geometric designs. They decorated their baskets with these designs, as well as their pottery, moccasins, skins, and jewelry. They identified these forms and designs with names. Not all the forms were symbolic. Many were simply Indian figures with no particular meaning. As mentioned earlier, the tendency to attribute hidden meanings to Indian designs can be romantic or commercial. Dramatic stories are ascribed to them to enhance their value. The gullible reach for hidden meanings, often themselves suggesting or guessing at the symbolism and asking the seller for confirmation, which they promptly get.

The symbolism of Indian ritual and ceremony can only be experienced, for it is expressed by the Indians themselves in motion, in song, in gesture, and in choreography in ritual and in dance.

The dress of Indian dancers is symbolic, and so of course are the objects they carry, the gourds and rattles, the evergreen branches. The "crowns" worn by the Apaches in the Mountain Spirits Dance (also called the Devils' Dance or Gahan) are symbolic, and so are the chalk-covered, almost naked bodies of the Navajos in their Fire Dance. The beat and the rhythm of the tom-toms are symbolic of other times and other events.

Smoking is deeply symbolic to the Indian. The long ceremonial pipe, the calumet, is a symbol of peace. Among the Sioux and other Indian tribes the pipe is regarded as divine, a gift of the sun to man. As such it is smoked only on occasions when momentous decisions hang in the balance. Indian pipes, like other symbols, are decorated with meaningful designs, and the pipes are protected and carried in bundles or in special bags, some of them richly ornamented.

Indian customs, like all other customs, were changed by contact with other tribes. So it was with the interrelationships of symbols. Taos, the northernmost of the pueblos, was on the frontier of the Plains Indians. Contacts among the tribes in trade and even in warfare wrought changes. Some of the characteristics of the Plains Indians were picked up by the Indians of Taos, and the influence of the symbols of the Plains Indians was gradually reflected in those of the Taos Indians. Among the warring tribes the influence of the symbols of the victor on the conquered was profound. Thus the symbols of many of the tribes are in some ways similar, and, although they have different meanings, time is obliterating the differences.

Yet another factor is that the true, pure symbolism of the past is vanishing with the passing of the elderly. When an old Indian dies, his knowledge of his tribe's symbolism is likely to die with him. What survives in symbolism has become almost incomprehensible even to the younger Indians.

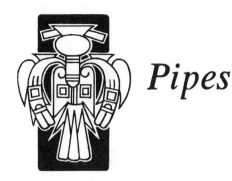

Pipes

What Columbus' sailors saw on that Caribbean isle stopped them cold. They gazed in amazement. The "Indians" were sucking on smoldering rolls of leaves, and smoke, actual smoke, was puffing out of their mouths. None of the sailors—nor indeed any European—had ever seen anything like it.

Columbus took some of the leaves (and some of the Indians) back to Spain. Within a century smoking had spread throughout the world, and within two hundred years tobacco was being grown in Portugal, Spain, Greece, France, Italy, England, Turkey, Egypt, Russia, and even China and Siberia.

Indian pipes. Top to bottom: a hatchet (tomahawk) pipe, an Indian stone reproduction of metal trade pipes made by the British, French, and Spaniards; a variation of the elbow pipe (sometimes called the squaw pipe); a crested pipe (eagle feathers and other decorations were tied to the crest); a modern adaptation of the claw pipe; another adaptation of the sacred claw pipe; a disk pipe, an early pipe found in Wisconsin; a Micmac pipe, of a design found from New England to the Rocky Mountains and as far south as Georgia. *National Park Service, Pipestone National Monument.*

Indian pipes. Top to bottom: A variation of the Plains pipe (the four rings on the shank represent the four winds); a redstone bowl with a wooden pipestem; a variation of the redstone bowl (the wood pipestem decorated with feathers); three sacred buffalo pipes, carved from redstone from the pipestone quarries of Minnesota. *National Park Service, Pipestone National Monument.*

By that time the Indians had been smoking for a thousand years or more. From South America or the West Indies its use spread across the Western Hemisphere. The Indians cultivated tobacco and blended it. It became part of their religion, part of their medicine, an indispensable symbol of their diplomacy.

In the beginning it is likely that they simply burned the aromatic leaves as incense. The fragrant smoke became a religious symbol. For ritual purposes they burned it in stone containers or urns. They learned to perforate the sides of the containers to admit air for a draft, and, when necessary, they blew through the holes to fan the smoldering leaves. Some of the early bowls had air holes all around the lower edge. Into these holes the Indians learned to insert hollow reeds, like spokes in a hub, and blew into them. As the

leaves smoldered, the smoke curled upward, and the Indians unavoidably inhaled some of it. It was a pleasant experience. The fragrance was rich. The smoke, their sacred offering, their message to the gods, was entering their very bodies. From this it was only a step to inhaling the divine smoke and devising pipes for the purpose. The early pipe bowls were huge, a foot or so high. Some weighed ten to twelve pounds or more. The bowls were hewn into many forms; some were effigies of animals and even human beings in sitting or crouching positions.

As the technique developed, so did the character of the pipes. Some were tubular, almost like giant cigar holders, a foot or more long. In time they evolved into smaller ones, the size of present-day cigarette holders. Into these the Indians stuffed the aromatic tobacco leaves.

The technique of smoking spread from tribe to tribe. Each developed its own style of pipes and cultivated its own tobacco. Planting, growing, and harvesting became ceremonial events. Most tribes had two stores of tobacco: one for sacred rites and the other for trading and ordinary use. They learned to blend different kinds of tobacco and to mix them with other aromatic leaves, such as sumac, and with the inner bark of dogwood. This mixture the Indians of the Ohio Valley called kinnikinnick.

The pipe styles also varied from tribe to tribe. The Indians fashioned them of whatever was handy—bone, sandstone, soapstone, slate, bauxite, quartzite, stalagmites, wood, clay, and pipestone (catlinite). But in one respect all were the same: all were sacramental and were believed to be of divine inspiration. The bowl was the altar. In it was burned the sacred offering, tobacco.

Making a pipe was a tedious task. The material it was to be made of was selected with great care. The hole of the bowl was drilled into the rough piece, usually with tools of chipped flint. Then the exterior was carved. The carving was almost classic. Stone pipes found in the Hopewell mounds of Ohio represented birds, squirrels, dogs, and other animals. These pipes had been made a thousand years before Columbus reached the New World. The early tubular pipes of the Indians of the Southeast were decorated with figures of ducks, wolves, and hawks. Out of the tubular pipes evolved many different shapes and forms. Disk pipes—flat, saucerlike disks with a bowl hole and stem—were once common. Now they are rare. Most of those on display today were found in Wisconsin, Iowa, or a broad area stretching from Michigan to Missouri.

The pipes of the Micmac Indians of eastern Canada had stubby decorated bowls. The style spread from the East Coast as far west as Montana and as far south as Georgia.

The pipestems were usually separate, and were often more highly prized than the bowls. Many were made of wood, such as ash. The wood was split, grooved, and glued back together to form a tube. Stems of sumac, their pithy core burned out with hot wires, were widely used, as were hollow reeds. The pipestems had as many forms as the bowls. Some were flat, some round, some even corkscrew-shaped. Some were decorated with feathers, quills, furs, and duck heads. Some were bound with horsehair. Others were beaded, painted, or ornamented with designs. The Arapahoes made pipes with stems three feet long and, like the Sioux and other Plains Indian tribes, wrapped them in bundles of buckskin or carried them in elaborately decorated pipe bags.

Wherever they roamed, Indians were on the lookout for pipe materials. Some three centuries ago the Sioux made a spectacular find. In the southwest corner of Minnesota they discovered quarries of pipestone, a rose-colored stone ideally suited for pipes. It was soft enough to be carved but hard enough to be strong. George Catlin, the painter who chronicled much of Indian life, visited the quarries in 1836. He described them in his writing as "the Classic Ground" (the Sioux believed that the red stone was formed from the flesh of their ancestors). Sensitive though Catlin was to the reverence of the Sioux for this sacred place, they mistrusted him and seized him, and he narrowly escaped death. Later the stone was named catlinite for him. Today the quarries are protected as the Pipestone National Monument, and their use is reserved to the Sioux. To the Sioux, to the Arapahoes, and to the other Plains Indians, as well as to the Indians of the Northwest and the Southwest, the pipe was an integral sacred part of their tribal life.

The Sioux calumet, often called the grand pipe, had a wooden stem of ash, two to three feet long, decorated with feathers and beadwork and painted with Sioux symbols. The catlinite bowl was polished smooth, sometimes in the form of a buffalo, a bear, or an eagle's claw. The decoration of the pipe was important. The color of the feathers meant peace or war. Many of the bowls and shanks had the four-winds design. The rings were sometimes around the bowl, sometimes around the shank. Each represented a wind direction.

The calumet was brought forth and smoked only on momentous occasions. It was used to mediate quarrels, to set the stage for negotiations, to solemnize treaties. To violate any treaty sealed with the smoking of the calumet was to invite catastrophic misfortune.

The very presence of the calumet implied the presence of the deities. This understanding transcended all tribal lines. To carry it was to ensure safety to the bearer and his party, even in the midst of enemies. It was an evidence of peaceful intent, a sort of passport, and as such was universally honored. Even the early white explorers carried "peace pipes" for protection in the event of encounters with hostile Indians.

But while the grand pipe of the Sioux was ceremonial, the Sioux made calumets that were less sacred. These were called trade calumets. They were made for trading and for smoking at social affairs and dances. Their use became so widespread that the events themselves often were called calumets, thus obscuring the sacred importance of the grand pipes.

Other tribes also developed pipes for pleasure smoking. One popular style was the elbow pipe, somewhat smaller and modified in form. These pipes were sometimes called squaw pipes, since women also smoked them.

Trade pipes profoundly changed the scene. Inexorably, enterprising whites pushed into the "market." When the Winnebagos of Wisconsin, like the Sioux, combined the tomahawk form with the long-stemmed pipe, white businessmen picked up the idea. In England and Europe they turned out metal tomahawk pipes by the thousands. Soon they were flooding the American frontier and filtering out into the wilderness. In time they penetrated clear across the country to the Pacific. Yet the true meaning of the Indian pipe continued to prevail. It continued to be an integral part of the Indians' political life, their intertribal conferences, their treaty negotiations. It continued at the heart of their religious life. It continued to be linked with their medicine and healing. Medicine men used it in their ceremonies to heal sickness and to ward off danger and trouble. Every medicine bundle contained sacred pipestems and tobacco. The pipe bowls were carried separately. The medicine tobacco was specially cultivated, nurtured, and guarded. It was harvested with ceremony. Some of it had narcotic qualities, and when it was used, the medicine man slipped into a trance and saw visions. In his rituals the medicine man taught the novices who would one day succeed him.

At death, the pipe was used in the last rites. When Chief Joseph, the great Nez Percé chief, was buried, the shaman blew smoke to each of the four winds and wafted the spirit of Chief Joseph whence it had come.

Beadwork

It has been said that the white man gave the Indian three things: the gun, the horse, and liquor. But the white man also gave him glass beads, or traded, bartered, and sold them, and in so doing changed the course of American history. Beads were involved in the discovery, exploration, and colonization of the New World, in western expansion, in the fur trade, and in more real-estate dealings than any man will ever know.

Long before the Indians sold Manhattan for a handful of beads, the pattern had been set. Indians were trading a beaver pelt, and sometimes several pelts, for a single glass bead. Soon they learned to trade beads for horses, food, and even slaves.

Today the situation is reversed. It is the white man, tourist, or collector who is eager to obtain Indian beadwork, trying to buy back the beads traded and sold to the Indians by white traders a century or more ago. To add to this irony, "Indian" beadwork from Hongkong and Japan is flooding the United States, even the reservations —and is being bought by unsuspecting tourists, who believe that it is genuine.

Of course, long before the first glass beads arrived from Europe, the Indians were stringing seeds and shells, stones, bones, talons, claws, and other materials. They made wampum of clam shells, cylindrical beads of white and purple. In time wampum became a form of Indian currency. The translucence and color of the glass beads fascinated them. To own glass beads became a status symbol. Their eagerness to acquire them made them easy prey for the Europeans.

Most of the early explorers brought glass beads and traded or sold them to the Indians. Columbus gave some red beads to the Indians. Francisco Coronado, Juan Cabrillo, Sebastián Vizcaino, and the Spanish missionaries Eusebio Kino and Junipero Serra all brought beads. By the time commercial firms like the Hudson's Bay Company had set up business on these shores, a century before the American Revolution, beads had almost become a staple, one item that almost always could be sold to the Indians.

The Indians recognized the trade value of beads almost as soon as the whites did. Beads arriving on the East Coast went out into the wilderness over the ancient trade routes, mostly across the northern half of the country. When one band of Indians encountered another, they traded for beads or, if the encounter was hostile, the winners took beads from the vanquished. Indian or white, the procedure was the same. Where there was movement of people or commodities, beads changed hands, and with them some of the skills of beadwork.

The beads moved westward by horse, by oxcart, along animal trails and traces, by wilderness road and highway. When the railways pushed westward, beads were transported on them. And when tribes were relocated out of the way of the white man, the tribes took their beads and their craftsmanship with them. Eventually the craft was passed along to other tribes whose paths they crossed.

It took the European tradesmen little time to assess the bead market in America. Soon the glass factories of Europe were tooling up for the boom. In Italy the makers of Murano glass, long experienced in bead making for European use, turned out beads for the Indians across the sea. Glass factories in England, France, Spain, the Netherlands, and Sweden entered the market.

The early trade beads, made in Europe expressly for trade with the Indians, were relatively large,

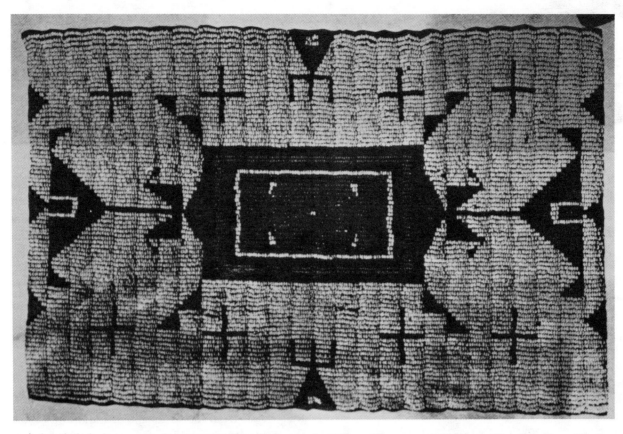

A beaded design on a pipe bag, Dakota Indians. *American Museum of Natural History, New York.*

the kinds used in necklaces. The Indians made necklaces too but soon were finding their own uses for the beads. They decorated their clothing with them and then their baskets and other items. They developed original techniques, discovering several ways to sew the beads onto skins and gradually incorporating beads in their loom weaving. They also wove them into their sashes and headbands. Glass beadwork began along the eastern seaboard around 1675. Seventy-five years later the Indians were embroidering with tiny beads, and by 1800 the craft had been introduced to the tribes of the West, and a number of them had become proficient in the craft.

By then many different kinds of trade beads were available. Tiny "seed" beads had become popular. "Pony" beads, so called because they were taken west in pony pack trains, were one-color glass beads. "Padre" beads were cerulean blue and opaque. As the demand for beads grew, so did the variety—new designs, fancier combinations of colors, different forms. These innovations were to continue for more than a century, as enterprising Europeans manufactured whatever they thought they could sell.

On the Great Plains the Sioux, the Arapahoes, the Cheyennes, the Kiowas, and the Comanches developed their own styles. Until the Civil War there were few differences in the beadwork of the tribes. After that time many styles evolved. Some were conspicuously artistic. Some followed the angular geometric designs. Others were derived from European styles—floral designs and double curves.

Two basic techniques emerged: beads woven on a small loom and two ways of stitching beads to skins. The first stitch is called "spot" or "overlay." In this technique the beads are threaded on a sinew. This sinew, with the beads on it, is then sewn to the skin. With a second sinew, the first sinew, with the beads on it, is sewn to the skin between every second or third bead. The needle never penetrates the skin but goes in and out just under the surface. When beads are sewn to cloth with this technique, the cloth is penetrated.

The second stitching technique is called the "lazy" stitch. The beads are threaded onto the sinew, and only the ends of the sinew are attached to the buckskin. This technique produces a rougher, corrugated surface, while the first technique produces a smooth, mosaic surface.

New varieties of beads continued to come into the Indian country. In the 1920's, Don Lorenzo Hubbell, of the famous Hubbell Trading Post at Ganado, Arizona, introduced a blue glass bead made in Czechoslovakia. It was a beautiful imitation of the finest turquoise and was readily accepted by the Navajos and widely used by them and others for the next several decades. Now it is as rare as many of the beads a century or more older. Today few of the old glass beads are around. Those that are repose in private collections and in museums.

Fine beadwork is still done by a number of tribes, among them the Bannocks and Shoshones of Idaho; the Kiowas, Arapahoes, Cheyennes, and Comanches of Oklahoma; the Turtle Mountain Chippewas of North Dakota; the Jicarilla and Mescalero Apaches of New Mexico; and the San Carlos and White River Apaches of Arizona.

Jewelry

Unlike basketry and pottery making, Indian jewelry making is flourishing in the Southwest. The craft has become more sophisticated and the work more refined, though it has lost its primitive vigor. The old, bolder designs are no longer made and are found mostly in collections, not for sale.

Today, the Navajo silverwork craft is highly developed. So is that of the Zuñis and the Hopis. Where once the Indians made it for themselves, now it is made almost entirely for commercial trade. It is more sophisticated, possibly prettier, but more reflective of the market than of the imagination and the skill of the maker.

The early Navajo silversmith made do with whatever tools he could devise. Squatting beside his forge and bed of cedar coals in his hogan, he used anything he could find that would serve as a crucible. He used a hollow fragment of broken pottery or a bowl or a dipper or a shovel. In this he melted down American dollars or Mexican pesos, an ounce of silver, or silver wire, sheets, or slugs. He heated his bed of coals by pumping hand bellows made of goatskin. As the metal became molten, he sprinkled it with borax for a flux. At just the right instant he poured it into a form and then hammered it on a chunk of iron that served as an anvil, reheated it, and hammered it again until he had the desired shape. Then he filed it smooth and polished it.

Such techniques are used no more. The present-day Navajo silversmith works with modern equipment, electricity, acetylene torches, and fine hand tools.

The style of Indian jewelry has changed almost as much as the craft of making it. The Navajos began working with silver about the time they were released from detention at Fort Sumner in the Bosque Redondo, several years after the Civil War. There is much conjecture about who taught them. Some say it was the Mexicans. While the Navajos were prisoners, they worked in other metals, fashioning crude bracelets and rings of brass and copper. By the time they returned to the Navajo country, they had learned enough techniques to work in many metals. After their return to the reservation, however, most of their work was almost entirely in silver, with no turquoise or stones of any kind.

At this point the Navajos' jewelry was the product of personal, individual effort. They used two techniques, the hammered silverwork described above and sandcast silverwork. Sandcasting was like molding. A form was cut into semisoft sandstone, and molten silver was poured into the impression. When it cooled, it was filed smooth and polished. Buckles, ketohs (wrist guards, worn as protection from the snap of the bowstring), bracelets, and rings were made in this way—and are still made this way.

Upon their release the Navajos took back to the reservation several designs that have since become classics. One such design is the ketoh, a wide bracelet that is now rare. Another is the *naja*, the crescent that hangs at the bottom of many Navajo necklaces. Sometimes these crescents are single; sometimes they have two or three tiers. In recent years some of them have been decorated with turquoise. They also took back the flower-like silver forms now called the squash blossoms. These are usually strung between the silver beads of necklaces. There are several theories about the origin of the design—one being that they were derived from a Mexican ornament. They took back designs for rings, bracelets, and earrings, as well as silver hatbands for use on their high-crowned black hats.

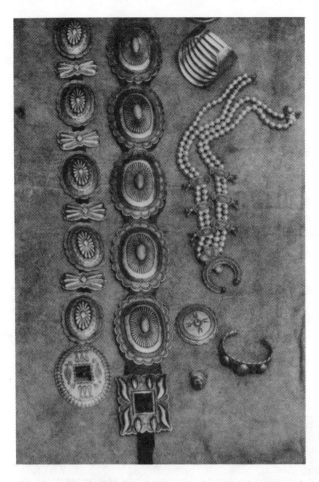

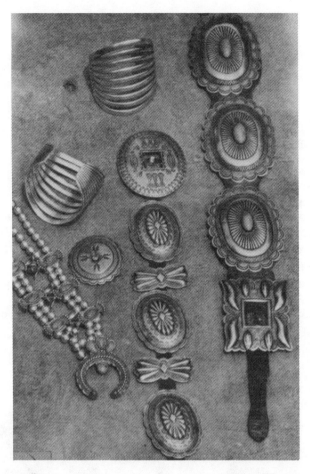

Silverwork of the Southwest. Left to right: Navajo hammered concho belt; Navajo concho belt with turquoise insets; Navajo hammered bracelet; squash-blossom necklace with *naja* (crescent); Navajo brooch with turquoise inset; Zuni bracelet and ring.

Navajo silverwork. Left to right: squash-blossom necklace with *naja*; a pair of hammered bracelets, a brooch; a small hammered concho belt; a large concho belt with buckle and conchos with turquoise insets.

When white traders saw the potential market for Navajo jewelry, they made arrangements with the more skilled silversmiths to make jewelry for sale outside the tribe. When they subsidized these silversmiths, the character of Navajo jewelry changed. It was no longer made by the Navajos for themselves. From then on it was made for trade.

In the meantime, the Zuñis had been developing their own jewelry craft. As early as 1830 they were making jewelry of copper and brass, and for centuries they had carved tortoise shells. About 1870, after the Navajos returned from the Bosque Redondo, the Zuñis came in contact with Navajo silverwork. They were fascinated by it, learned the craft, and developed their own styles. The Zuñis specialize in inlay and mosaic work, setting various stones together in patterns.

When the Navajos began using turquoise in their silverwork about 1890, the Zuñis did the same thing. The Zuñis, however, developed their own techniques and designs. They tended to use more stones, more elaborate settings, even clusters of miniature settings. The Navajos tended to use more silver and fewer inlays. This difference in styles continues to this day.

Today the Zuñis set various stones together in patterns, using turquoise, jet, coral, and even mother-of-pearl. In this style their work is almost unique, and they have developed modern and efficient techniques for the production of popular Indian jewelry. Nearly a thousand Zuñis are engaged in the manufacture of jewelry.

The first Zuñi silverwork was heavy, almost bulky. Today it is streamlined. Until about 1920 they sold all their work to other Indians. Today their jewelry is sold far and wide, far beyond the borders of the Indian country.

Like the Navajos, the Hopis have produced outstanding silverwork for many years. They too developed their own styles. They are particularly known for their overlay work. Designs are cut through a sheet of silver, which is then soldered to another sheet, and the cutouts are decorated with black. With this technique the Hopis make fine bracelets, rings, bolos, and other items.

In silverwork the Navajos led the way. They had been using turquoise for years before they started working with the white man's silver. It was natural that the other Indian tribes would copy them. The Santo Domingo Pueblo Indians did so. They are best known for their shell and turquoise beads, but for years now they have also produced some silverwork. The Santa Ana and Jémez Indians copied the Navajos, and the Indians of Acoma and Laguna also produce silverwork.

The Indian jewelry of today has its own worth, its fine workmanship, its popular designs. Compared with it, the older work is crude, but, as in all art, therein lies its vitality and its true value.

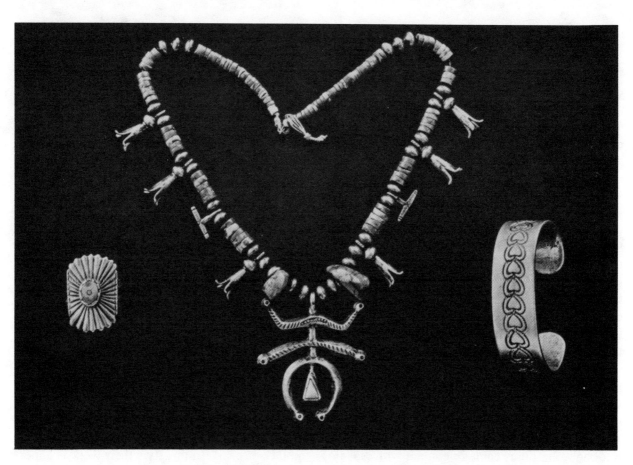

Navajo silverwork. *American Museum of Natural History.*

Pawn

It has not been long since just about every trading post in the Indian country of the Southwest had a pawn rack. Behind the counter in the least accessible part of the trading post hung the pawn—beautiful Indian silverwork: ketohs, elegant concho belts, most of them set with turquoise, bridles, belts, rings, necklaces—every kind of Indian jewelry and decoration. In a way all of this was "in hock," although the arrangement was actually somewhat different.

An Indian's silverwork represented his wealth, or economic worth. He regarded it as negotiable, which in most cases it was, although rarely negotiable for money. Usually it was collateral for food or merchandise. It was put up as security and was redeemed not for money but for wool, lambs, or piñon nuts and sometimes for labor. It was also sometimes pawned for safekeeping. When an Indian was to be gone from the area, herding his sheep in the high-country grazing grounds, he would bring in his most valuable silverwork. He would take a small loan—no more than a token sum—and leave his bracelets, necklaces, belts, squash blossoms, or silver buttons. The trader then became responsible for them. When the Indian returned some months later, he redeemed them and paid the going interest, usually 10 per cent.

Under the regulations of the Bureau of Indian Affairs the trader accepting silverwork or anything else for pawn was required to hold it for at least a year and to inform the Indian when his time was up. If the Indian needed more time, usually it was granted. But if he did not redeem his pawn or did not try to reclaim it, the trader could then sell it. However, the trader was required to sell it for no more than the amount on the pawn ticket plus 10 per cent. In this way the trader—in theory at least—was enjoined from selling an Indian's silver-

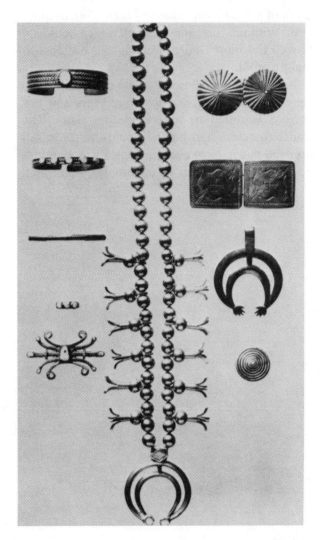

Navajo silver ornaments. *Smithsonian Institution National Anthropological Archives, Bureau of American Ethnology Collection.*

work or any other pawn without giving the Indian the opportunity to reclaim it. In practice it did not always work out that way. When the unreclaimed pawn became "dead pawn," traders sometimes sold it for far more than they had loaned on it.

For the trader such dealings required a solid knowledge of the intrinsic value of the items brought in for pawn. They also required a high order of personal evaluation of the Indian in question. Without such judgment a trader could go broke, and most traders were in the business to make a profit.

In early-day trading posts the pawn rack was heavily laden. Until not so many years ago few persons ventured to remote trading posts. The trader therefore had limited opportunities to sell his dead pawn. Now even the most distant and inaccessible trading posts are accessible by car—and today most pawn racks are bare. Collectors have cleaned them out. Also, today's Indians are unlikely to place their valuables in pawn. While in times past the loan on Indian pawn was a small percentage of its value, today the pawn tickets show a much higher percentage. Moreover, the truly old silverwork the Indians still own is cherished. They wish to keep it, if not for themselves then for their tribes. Conversely, they do not "convert" their money into silverwork to make it negotiable as pawn. What money they have they use as money, demonstrating the same level of skill in money management as most whites.

Old pawn, and old Indian jewelry that never was pawn are becoming increasingly valuable, not because it is fine, or even good, work but simply because it is old. In its historic value lies its true worth.

Indian Relics in Europe

Almost from the day the first white men set foot in America, they began shipping Indian "souvenirs" back to Europe. Early explorers and missionaries took or sent home Indian arts and crafts. While today it is virtually impossible to remove ancient treasures from Egypt and Greece, the practice of combing the United States for Indian artifacts for European collections goes on. Some of the finest collections of American Indian relics are to be found in European museums. From the beginning Europeans were fascinated by Indian culture. They were enchanted by the charm and beauty of Indian artwork. They used every means, some honorable, some considerably less than honorable, to acquire the things of American Indian life. The paradox is that the countries of the early explorers, Spain, Portugal and Italy, have the fewest and the smallest collections. England, Germany, Sweden, and Denmark have extensive collections.

First it was the royal European adventurers who cadged, bartered, or stole. With the western expansion, enterprising Americans bought up Indian goods and sold them to European collectors. Thomas V. Keam (for whom Keam's Canyon in the Hopi Country of Arizona is named) made it a business to collect Indian goods for sale to Europeans. Wealthy Europeans visiting in the United States acquired collections and shipped them home. In time many of the private collections were placed in museums.

The Germans and the Austrians especially took a lively interest in American Indian goods. Today there are Indian collections in sixteen German museums. The Museum of Ethnology in Berlin has about eight hundred Indian items. This museum acquired whole collections from Americans. It has such items as a quiver, a bow case, and arrows of

the Jicarilla Apaches, a good deal of pottery and flutes of the Pimas and Papagos, and rattles of the Yumas.

There are also major Indian collections in Hamburg, Bremen, Munich, Dresden, Stuttgart, Zurich, and Mannheim. Some excellent Indian specimens in Cologne were destroyed by the bombing in World War II. Interestingly, although many of the European museums have collections of items of the Indians of the American Southwest, quite a few concentrate on the Indians of America's Great Plains—the Sioux, Crows, Cheyennes, Shoshones, and Arapahoes.

The Museum of Ethnology in Vienna has some excellent specimens of Pueblo pottery made by Santo Domingo, Zuñi, Cochití, Acoma, Laguna, and Hopi Indians. They also have fine Navajo rugs and blankets and shell and turquoise ketohs and necklaces.

England has American Indian collections in the British Museum (a vast collection) and in Bath and Cambridge. The Oxford Museum has more than a thousand Indian items.

In France the largest collection is in the Museum of Man in Paris, numbering about six hundred items, such as pottery from Cochití, Santa Clara, and Tesuque, stone axes from Zuñi, Hopi woven belts, rabbit sticks and weaving boards, and even a polychrome deer effigy from Laguna Pueblo.

In the latter part of the nineteenth century and the first quarter of the twentieth century foreign diplomats, particularly consuls, took a great interest in Indian relics and artifacts. They used their contacts to seek out and acquire collections and ship them back home. In this way many of the finest and rarest items found their way into European museums. The interest in Indian items became contagious, and presently the Europeans were competing with each other. Small wonder that today, while Americans are scouring the countryside, much Indian material reposes in museums in Stockholm, Helsinki, Copenhagen, Norway, Holland, and Scotland. The City Ethnographic Museum in Stockholm has a collection of almost seven hundred items—fine Pueblo pottery, Navajo bowls, silver earrings, bracelets, and items of copper and turquoise.

But the true measure of the interest of Europeans in the American Indian is not simply that they have been collecting his relics and artifacts, his utensils and tools, his arts and his crafts for nearly five hundred years but that they have been studying and writing about him all that time. For example, books about American Indians, written by German scholars and illustrated by German artists, compare favorably with books about American Indians by American historians and anthropologists.

Tribal Government

Indians number about four-tenths of 1 per cent of the population of the United States, fewer than one million people. Probably no other group so small has had so great an influence on the American government. The Iroquois Confederacy, sometimes called the Five Nations, of central and western New York was organized centuries before the framing of the United States Constitution. Each of the five tribes, the Cayugas, Mohawks, Onondagas, Oneidas, and Senecas, had the status of a state. (Later they were joined by a sixth tribe, the Tuscaroras.) Each governed its own affairs. Each sent representatives to the league council, and each tribe voted as a unit, one vote for each tribe. Federated for "common defense and offense" in matters of war and "foreign" affairs, the league council prevailed. The vote had to be unanimous. Democracy—government by consent of the governed—was the touchstone of tribal government then and remains so today.

Indian self-government has many forms. It may control several hundred tribes or subtribes, bands, and groups. In principle tribal governments are sovereign, yielding only those rights pre-empted by the United States Congress and in some instances by the states. Yet the tribes have higher status than states. They are subordinate to the federal government but nevertheless are sovereign. Unlike Congress, tribal governments often encompass both the legislative and the executive branches and in some cases even the judicial branch. In addition, some tribes have corporate status. Today many tribal governments are similar to the government of the Five Nations and to that of a number of other tribes that were prospering at the same time.

In 1620, the year the Pilgrims founded their first colony in Massachusetts, the Pueblo Indians across the continent were electing their first officers. The territory that is now New Mexico was under Spanish rule. The king of Spain had ordered that each pueblo elect a governor and a lieutenant-governor. The Indians complied, but they did not discard their own governments. They accommodated them to the Spanish "civil" government. Even at that early time the pueblos, though autonomous, had a central council of tribal governments. They still have today—the All-Pueblo Council. Although the Pueblos, like nearly all other Indian tribes, had no written language, they have an unwritten tribal code, a system of rules and regulations understood and accepted by all. The lengthy oath of office is the same today as it has been for eight hundred years or more, handed down by word of mouth.

The pueblo tribal councils function as they have for many centuries. Decorum is strict. Visitors are barred except on rare occasions. In some pueblos the councils also act as courts of law. Thus the councils make the laws, enforce them, and adjudicate in trials.

Nearly all Indians govern themselves through some form of council. Every four years the Navajos elect a tribal council of seventy-four members —four councilmen for each of eighteen land-management districts. The chairman and vice-chairman are elected at large by all the districts. The tribal council has the authority to speak and act for the Navajo tribe. It meets in the Navajo Council House in the capital, at Window Rock, Arizona.

The Crows of Montana have a different form of tribal government, a general council. When the council is summoned, all adult members of the tribe assemble in a sort of town meeting. All adults are entitled to vote. Four times a year they elect delegates to go to Washington, D.C., to confer with officials of the Bureau of Indian Affairs, with members of Congress, and with other officials involved in their affairs. In other tribes the elected members of the tribal council elect a governor or president of the group. The term of office varies from tribe to tribe.

Rarely has a chief's status been based on heredity. Indian dynasties are almost unknown. In times past an Indian achieved the status of chief by virtue of his ability, wisdom, and leadership. More often than not the chief was not a military figure. Subchiefs, men of special talents and experience, were the battlefield commanders. Some of the "chiefs" who made treaties were self-appointed—sometimes to their regret. Decisions were generally made by consensus vote, often by a unanimous one. This practice is generally followed today.

Most modern-day reservation Indians take an active interest in politics. In fact, a far larger percentage of Indians turn out for their elections than white Americans do for theirs. In a recent Navajo election 80 per cent of the Navajos voted. That is a greater percentage than that ever posted by whites in any presidential election since the founding of the United States. Interest in the reservation elections extends to Navajos who no longer live on the reservation. They are permitted to vote by absentee ballot. In order to vote, all Navajos, both on and off the reservation, must register. Voting is facilitated by photographs of the candidates printed on the ballots. In this way Navajos can vote for their choice, whether or not they can read. The Navajos, the largest tribe in the United States and owners of the largest reservation, have no constitution. The tribal council conducts the tribe's extensive business and governmental operations under a code of guidelines. Only three of the nineteen pueblos of New Mexico have adopted constitutions: Isleta, Laguna, and Santa Clara. The other sixteen pueblos utilize the traditional unwritten form of government. With this understanding they conduct both their internal and their external affairs. However, the All-Indian Pueblo Council, to which all the pueblos belong, does have a written constitution.

The Hopis, like the Pueblos, retain autonomy in each of their villages but have a central council to which all the villages belong. Each village has votes in proportion to population. In order to vote, an individual Hopi must have lived on the reservation at least six months. No absentee voting is permitted.

Nearly all the tribes have written or unwritten bills of rights providing equal political rights and opportunities, freedom of worship, freedom of conscience (the right to speak and write their opinions), the right to assemble, and the right to petition. All Indians cherish and have long fought for these rights.

Indian justice, meted out by tribal councils, is often severe. In many tribes penalties are spelled out. For example, on the Standing Rock Reservation of the Dakota Sioux a councilman or officer convicted of a felony forfeits his office.

A number of tribal governments provide for naturalization of outsiders as members of the tribe. In Santa Clara Pueblo an Indian from another pueblo or reservation who marries a member of the pueblo may also become a member of the pueblo with the assent of the tribal council, by a form of "naturalization." The candidate is required to appear before the council, petition for acceptance as a member of the pueblo, and renounce allegiance to any other pueblo. A year later he is required to appear again and is questioned whether he has kept his promises. If he has, he is permitted to swear allegiance to Santa Clara, and in due course he receives his membership papers.

The Hopis have similar provisions for naturalization of certain persons of Indian blood. As members they can hold office in the tribal council. But representatives of the United States or state or local governments are barred from holding any tribal office.

The Red Cliff Band of Lake Superior Chippewa Indians operates under a federal charter with a constitution. Their bylaws provide that "all persons of Indian blood whose names appear on the official allotment roll of 1896 and on the census roll of 1934" are members of the tribe. All children of any member of the Red Cliff Band "who is a resident of the Reservation at the time of the birth of such children" are members.

In addition to their citizenship within their tribes all Indians born within the boundaries of the United States are American citizens and may vote on the same basis as other citizens. They are *not* wards of the government.

Police and Judicial Procedures on the Reservations

Matters involving policing the reservations and judicial procedures are complex. On some reservations the state supervises police activities. On others tribal laws or regulations imposed by the Department of the Interior apply. On still others a combination of federal and tribal regulations is followed. On many reservations the officers of the law are Indians, most of whom are employed by their own tribes.

The judicial system is equally complex. By and large, offenders who have violated tribal laws are tried by tribal courts, many of which were modeled on state courts. For more than a century a major problem has been how to make these Indian courts effective. Many of the judges were not qualified by white standards. Many Indian judges had no courtrooms or furniture or the staff necessary to operate a court. To compound these problems, an Indian's idea of justice is often different from that of a white man. Not so long ago in many Indian courts it was a common practice for innocent Indians to plead guilty, hoping thereby to ingratiate themselves with the judge and get off with a lighter sentence.

Indian judges with no training—and no access to any—were obliged to rule in Indian matters according to the white man's law. To the Indian this practice was unfair, unrealistic, and unworkable. The white man's view of the white man's law was not and is not the Indian's view. To the Indian judge his tribal law—his tribal tradition— is a sounder criterion for making judgments.

For decades the Indian court system was actually hampered by government regulations. One of the intents of the Indian Reorganization Act of 1934 was to give the Indians a practicable Indian judiciary. Tribal courts would try only misdemeanors, and each tribe would select its judges

from its own group. Moreover, each tribe was encouraged to adopt its own codes. The system did not work. Since the judges had to be selected from the local tribes, the choices were few. Often only the unqualified were eligible.

Then the federal and state courts began transferring complicated civil cases involving Indians to the Indian courts. The judges, again without training, lacked guidance. To add to the problem, the lines of jurisdiction among the government, the state, the Bureau of Indian Affairs, and the tribe were blurred. The Indian judges did not know the extent of their authority. The system bogged down.

Another factor made the situation even worse. Most judges were appointed for periods of one to four years, which meant a rapid turnover. Hardly had the ablest of judges learned his duties when his term expired. His experience was lost, and he was replaced by another inexperienced Indian. The Navajos solved this problem by electing judges for life, with removal only for cause.

To aggravate the situation, some tribes took the position that the judges should not be paid at all—that service was part of their duty as members of the tribe. Other tribes paid the judges stipends that were not enough to live on. The Bureau of Indian Affairs paid some judges, but even the top pay was only about $3,600 a year. After more than thirty years under this system some Indian courts had become virtually white courts, some had evolved into a mixture of white and Indian courts, and some were operated almost entirely according to tribal traditions.

This was the situation when the Civil Rights Bill was enacted in 1968. Under this law it became the responsibility of the Indian judiciary to guarantee the civil rights of Indians. It is now government policy that Indian identity must be honored and preserved so that tribal traditions will not be lost.

In the same year the Indians themselves took a big step when they organized the National American Indian Court Judges Association. This was a significant move. The objectives of the association are to upgrade Indian courts through ongoing education and training of judges and staff and to achieve uniform court practices throughout the Indian court system. In training Indian judges, due regard is given to tribal practices. When those practices run counter to due process, however, especially in civil-rights issues, then the United States judicial system prevails.

Today virtually every reservation has tribal police, tribal courts and Indian judges. Many have criminal investigators. Every reservation has a jail and a prosecutor.

The jurisdiction of tribal courts is still limited to misdemeanors and to offenses against tribal laws. The more serious offenses (such as murder, rape, robbery, larceny, and manslaughter) are tried in state and federal courts. Civil cases are tried in both tribal courts and state courts. Where necessary, the FBI, the Treasury Department, and postal inspectors work with BIA officials on the reservations.

Only federal and tribal laws apply on reservations, except in those states that have assumed jurisdiction over the reservations: Alaska, Iowa, Kansas, Minnesota, Nebraska, New York, Oregon, Wisconsin, Florida, Idaho, Nevada, and Washington. In these states the laws of the states also apply on the reservations.

Under the Civil Rights Act of 1968 due process must be observed in all Indian courts. In Indian courts no person, Indian or non-Indian, can be deprived of his civil rights. The law spells out the right of any Indian who feels that he has been illegally detained to file a writ of habeas corpus in a federal court. The ultimate purpose of this act is to assure the Indian of due process in the tribal courts so that it will not be necessary to appeal to higher federal courts. To help achieve this goal, Arrow, Inc., Washington D.C., has launched two important programs. The first is a research project that will culminate in a manual on court procedures for Indian judges. The second is a training project to instruct Indian judges in the law.

Treaties with the Indians

The United States was not yet a nation when it made its first treaty with the Indians. The year was 1778, and the treaty was with a strategic tribe, the Delawares. The colonists and the British were at war, and in some regions the Indians held the balance of power. Since 1775 both the colonists and the British had sought the active help of the Indians, or at least the assurance of their neutrality. Both sides made unrealistic promises to the Indians.

In the first treaty, which was signed at Fort Pitt, in return for guarantees of the Delawares' support in the war, the Revolutionary government of the United States recognized the Delaware tribe as a sovereign nation and guaranteed its territorial rights. As added inducements the colonists promised the Delawares food, clothing, utensils, and even implements of war. Further, they invited the Delawares and other friendly tribes to form a state of their own, join the newborn nation, and even send their own representative to Congress.

In the next ninety years the United States government made more than 370 treaties with Indian nations. The Fort Pitt Treaty was the first of 45 treaties made with the Delawares. In those early days and later, 22 treaties were made with the Cherokees, 39 with the Sioux, 47 with the Chippewas, and 47 with the Potawatomis. Between the years 1789 and 1850 alone the United States negotiated and ratified 245 treaties. Many more, signed in good faith by the Indians, were never ratified by the United States Senate.

About one-third of the 370 treaties were peace treaties. Two-thirds were land cessions. In the 245 ratified treaties the Indians ceded some 450 million acres in return for less than $90 million —less than twenty cents an acre. Many of those treaties have been in litigation for years.

None of the treaties was observed for long. Yet they remain today the legal and moral bases for Indian claims against the government.

The Revolutionary War was scarcely over when the new nation made its first treaty with the Cherokees. In the Hopewell Treaty of 1785 the Cherokees acknowledged the sovereignty of the United States and gave up land that had been occupied by settlers and squatters. In return the United States agreed to recognize the strictly defined new boundaries of the Cherokee lands. It also gave the Cherokees the right to send a deputy to represent them in Congress. Fifty years later, after more than twenty additional treaties, the Cherokees were rounded up and marched over the Trail of Tears to exile in Indian Territory.

In the meantime scores of treaties had been made with other Indian nations. In 1794, President George Washington sent his secretary of war, Timothy Pickering, to make a treaty with the Seneca Nation of the Iroquois. In return for peace and friendship the government promised to respect the lands and boundaries of the Iroquois and never to disturb the Indians in their use of their lands. "The United States," the treaty stated, "will never claim the same, nor disturb the Seneka [sic] nation."

In the 1950's a dam was projected that would flood much of the Seneca Reservation in New York. The Senecas hired a staff of engineers, who offered an alternative site for the dam that they claimed would cost less and be more efficient. Their claims were to no avail. In 1960 the dam was built, and a major portion of the Seneca Reservation was flooded.

Between 1778 and the outbreak of the Civil War the government made 45 treaties involving the Delawares. In their homeland in New Jersey and Pennsylvania the Delawares numbered ten thousand. In the next 150 years they were displaced seven times—to the Ohio country, to Ontario, to the Ozarks, to the Plains states. Some bands ended in the Pacific Northwest. Once the Delawares had been displaced from their indigenous lands, they were without a land base. Thereafter, homeless, they could establish no secure base anywhere. When the remnants of their tribe were at last settled in Indian Territory, only one-sixth of them had survived.

Nor were they secure in Indian Territory. Robert J. Walker, territorial governor of Kansas, was soon urging that they and all the other Indians settled in the eastern part of Indian Territory be moved on to the supposedly worthless western part of the Territory. "The Indian treaties," he declared, "will constitute no obstacle, any more than similar treaties did in Kansas."

In the Revolutionary War and in the War of 1812 many eastern tribes sided with the colonists. Although the wars were not their wars, as allies of the colonists they suffered heavy casualties. Despite their support the movement to remove them from their ancestral lands went on. By 1834 the United States had cleared the eastern states of all the tribes that had been their former allies.

During Andrew Jackson's presidency more than ninety treaties were concluded with the Indians. By those agreements they were compelled to surrender millions of acres and move westward beyond the Mississippi. The Indians protested that many of these treaties were fraudulently concluded—that the American government had set up puppets within the tribes and signed unauthorized treaties with them. One such figurehead was William McIntosh, a Creek chief. McIntosh was a half blood. Closely identified with the whites, he organized sorties to capture fugitive black slaves and return them to their white owners for bounties. When, without authority, he signed a treaty relinquishing Creek lands, he was seized and killed by his tribesmen for violating tribal law.

In 1837 a treaty was concluded with certain members of Wisconsin's Winnebago tribe, who ceded their land to the government. The entire tribe opposed the cession, charging that unauthorized Winnebagos had been pressed to sign the treaty. The government insisted that the treaty was valid and sent troops, rounded up the Winnebagos, and removed them to Nebraska. But they refused to stay. They drifted back to their homeland in Wisconsin. Again the soldiers rounded them up and moved them to Nebraska. Again they went back. After their fourth removal, in 1874, the three thousand who returned once again to Wisconsin were permitted to stay there, under the Homestead Act of 1875.

About seven hundred Winnebagos remained in Nebraska. They are now a separate tribe, a people fragmented by removal.

The controversial New Echota Treaty of 1835 provided for the removal of the Cherokees from Georgia to Indian Territory. The treaty was signed by a handful of Cherokees selected by the council as a committee representing a few hundred people. The overwhelming majority of the Cherokees, some sixteen thousand, protested the signing as treason. They sent an authentic delegation to Washington, D.C., to oppose the ratification of the treaty. The Senate ratified it by a majority of one, and the Cherokees were driven from their lands. Most were exiled to Indian Territory. Some escaped to North Carolina, where they are recognized today as a separate tribe, the Eastern Cherokees.

Three years after the Cherokees moved west over the Trail of Tears, three of the Cherokees who had signed the New Echota Treaty were slain. The killers were never found.

The controversial Nez Percé Treaty of 1863 led to war and to the virtual destruction of the tribe. In a prior treaty, signed in 1855, the United States had confirmed the rights of the tribe to its ancestral lands and had promised to protect it from encroachment. The Nez Percés signed this treaty, but the Senate failed to ratify it or carry out its promises. Intruders, white settlers, miners, and renegades invaded the Nez Percé lands.

By the time the treaty was ratified four years

later, in 1869, the Nez Percés had deep suspicions about the motives of the American government. Even the most ardent supporters of the treaty among the Nez Percés denounced the government for failure to carry out its promises.

In 1863 the government appointed a new commission to negotiate a new treaty with the Nez Percés. Four bands of the tribe refused to participate and seceded from the Nez Percé Nation. Young Chief Joseph, whose band had lived for generations in the Wallowa Valley (Valley of the Winding Waters), was the leader of one of the dissenting bands. But two other chiefs, Lawyer and Big Thunder, signed the new treaty. They ceded Chief Joseph's Valley of the Winding Waters to the government but kept their own homelands at Kamiah and Lapwai. When the government sent troops to enforce the treaty, Chief Joseph resisted. In the bitter war that followed, Chief Joseph lost his homeland, the Nez Percés were removed to reservations, and Chief Joseph spent most of the rest of his life in detention.

The policy of treating with the Indians as sovereign nations lasted about ninety years. In the beginning it was a matter of expedience. Later the aim was the cession of Indian lands and protection of the official government policy on slavery. From 1787 until 1860 all treaties with the Five Civilized Tribes contained a clause providing that "all fugitive slaves belonging to citizens of the United States must be restored to their owners."

After the Civil War the United States government was free to deal with the Indians on different terms. In the Indian Appropriations Act of 1871, Congress ended the practice of treaty making with the Indians. But the act did provide that the obligations of the treaties already made would remain "unimpaired and in effect." In its more than 370 treaties the United States had gained nearly a billion acres of territory.

The Constitution of the United States provides that treaties are the supreme law of the land. The Medicine Creek Treaty of 1854 provides that the Indians are entitled to half of the salmon caught in the waters of the state of Washington. Litigation over this issue has been going on for years.

Further, the United States Supreme Court has ruled that "treaties made with Indian nations are the most sacred obligations of the Federal government" and that "if interpretation of an Indian treaty is doubtful, it should be decided according to what it meant to the Indians." Most Indians believed that their treaties were for as long as the sun shines and the rivers run. Most believed that the basis of their treaties with non-Indians was *mutuality of interest*—that neither party was free to dictate the terms or ignore the terms, or to abridge or violate the terms implicit in the agreements.

The more sophisticated Indians sensed that the treaties were mere scraps of paper and that nothing had halted or could halt the western expansion of the whites. They also knew that, having little power to enforce the treaties, they had to rely on the good faith of the other party. Thus enforcement has become the prerogative of only one party to the treaties, the United States government. If the government does not or will not enforce the treaties, the Indians can only seek relief in the courts.

Further, while the government can assess penalties or threats of penalties against the Indians for noncompliance, the Indians are powerless, save by going into court, to hold the government accountable or to seek redress.

Historically the Indians have perceived that the government has disregarded its most solemn obligations and promises to them. Chief Red Cloud, the Oglala Sioux, said: "They made us many promises but they never kept but one. They promised to take our land, and they took it."

The Pan-Indian Movement

Why don't the Indians get together? Why don't they unite in their efforts to improve their lot? Indians have been striving to achieve unity for more than five hundred years. Long before the white man arrived, farseeing tribal leaders sought to organize alliances to defend themselves against encroachments by other tribes. After the whites came, they strove to organize alliances to maintain their rights. The effort is still going on, through the Pan-Indian Movement.

In earlier times alliances of Indians went on the warpath. Now they exert pressure in other ways, but in effect the "Indian wars" are still going on. Today, as in the past, they are mainly local or area efforts. The alliances are striving for unity but have not yet achieved it. Within the movement, today as in the past, are activists and conservatives, firebrands and sage counselors. Some are for Red Power—for throwing down the gauntlet. The more conservative are for working through established channels.

The fact that so many organizations are working for Indian unity suggests the nature of the problem. The Indians are not one people. They are many peoples. Indians are strongly individualistic, and tribal identity and loyalty remain barriers to effective unity. About half of all the Indians in the United States live on 284 reservations and in pueblos, rancherias, and colonies. To some extent the tribes are isolated from one another. The Navajos remain Navajos, the Pueblos remain Pueblos, the Sioux remain Sioux. Those who leave the reservations for the cities tend to think of themselves first as members of their tribes and only secondly as Indians. Such an attitude hinders coalition. Language differences are also formidable barriers.

Yet despite these frustrations many efforts have been made to bring the Indians together. As early as 1570 the Iroquois tribes of the Northeast were ravaged by internecine war. An Iroquois chief, the real Hiawatha, preached that the tribes were destroying each other and urged them to join in an alliance for the common good. Hiawatha's proposal stirred so much opposition that he had to flee for his life. In the wilderness he found an ally, another refugee, a Huron named Dekanawida. Together they visited the warring tribes and promoted the alliance. The result was the Iroquois Confederacy mentioned earlier. The tribes adopted a constitution and called their entente the "Great Peace." Each of the nations retained its autonomy but became a member of the alliance for "common defense and common offense."

In the meantime Indians in other areas were making similar moves. By 1600, hundreds of miles south, Powhatan had become chief of a confederation of about twenty-five tribes in the Tidewater region. And before the close of the century the Wampanoag chief called King Philip had united many of the tribes of the Northeast. His was among the first of many Indian alliances formed expressly to fight the whites. The alliance was ultimately crushed, and King Philip was killed.

At almost the same time, on the other side of the continent, a Tewa medicine man named Popé united the Pueblos, Apaches, and other southwestern Indians against the Spaniards. In a score of scattered villages the Pueblos struck all at once. They killed over four hundred Spaniards and drove the rest out of the area. Though the Spaniards ultimately returned, for thirteen years the Pueblos' land was free.

The spirit of confederation was in the air. In what are now the states of Georgia and Alabama fifty Indian communities joined in the Creek Confederacy, overcoming the barrier of six distinct tongues. In the Great Lakes area the Ottawa chief Pontiac undertook to ally all the Indians from Lake Ontario to the Mississippi River. "Why do you suffer the white man to dwell among you?" Pontiac asked. "My children, you have forgotten the customs and traditions of your forefathers. Fling all the white man's things away. Live as your wise forefathers did before you."

In 1763, Pontiac's warriors attacked all the English forts in the area simultaneously. The Ottawas and Chippewas attacked Detroit. The Delawares, Mingoes, Shawnees, and Hurons attacked Fort Pitt. What Pontiac did not know was that the commanders at Detroit, Fort Pitt, and Fort Niagara had been warned. They held, but the other forts fell. The victory was short-lived. Pontiac lost favor among his allies, and he was assassinated.

Joseph Brant, the Mohawk chief, united the Senecas, Cayugas, and Onondagas with his own tribe and joined the British in the Revolutionary War. His effort to unite the tribes failed, however: two other Iroquois tribes, the Tuscaroras and the Oneidas, fought on the side of the American colonists.

Tecumseh, the great Shawnee chief, dreamed of "uniting all red men" and establishing an Indian state. He visited tribes in the Ohio Valley and the Great Lakes region and traveled as far as the Gulf of Mexico and west of the Mississippi River to consult the leaders of the Osages and other tribes. He said: "The way, the only way, to stop evil is for the red man to unite in claiming a common and equal right in the land as it was at first, and should be now, for it was never divided but belonged to all. No tribe has the right to sell, even to each other, much less to strangers. Sell a country! Why not sell the air, the clouds, and the great sea, as well as the earth? Did not the Great Spirit make them all for the use of his children?"

Tecumseh united the Shawnees, Delawares, Wyandots, Ottawas, Chippewas, and Kickapoos, but the Cherokees refused to join the alliance. Tecumseh was in the South trying to unite the Creeks, Choctaws, and Chickasaws when his warriors were defeated at Tippecanoe, Indiana. He retreated to Canada with the British forces. He was killed in the War of 1812, fighting on the side of the British.

In Wisconsin and Illinois the Sauk chief Black Hawk, who passionately hated the whites, envisioned an Indian confederacy strong enough to drive them out. He tried to organize the Winnebagos, the Potawatomis, and the Foxes. They were defeated in the Black Hawk War of 1831–32.

But efforts to unite continued. In the Northwest, Seattle, the Suquamish chief, organized the six tribes of the Duwamish Confederacy in the 1850's to resist the "horse tribes" pushing into his territory from the east.

In the 1870's, Quanah Parker, the half-white Comanche chief of the Quahadis, led a band of some seven hundred Comanches, Cheyennes, and Kiowas against the white buffalo hunters who had invaded their territory. Though defeated, he did not yield his dream of Indian confederation.

Two other powerful Indians rose on the Great Plains. Sitting Bull, the great Sioux leader, united the Teton Sioux and the Northern Cheyennes. Crazy Horse, the Oglala Sioux chief, united the Oglalas and the Cheyennes. They joined forces to help defeat Custer at the Little Big Horn in 1876.

Thus the roots of the Pan-Indian Movement are deep. The passing years have drained none of its vigor, none of its intensity. But the movement is still amorphous, with many organizations having many of the same ultimate goals but different approaches and attitudes. Unity is their common goal, and yet it still eludes them. Why?

The answer is a complex one. It lies in the nature of the Indian and his relationship to the land —an affinity for Mother Earth that white persons cannot fully share. Much of the mischief lies in the word "Indian." The term implies that the Indians are one people. They are not. If they were one people, all the Indians of the United States would react as one people, resolve their differences, and join forces. But each group has its own problems and, moreover, its own attitudes toward "other Indians." What is important to one group is unimportant to others. While all tribes are in their own ways religious, their religious values vary.

Despite ages-old efforts at unity, factionalism—divisiveness—is a major factor of Indian life. Long before white men appeared on the scene, closely related Indian groups were splintering, each one not only going its own way but frequently fighting each other. The Athapascans split into groups that ultimately became the Navajos and the Apaches. The Apaches themselves split into many groups: the San Carlos, the White Mountain, the Mescalero, the Jicarilla, the Chiricahua, and several smaller groups. Similarly there are a number of Sioux groups. Many other tribes have split into factions. Indians within one pueblo split and even built a wall to separate them within the village.

Yet the strong undercurrent toward unity persists. In the very territory where the first powerful Indian league was born, today another pan-Indian effort is taking form. The Iroquois tribes are still seeking to unite "all the tribes of the Western Hemisphere."

Urban Indians

Since World War II about half of all the Indians of the United States have moved to the cities, and they are still doing so. Statistics rarely tell the whole story, but in the last decade they have told a great deal about the Indians. In 1960 about 170,000 Indians were living in cities. In the following six years this number increased by nearly 230 per cent, and the trend continued. As of 1970 almost 500,000 Indians were living in cities.

The greatest concentration is in Los Angeles, where more than 60,000 Indians live, almost 10 per cent of the Indian population of the United States. In San Francisco and the Bay area there are about 20,000 Indians; in Chicago, about 15,000. Minneapolis, Denver, Tulsa, Phoenix, and Milwaukee each has an Indian population of more than 10,000, and there are large Indian populations in Seattle, Oklahoma City, Portland, Albuquerque, Rapid City, Duluth, and Buffalo.

The movement toward the cities accelerated during World War II, when great numbers of Indians joined the armed forces or left the reservations for wartime jobs, thus breaking their ties with their traditional lives. At war's end, with new perspectives, they began moving to urban centers in search of better jobs, better opportunities, better education, better housing, better health care. Instead they found frustration and hardship, open discrimination, sometimes cruelty. They still find it.

The frantic pace baffles Indians newly arrived in the city. They are stunned by the anonymity of life there. They suffer from the language barrier and from their separation from the only culture they know. They suffer from their broken contacts with family, tribal life, and deep spiritual relationships. Economically they are unable to compete on white terms. They lack schooling, job training, and the kinds of experience required for successful city life. Even worse, in the city they are no longer Indians as such. They are simply indigent persons—and members of one of the smallest minorities at that. On the reservation they had an agency to turn to, an agency set up to serve only them. In the city they are on their own. What services they get are from the community or the state. Often these services differ from what they have been used to on the reservation. Such problems have raised the question whether the government should provide the same services to city Indians as to reservation Indians.

Looking for jobs and a better life, many urban Indians drift from neighborhood to neighborhood. Frustrated, they move to other urban areas, from city to city. Finally, in despair, about 40 per cent move back to the reservation. As they return, they meet others venturing out, determined to make it in the cities, a heartbreaking cycle. Yet the agony of the move does not discourage the migration. The Indians continue moving to the centers of white culture. Both the Indians who move and those who stay behind are affected. Those left on the reservation are deprived by the "brain drain," since many of their young and better educated, the very ones whose talents and energies are most needed at home, are moving away. Those who leave tend to lose their tribal affiliations and also their "Indianness." Still worse, the Indians on the reservation feel that an Indian who leaves for the city and perhaps marries a white is almost irretrievably "lost." Thereafter, they feel, for all practical purposes, he is less likely to be in tune with them and less likely to take part in their struggles.

On the reservation the Indian's tribal status is important. In the city it is not. On the reservation he "belongs." In the city he does not. In fact, his

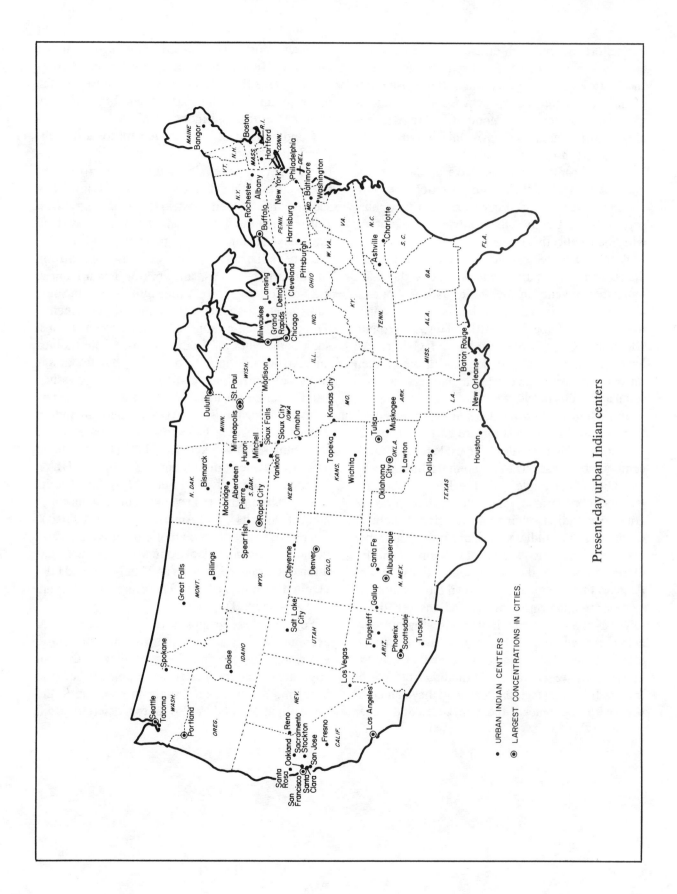

Present-day urban Indian centers

• URBAN INDIAN CENTERS
◉ LARGEST CONCENTRATIONS IN CITIES.

very effort to band with others of his tribe in the city works against him. For even though all city Indians are in the same situation, the divisiveness of the tribes often keeps them from working together for the common good. Los Angeles has about thirty Indian groups. Only about twenty have joined in coalition movements.

Just the same, the basic drive of the city Indians is unity. In their detribalization they are coming to see that in order to survive they must organize—that unity is their only means of coping with their collective despair.

Wherever there are concentrations of urban Indians, there are Indian centers. Today there are more than seventy in such cities as Los Angeles, Chicago, San Francisco, Milwaukee, Minneapolis–St. Paul, Phoenix, Seattle, Tulsa, Portland, Oklahoma City, Albuquerque, and Gallup. All have the same goals: to help the urban Indian make the transition to city life and to serve his personal and social needs.

In addition, wherever there are service centers there are Indian associations to carry out special functions, such as medical clinics, legal-assistance centers, organizations to rehabilitate Indians who have been in trouble with the law, alcoholism-treatment programs, and clubs that promote American Indian singing and dancing. Wherever there are urban Indians there are Indian churches and Indian athletic associations. Many of the Indian centers have their own publications. In Los Angeles they even have their own blood bank.

In economics most urban Indians see themselves as the forgotten minority, ranking not only below the white population but also below all other ethnic or racial minorities. That is why urban Indians are seeking direct funding from Washington. It is, they feel, the only way they can compete with the blacks, the Chicanos, and other stronger minorities. Presently most urban Indian efforts are funded to some extent by the Department of Health, Education, and Welfare, by the local community chest or United Fund and by churches, clubs, and individuals.

Hand in hand with the movement toward coalition is the conviction of a growing number of Indians that they can make their most effective stand in the cities rather than on the reservations. They see the cities as their most strategic battlegrounds. But to wage the fight in the cities they know they must have strong urban organizations. Gradually the city Indians are overcoming tribalism. Strong Indian urban groups, all working toward unity, are proliferating around the country, and in some cases are expanding into national movements. The older, well-established Indian organizations, such as the National Council of American Indians and Arrow, continue to be active, but the newer Indian organizations tend to be more aggressive. San Francisco has its UNA (United Native Americans); Minneapolis, its AIM (American Indian Movement), which has spread to many areas of the country; Milwaukee, its CTAI (Consolidated Tribes of American Indians); Seattle, its UIAT (United Indians of All Tribes); Los Angeles, its UIDA (Urban Indian Development Association); and Chicago, its UIA (American Indians United). There are many others, among them NAIC (National American Indian Council), COINS (Coalition of Organized Indians and Natives), and UIT (United Indian Tribes). There are many others (see Appendix B).

Some of these groups have come into national prominence. All are working for the same basic goals, yet the very number—each with its own approach—underscores the complexity of the problem. But what they share in common is the same plight. What they also share is determination.

Indian Journalism

In terms of communications the Indians have come a long way since the whites first reached American shores. Today the Indians of the United States publish hundreds of newspapers, magazines, quarterlies, and annuals. There is a growing body of talented, trained, skilled Indian journalists. Indians have their own press service, the American Indian Press Association, which maintains a news bureau in Washington, D.C., where their future is being determined.

Almost from the first encounter with the whites, Indian leaders saw the need for better means of communication than they had. They quickly perceived the value of writing—how the whites used it for treaties, commands, instructions, and a hundred other purposes. They saw the printed word. They saw pamphlets, booklets, periodicals, and books. They saw the advantage such means of communication gave the whites. They sensed their own disadvantage in not having written languages, not having books, not having the means of publishing their point of view or even of communicating by writing, Indian to Indian.

Most of the pro-Indian associations that came into existence in the nineteenth century published some kind of organ, or "voice." Through these journals they enunciated what was all too clear to them but what few whites were willing to admit. The pro-Indian publications gave the Indians' view of what the federal government was doing to them. They discussed politics, white encroachment, the growing efforts to detribalize and acculturate them. They pleaded for restoration of their rights. They attacked white pro-Indian associations that ostensibly were organized to "help" the Indians. These organizations, they held, were "integrationist" and "antitribal," not so much because of cunning and deceit on the part of the organizations as because of their naïveté. The fault, they believed, lay in the incapacity of the do-gooders to understand the Indian ethos. Actually, they were working against the welfare and the rights of the Indians, hampering rather than helping them.

Still the pro-Indian press was only a feeble voice in the wilderness. In addition to its struggle to survive, it had to compete with the better-financed, deeply entrenched white press. The white writers, editors, and publishers, intentionally or unintentionally, invariably presented the white man's version of Indian affairs. In the view of the Indians the white press neither understood nor properly interpreted the Indians' problems.

The Indian press was short of resources and, even more frustrating, was confronted with the language barrier. The educated Indian journalists wrote in English, but how many Indians could read English? Yet the Indian press survived and grew. It became an extension of the whole Indian struggle, an additional manifestation of Indian resistance. It became a rallying point against "conquest and colonialism."

In 1911 a group of forty-four Indian intellectuals gathered at Ohio State University to organize the Society of American Indians. One of their purposes was to prove that Indians could be as "civilized" as whites. They founded the *Quarterly Indian Journal,* edited by Arthur C. Parker, a distinguished Seneca scholar. They set as their goals an end to the abuses by the Bureau of Indian Affairs and improvement of the quality of Indian education.

Most of the members of the society agreed on these goals, but there was not the same agreement on how to achieve them. Disagreement led to bickering and then to dissension between the con-

The logo of Dr. Carlos Montezuma's crusading magazine *Wassaja*.

servatives and the activists. Dr. Charles Montezuma, a Yavapai physician practicing in Chicago, declared that the reservations had become colonies run by white agents of the government and by white missionaries who were tools of exploiters. He resigned, and the dissension tore the society apart.

In order to wage a more vigorous fight against the government, Dr. Montezuma and his followers founded a militant Indian journal, *Wassaja*. *Wassaja* became the voice of the Indian activists of the day. In its articles it spelled out the Indians' hatred, distrust, and contempt of the government. It called for Indian unity, tribalism notwithstanding, as the only hope of the Indians.

Both *Wassaja* and the *Quarterly Indian Journal* are now long gone (a later publication called *Wassaja* is published in San Francisco), but the goals both fought for are still the goals of the Indian press. The American Indian Press Association serves more than 150 Indian publications. It is dedicated to improving the quality of Indian journalism and improving communications among the tribes. From its Washington bureau the AIPA sends weekly reports to its client papers about what is going on in Indian affairs. It also covers the major national and regional Indian conferences. With this service Indians on even the most

remote reservations have access to news that concerns them. Moreover, the news is reported by trained Indian journalists.

On the reservations the Indian publications enunciate their own aims. The Oglala Sioux of South Dakota "work to inspire tribal awareness and unity with (their) brother tribes."

The Indian dilemma is "unity or tribalism." Tribalism is still strong, and so far tribalism remains a barrier to Indian unity. Indians still tend to think of themselves first as members of their tribe and secondly as Indians. As attractive as the ideal of unity seems, it appears to mean a loss of tribalism. Many Indians equate detribalism with loss of their culture. They cling to tribalism as the bulwark of their culture. Yet, vis à vis the whites, tribalism results in divisiveness and therefore impedes unity.

Almost from the beginning the whites have tried to destroy traditional Indian tribal life. They are still trying. The Indians are still resisting, and the voice of resistance is the Indian press. While many Indians have settled for a certain measure of acculturation, in practice they continue to oppose it. The Indian press speaks out against the dissolution of Indian culture by the white man's technology. Indians buy television sets and washing machines and refrigerators, but that does not mean that Indians wish to become whites. The Indian point of view is that Indians are Indians and that they wish to remain Indians.

Indian publications, like white publications, vary in quality. But they have one quality in common: they are dedicated to the Indian viewpoint. This viewpoint, they hold, is often blurred if not obscured in the white press. Within its capabilities, the Indian press covers the full range of Indian interests—news about the major issues concerning Indians, feature stories about Indian interests, coverage of social events, and sports, poetry, philosophical pieces. Scholarly Indian journals are devoted to history, archaeology and other sciences, and the humanities.

The Indian press reflects what is on the mind of the American Indian. Possibly the truest way for the non-Indian to gain some understanding of the "Indian problem" is to read what the Indians themselves are writing.

A directory of Indian publications appears in Appendix C.

St. Anthony Mission, constructed by the Zuñis under the direction of Spanish missionaries in 1629. The mission was rebuilt in 1922 and was rededicated in 1972. *Troy Gruber, Bureau of Indian Affairs.*

PART TWO

VISITING INDIAN COUNTRY

Kah-Nee-Ta Vacation Resort, Warm Springs Indian Reservation, Oregon. *Bureau of Indian Affairs.*

Visiting Reservations

In the last five hundred years Indians have learned a good deal about "visitors" and their ways. Still, like most persons, they respond warmly to good manners and courtesy. Most Indians are patient and gracious. But they are justly sensitive to invasion of their privacy. One wise old Indian put it this way: "We are not saints, but we are not savages."

Like people everywhere, some Indians are easy to get along with, and some are not. Some reservations have strict regulations. Some are more permissive. Most of them are somewhere in between. It helps to smooth the way to know something about a reservation and its people before visiting them.

First, the visitor should bear in mind that he is a guest. A reservation is the Indians' domain. It is their home. Besides, it is their most important resource and, in many cases, the main sources of their tribal income.

The visitor should bear in mind that Indians have their own scale of values, their own standards. These standards are different from those of most whites. Deep within the Indians' spirit is the knowledge that they were in America first and that they managed to live off the land for thousands of years before the white incursion. They expect whites to obey tribal laws, just as they obey the laws of the state and of the nation.

On many reservations signs and billboards inform the visitor where he may go and where he may not. The thoughtful visitor will exercise the same consideration while visiting a reservation that he does when he is a guest in the home of friends. He will restrict himself to the public areas and stay out of those that are off limits.

On some reservations the Indians defray operating costs by charging modest parking fees, which

are in effect admission fees. Some reservations have extensive parking areas.

Since the communities and the Indians themselves are so colorful, the temptation to photograph them, or to make sketches or paintings is almost irresistible. The visitor should be aware that some Indians require a fee to make pictures of any kind. In some places no photography or picture making is permitted. In others permission to photograph, paint, or sketch is granted for a fee by the tribal headquarters. If the fee is not paid, the visitor is usually not permitted to carry his camera, sketch pad, or painting equipment while he is on the reservation. In addition, the visitor should offer to pay any individual he wishes to photograph, draw, or paint. No Indian should ever be photographed without his express personal permission. In some of the pueblos the churches and the kivas (ceremonial chambers) may not be photographed at all. The thoughtful visitor will respect these regulations and strive for the best possible rapport with the Indians.

The more the visitor knows about the reservation and the tribe the more satisfactory his visit will be. Moreover, it will save him time and enable him to see and learn more.

Having faced a steady flow of visitors for years, the Indians are often passive, but they almost always respond readily to courteous and considerate visitors. On most reservations the Indians go out of their way to make visitors welcome and comfortable. Many reservations have picnic grounds, and some have campgrounds.

The chiefs, governors, or chairmen of the tribal councils are busy persons. They are courteous, but they rarely have time for idle conversation. The visitor should respect them as he would other busy executives. Many reservations have their own enterprises, arts and crafts, industries, power plants, sawmills, and cattle ranches. The workers are also busy at the necessary tasks for living.

The watchword in visiting Indians on their lands is courtesy. Remember, you are a guest.

Ceremonials

Indian ceremonials are attracting more visitors every year. Indian ceremonials take place somewhere in the United States every month of the year. As more white tourists visit the reservations, more are coming to understand the sacredness of these rites.

A number of events billed as ceremonials are not, in the true sense, ceremonials at all. They are performances, organized and staged as shows. True Indian ceremonials are religious ceremonies and are executed by the Indians in the same spirit as religious ceremonies held anywhere in the world. Some Indian ceremonials are open to the public. Some are not. The annual fiesta at Santo Domingo Pueblo in New Mexico is held early in August. About five hundred Indian dancers, singers, and clowns execute a number of religious rites, including the Corn Dance. On one day during this period the dances are open to the public. But when the Plains Indians do their Sun Dance and the Hopis perform their rites in their kivas, these events are held strictly for their own people, and are in no way shows.

The one basic principle that pervades all Indian ceremonies is that man must live in harmony with nature. The Indians knew this long before the white man came. They learned to study the sun and the moon and the stars. They adapted their lives to the winter solstice and the summer solstice and to the divisions of the year. By observing the sun and the solstices and the seasons, they set their ceremonies to follow the natural calendar.

In spring their ceremonies were held to assure success in planting, germination, and growth.

In summer they carried out rites for the protection of their crops and to bring rain.

In fall they gave thanks for the harvest and prayed for continued fertility in the seasons to come.

In winter they prayed for snow so that the rivers would be full in spring. At the same time they prayed for protection against the cold, the winds, and the blizzards.

All these were annual rites. In addition special ceremonies were held, among them the ceremonials for the hunt. In these rites they asked the Great Spirit to protect the hunter and to bring him good fortune, and they supplicated the animals to permit themselves to be killed for food.

In time the ceremonials became stylized in a series of formal acts, performed in a certain routine, each designed to bring about a certain response.

The Indians of the Southwest performed these rituals for centuries before the Spaniards brought Catholicism. In time the Indians of the Southwest adopted their own version of Catholicism but did not drop their own faith. The two religions went hand in hand. As a gesture of compromise the Spaniards assigned a patron saint to each of the pueblos and set aside a day for the veneration of the saint. Acoma annually celebrates a fiesta on Saint Stephen's Day. Isleta Pueblo celebrates Saint Augustine's Day; Tesuque, the Feast of San Diego; Jémez, the Feast of Saint Guadalupe; Laguna, Saint Joseph's Fiesta; Picurís, San Lorenzo Day; Santa Clara, Saint Clara's Day; and so on.

In all these celebrations the Indians combine their style of Catholicism with their native faith. Either the priest of the community or a visiting priest conducts mass, and the Indians come to the church to pray. In some pueblos, when this service is over, the Indians carry the statue of their patron saint out of the church and around the plaza of the pueblo, beating drums and reciting chants as

Choctaw dancer, Plains style.

An artist's rendition of a Shalako dancer. *New Mexico Department of Development.*

The kiva at San Ildefonso Pueblo, New Mexico. The kiva is oval in shape. The banner is a sacred symbol, used during harvest dances.

they go. After a while the statue is placed in a bower of cornstalks and greenery, and the Indians dance before it, singing prayers and chants of thanksgiving.

These are ceremonies of celebration. Others are held for varying purposes. They may last for one day to many days. Some Hopi ceremonials last nine days, and some in the Pacific Northwest last four days. Some tribes have only a few ceremonials a year. Other groups average one or more a month.

Many of the ceremonials of different tribes have evolved into almost identical forms. Basically, a ceremonial consists of a retreat and in the last stages a dance or drama. The retreats are always private. During this stage the Indians taking part practice abstinence. For the first part of the retreat they eat no meat, usually nothing containing grease, and no salt. Toward the end of the retreat they eat nothing. In the pueblos the Indians usually carry out their retreats in the kivas. In these semisubterranean chambers they are virtually im-

prisoned. In other areas the retreats are held in lodge halls.

The retreat is followed by the dancing. The Indians come out of the kiva in costume, their faces and bodies painted, sometimes wearing masks, and attired in symbolic regalia. By this time they are weak from hunger, but they dance. Sometimes the dance lasts only a few minutes; sometimes it lasts for days. Each family has its own ceremonial costumes, which are cherished and guarded by them. Some families are keepers of regalia for the whole pueblo, or group, and this responsibility is considered an honor.

The degree of secrecy in ceremonials varies from tribe to tribe and community to community. Each group makes its own decisions about what portion of the ceremonial, if any, may be witnessed by the public. Often the public is welcomed to the latter stages, a dance or a drama in which certain traditional myths or legends are acted out. The public is sometimes permitted to see the processions of the priests and may be present for the singing of the traditional songs, the rites of smoking and sacrificing of food, and the offering of prayers.

Aside from the pueblo fiestas, many other ceremonials are staged. Some are held annually, some biennially, and some seasonally within the year. Some are unscheduled, held whenever the occasion demands. The medicine man sends out a summons for a ceremony, often a sing and a dance, when there is an emergency. The visitor lucky enough to be in the vicinity may sometimes see these extraordinary, almost extemporaneous ceremonies.

Because of the widespread interest in Indian ceremonials, major powwows are staged for the public each year. Although the dances and ceremonies are, in a sense, always religious, in the major events they are staged as demonstrations or exhibits.

Among the best known southwestern ceremonials are the American Indian Days celebration at Sheridan, Wyoming, held at the end of July; the Mescalero Apaches' Mountain Spirits Ceremony, held on the reservation in July; and the three-day celebration of the Jicarilla Apaches, including the Ghost Dance and Fiesta, held on the reservation in September.

The annual Shalako Kachina Ceremony held at Zuñi Pueblo in December is a major event. The first part of it is barred to the public; the latter part is open.

Other important religious ceremonies are the Hopi Snake Dance, held in the Hopi pueblos in August; the Comanche and Horse-tail Dances, held at Taos in February and March; and the various ceremonies of the Navajos, in which the men do the dances to find food, to protect them from the elements and from their enemies, to exorcise evil spirits, and to regain health. The Navajos also stage their own tribal fair at their capital, Window Rock, Arizona, late in September.

According to the season, Indian ceremonials and events are taking place continually in some part of the nation. Alaska Indians celebrate the Polar Bear Season at Kotzebue and the Walrus Carnival at Savoonga. Their biggest winter celebration is held at Anchorage.

Across the continent, the All-Choctaw Fair is held in Mississippi in July. Many Indian ceremonials are held in Oklahoma and the Dakotas, and a number are also held in Colorado. One of the most interesting Indian events is the annual Indian Arts and Crafts Market, held in Santa Fe on the third Saturday and Sunday in August.

Information on these and many other Indian ceremonials and events will be found in Part Three of this book.

Linda Willis, Choctaw Princess, 1973.

When Indians Dance

Scarcely anything depicts the American Indian more eloquently than his dancing. It manifests all that he is, his attitude toward life, his relationship to nature, his convictions, his faith, his expressions of joy. He dances to bring rain, to give thanks, to propitiate his deity, to pray for a bounteous harvest, to protect him from evil, to promote the fertility of his crops and animals, to help him face the dangers of his existence, to help him in his hunting.

To the whites, Indian dancing often does not seem to be dancing at all. It is ceremonial, ritual. The Indians dance for sheer entertainment too and to demonstrate skill and endurance, but usually they do so for deeply symbolic reasons.

Not all Indian dances are open to the public. Those held on reservations, on Indian lands, and at pueblos are usually part of the communal life of the Indians. They are sacred dances, and the public is barred. On such occasions the thoughtful visitor will not intrude. Dances held at public affairs are, of course, secular performances. They are for the public.

Time is slowly destroying true Indian dancing. As the Indian legends and traditions grow dim, gradually the authentic Indian dances are "lost." Today they are mere fragments of what they were in times past. Yet the real Indian dances seen today are valid representations. The details are lost, but their symbolism remains. Authentic Indian dances can still be seen on or near the reservations and Indian lands.

Nearly everyone has heard of such "standard" Indian dances as the War Dance, the Rain Dance, the Corn Dance, and the Snake Dance, but there are countless others. Some of them have become classics. All are integral parts of Indian life. The Hopi Snake Dance mentioned above is a rain dance. The whole ceremony lasts about eight days. The rituals of the first days are secret, barred from the public. When the pageantry and the dancing commence, the public is permitted to look on. The snakes are carried in the mouths of the participants, and after the songs and the dances the snakes are taken to designated places, released, and bade to bring back rain. When the ceremonies are completed, everyone in the pueblo takes part in the dancing, feasting, singing, and games.

One of the most interesting Indian dances of the Southwest is the Apache Mountain Spirits Dance. The dancers, representing the Gahans, supernatural beings, wear mysterious black masks that cover the entire head. Atop the masks are tall cut-out symbols, fantastic headdresses often called crowns, for which the dance is often called the Crown Dance. Each dancer gestures with symbolic sticks in his hand as he dances around the bonfire at night, chanting. The dance steps are stylized, and as the dance progresses, young maidens join in.

The Navajo Yei-bi-chai is also a night dance. The chant is a mysterious, plaintive litany. As they dance around giant bonfires, their shadowy faces and bodies cause grotesque shapes in the flickering light of the flames.

The Indians of San Juan Pueblo in New Mexico perform the Deer Dance, a realistic simulation of the deer hunt. They pray for a successful hunt and for a bountiful supply of venison.

Many Indian dances honor animals. The Utes do the Bear Dance at Ignacio and Towaoc in Colorado and at the United and Ouray Reservation in Utah. The Hopis do the Buffalo Dance, in which the bison, impersonated by Indians, are "killed." The Indians of Picurís Pueblo in New Mexico perform the Elk Dance, and the Taos Indians per-

A Greyhorse Osage war dancer, near Pawhuska, Oklahoma. *Fred W. Marvel, Oklahoma Tourism and Recreation Department.*

form the Horsetail Dance, which honors the horse for his service and fidelity to mankind. In their dances the Indians honor many other animals, among them turtles and dogs.

Dances are also held for birds and insects. In the Eagle Dance the Pueblo Indians, cleverly dressed to simulate the eagle, "soar" as the noble birds do. The Indians of Tesuque Pueblo do the Thunderbird Dance for rain, and the Zuñis do the Night Bird Dance foretelling the coming of nightfall. The Jémez Pueblos perform the Crow Dance, which depicts the crows swarming over their cornfields. This dance is usually held for entertainment. The Pueblos do the Parrot Dance, and the Hopi maidens perform the Butterfly Dance, their hairdress representing a butterfly.

The dances of the Indians reveal their interrelationships. Each tribe, each band, has its own dances, and each relates its own legends and traditions and faith. The Navajos perform the Riding Song Dance on horseback. As they ride slowly through the night, they chant a soft, melodious song. It serves to occupy them in their loneliness and protects them. The Pueblos hold a number of Basket Dances. These dances symbolize the foods that the baskets contain, the substance of life, and the endless chain of existence.

The Zuñi women do an almost formal dance, bearing beautifully decorated jars on their heads. Clothed uniformly in deep-blue dresses with embroidered sleeves and wearing the characteristic bulky white leggings, they move through the formations with skill and grace, never touching the exquisite jars on their heads.

The Harvest Dances of the Pueblos are dances of thanksgiving. In basic ways all the Harvest

Taos Pueblo Indian children doing the Hoop Dance, for which they are famous.

Dances are similar, and yet each pueblo expresses its gratitude in its own way.

Many dances tell stories and legends, and some relate history. The San Ildefonso Comanche Dance commemorates the coming of the Comanches and other Plains Indians to the Pueblo Indian country. It tells of their remorseless warfare, of the many fierce battles. The Taos Indians, who first felt the brunt of the Comanche attacks, do their own version of the Comanche Dance. The strong mark of the invader is on many Pueblo dances.

Some of the dances were cruel. One such was the famous Sun Dance performed by the Sioux, by the Cheyennes, and by other Plains tribes. It was a ceremony of penance and self-torture. The skin or the muscles of the brave's breast were pierced with a skewer. Pegs were forced crosswise into the wounds, and long rawhide thongs were attached. The other ends of the thongs were attached to a pole, or sometimes to the heavy skull of a buffalo. The Indian pulled against the thongs until his flesh gave way or until it would not yield. In this way his courage and endurance were tested. The ceremony lasted eight days. The first phases were held in secret. When the dance was finished, the onlookers were permitted to take part in the smoking and feasting that followed. The Sioux chief Sitting Bull was proud of the scars he bore from taking part in the dance.

All these dances and countless more have been depicted by the Indians themselves in their art. Indian artists make beautiful and impressive pictures of what is important to them—their ceremonies, their hunting, their dancing. So it has been through the ages. In the Indians' art of the last several centuries they graphically show themselves in dance, sometimes in mass ceremonials, sometimes with only a few dynamic figures in action. But all underscore the meaning and the importance of the dance in their lives. All throb with the vitality of a people using every creative means to express what they really are.

Happily, with a little planning, good representations of genuine Indian dances still may be seen. They are listed in Part Three of this book.

The Apache Mountain Spirits Dance, American Indian Exposition, Anadarko, Oklahoma. *Fred W. Marvel, Oklahoma Tourism and Recreation Department.*

Buying Arts and Crafts

Genuine fine Indian arts and crafts and relics are rare and expensive today and becoming more so. An Indian piece that is genuine and fine either is old or was handmade in modern times. If it is *old* and *good*, it is expensive because it is rare, likely a collector's item. If it is *new* and *good*, it is expensive because it was laboriously made by skilled Indian craftsmen.

Today nearly six thousand Indians, Eskimos, and Aleuts are earning their living, or part of it, in arts and crafts. About 15 per cent of the population of the Eastern Cherokee Reservation in North Carolina is engaged in making fine baskets and wood carvings, doing beadwork, and weaving linens and woolens.

On some reservations the Indians have given up the old handicraft methods and have learned modern techniques of manufacture. The Zuñis have switched from pottery to jewelry. Today Zuñi silversmiths number about one thousand.

Jewelry is also a prime craft of the Navajos and of the Hopis (see Part One, "Indian Arts and Crafts").

Fine Indian work is still available, but the buyer should know that in some places imitation Indian arts and crafts from Hong Kong or Japan or from domestic factories are offered alongside genuine Indian work. Markings such as "Indian style" or "Indian type" may deceive the unwary buyer. Authentic work in most cases bears a marking proving that it is genuine. Often it will be the emblem of one of the Indian Guilds. For example, the emblem of the Hopi Silvercraft Guild, a sun shield, may be found on the back of this fine Indian work.

Japan turns out plastic and clay kachina dolls (carved from wood by the Hopis), and some "Indian-style" fabrics are the products of American textile mills and are not woven by the Indians.

Turquoise is synthesized, some of it so well done that only an expert can detect it. Also, some turquoise stones are treated with oil to give them a luster which soon fades to dullness.

Similar conditions occur with pottery. True pottery is decorated before it is fired. Some of the Indian pottery offered today is painted with ordiary poster colors *after* it has been fired, and the colors soon fade or wear off. Some of the so-called "genuine" Indian pottery items are seconds or rejects.

Collectors are advised to buy with great care from peddlers on the streets. Also, care is required in selecting Indian merchandise in stores where imitation is mixed with genuine.

Some Indian arts and crafts have evolved into modern forms. The style of some of the pottery of Jémez and Tesuque Pueblos has become modernistic. Some are even decorated with psychedelic poster paints. The use of modern synthetics has become so pervasive that experts foresee the disappearance of the wool, the fibers and grasses, the clays, stones, and minerals in the making of Indian crafts. The true Indian crafts are disappearing. Most of the old Indian crafts repose in museums and private collections. Little is available anywhere else.

Just the same, a genuine effort to produce fine crafts goes on. In some places it flourishes. For years now, Indian leaders have strived to save their arts and crafts, to try to prevent its complete extinguishment. At the Institute of American Indian Arts at Santa Fe, young Indians are taught the arts and crafts—painting, sculpture, and ceramics. They are instructed in lapidary and textiles, in drama, music, and the dance, and even in creative writing.

Indian arts and crafts today generally fall into these classes:

1. Authentic antiques, genuine old pieces
2. Fine modern handicrafts, authentically made
3. Run-of-the-mill tourist-trade items
4. Trinkets, curios, souvenirs

Today there is a sharp line between genuine Indian arts and crafts and the counterfeit. A hard line has been laid down by the Indian Arts and Crafts Board. Fines and punishments may be imposed for misrepresentation of Indian arts and crafts. The effort is to authenticate the genuine and to discredit the imitation.

Camping with the Indians

The Indian latchstring is out. Today, instead of resisting the presence of visitors on their lands, most tribes are inviting them to camp on their reservations. The sites of many campgrounds now open for public use are historical and ceremonial sites where the Indians themselves once made encampment. In addition, some of the tribes have set up multimillion-dollar resort complexes. The operation of these enterprises is strictly Indian. The campgrounds are supervised and managed by Indian officers. Indian rangers perform the same functions as forest rangers or national-park rangers.

On most reservations, camping is restricted to established campgrounds. On some visitors are permitted to camp anywhere except in posted areas. Some of the Indian campgrounds are in the desert, some on rugged plateaus, some in the mountains, many around lakes and streams, some in canyons and dense forests.

Some of the campgrounds are primitive. In these the visitor should expect to rough it. Most, however, have all the standard facilities. Some even have trailer hookups. Usually water is available, piped to the site or available from springs or wells. The prudent camper will, however, take along his own water supply. Except in the most primitive camps there are toilets, and some have flush toilets and showers.

Campfires are usually permitted. In some campgrounds firewood is free, already cut and ready for use. Down or dead wood may be gleaned and burned in the fire holes.

Why are the Indians now encouraging the public to camp on their lands? It represents a realistic use of their greatest resource, their land. It also enables them to cope with the challenge of white pressure. The pressure on Indian lands is different today from what it was in frontier times, but it is still present.

Today non-Indians are penetrating farther into the wilderness, seeking camping sites and recreation. In recent years this trend has taken them onto the reservations in staggering numbers. For years Indians were almost passive about visitors. Visitors came and visitors went. If there were places for them to camp on the reservations, they camped there. If not, they camped anyway, often to the dismay of the Indians. Their presence posed problems for the Indians—protection and maintenance of their lands, custodial services, facilities. All of this was costly in both manpower and money. Besides, with inadequate facilities to control the growing number of visitors, their most important resource was endangered.

A reservation is not merely a living space reserved for Indians. It is also the source of their tribal income. Some tribes use portions of their lands for raising stock. Some with forest acreage run sawmills. Some lease acreage for mining. But many, observing the influx of recreation seekers, saw clearly their dilemma: either bar the tourists from the reservation or accommodate them and control their presence.

The major tribes throughout the country have chosen the latter course. With established campgrounds they can maintain and protect their lands. At the same time they can realize some tribal income. For the tourist exciting new areas have been opened for his use. This development coincides with the surging interest in everything Indian, arts and crafts, museums, politics, life styles.

On some reservations the tribes have made recreation a major enterprise. One of these is the Fort Apache Reservation in east-central Arizona. This reservation sprawls over a rugged mountain country of more than a million and a half acres. It is the largest privately owned recreation area in the West, with about 1,900 campsites in 18 camp areas. Here campers are welcomed with the Apache words "Hon Dah" ("Be My Guest").

The Mescalero Apaches of New Mexico have about 265 campsites in four campgrounds, plus about 300 picnic sites. They also operate a modern ski resort, Sierra Blanca, with a lodge and restaurant.

In Oregon the Confederated Warm Springs Tribes own and operate a multimillion-dollar vacation resort, Kah-Nee-Ta.

Besides all these, owned and operated by the Indians, there are many public campgrounds near or adjacent to Indian reservations. Navajo National Monument, just west of Tsegi Canyon, operated by the National Park Service, has a splendid campground right on the Navajo Reservation.

Visiting an Indian reservation—particularly camping on one—is a little like visiting another land. Indeed, it *is* visiting another land. A reservation is in fact Indian country. It belongs to them. This fact requires good manners on the part of visitors—the same common courtesies practiced by guests in any social situation. The reservation —all of it—is private property. It is the land and the home of the Indians who live there. A reservation is not a public park on which Indians happen to be present.

In Indian campgrounds, as in Indian villages anywhere, some Indians are fairly strict about behavior. They are particularly sensitive about photography. The thoughtful visitor will respect the privacy of the Indians. They usually will cooperate if asked to pose, but no visitor should presume to photograph an Indian without his express permission. If he agrees, he should be offered an appropriate honorarium. Visitors to the pueblos should not even make sketches or paint pictures without permission from the tribal headquarters. The Navajos have an almost poetic way of admonishing visitors to their lands: "Leave only footprints, take only photographs."

The visitor planning to camp on an Indian reservation should learn something about the camping facilities before he arrives. Information about the campgrounds is provided in Part Three. The tourist can obtain further information by writing or telephoning the reservation.

A number of attractions will reward the visitor to most Indian reservations:

Recreation: On most reservations there are hiking trails and hunting and fishing facilities. On some there are lakes and streams for boating. Tribal hunting and fishing licenses are usually required.

Scenery: Spectacular scenery is to be seen in the vicinity of many reservations.

Tours: Most major reservations have charted self-conducted motor tours to the points of interest, particularly the historic sites, on or near the reservation.

Perhaps most important of all is the appeal of Indian life and Indian customs and the adventure of seeing the Indians on their own home grounds. Here the visitor may see the Indian in his own, not the white man's, milieu. The Indian "at home" is far more interesting than the scenery, the historical sites, or the arts and crafts. For a bonus the enterprising visitor may be able to time his visit so that he may see the Indian ceremonials, festivals, dances, or fairs.

Kah-Nee-Ta Vacation Resort, Warm Springs Indian Reservation, Oregon. *Bureau of Indian Affairs.*

PART THREE

GUIDE TO INDIAN COUNTRY

A guided tour of Tonto National Monument, Arizona.
National Park Service.

THE FIVE REGIONS

For practical purposes, in this part of the book the Indian tribes are presented geographically in the following order: the Southwest, the Central Region, the Northwest, the Southeast, and the Northeast.

Because of many factors—primarily government-enforced removal—Indians of the same tribes and linguistic groups are today found in widely scattered parts of the country. Where they live now may have little relationship to their tribes, their languages—or their wishes. Most of the Cherokees live in Oklahoma, but a considerable band of Cherokees live on a reservation in North Carolina. The Apaches have reservations in Arizona and New Mexico, but some also live in Oklahoma. The Seminoles have four reservations in Florida, but many also live in Oklahoma. The Oneidas, who once lived in the East, now have a reservation in Wisconsin. There are bands of Potawatomis in Wisconsin, Kansas, and Oklahoma. And so on.

In few cases do most of the Indians of any tribe live together in one area. A notable exception is the Navajo tribe, nearly all of whom live on the Navajo Reservation.

Each of the regions listed above is treated as a unit. Each section below contains a directory of the tribes and reservations in the region, together with brief accounts of the major tribes, their history, and their present status. Suggestions are provided about where to go and what to see in each region, together with descriptions of the main attractions, including historical sites, natural phenomena, and significant tribal events.

Each section also contains a calendar of Indian events—ceremonials, dances, dramatizations, feast days, and fiestas—all listed by months. Persons planning visits to the Indian country can schedule their arrivals accordingly. Further to assist the visitor, each section contains directories of Indian reservations and campgrounds in the region, listed by states.

The purpose of this part is to help orient the reader to the world of Indians. It is designed to brief him specifically on where to go and what to look for. The chances are that he will find more than he ever dreamed.

The Cliff Dwelling from Speaker Chief Tower, Mesa Verde. *Jack Boucher, National Park Service.*

THE SOUTHWEST

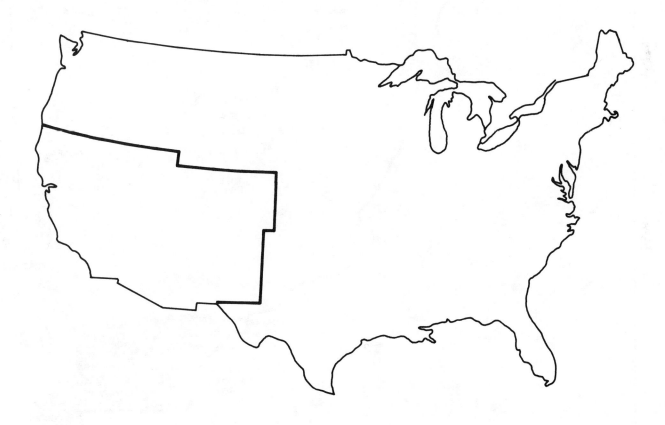

Montezuma Castle National Monument, Arizona. The castle is a five-story structure with twenty rooms. It accommodated twelve to fifteen families (about fifty people). *M. Woodbridge Williams, National Park Service.*

Tribes and reservations of the Southwest

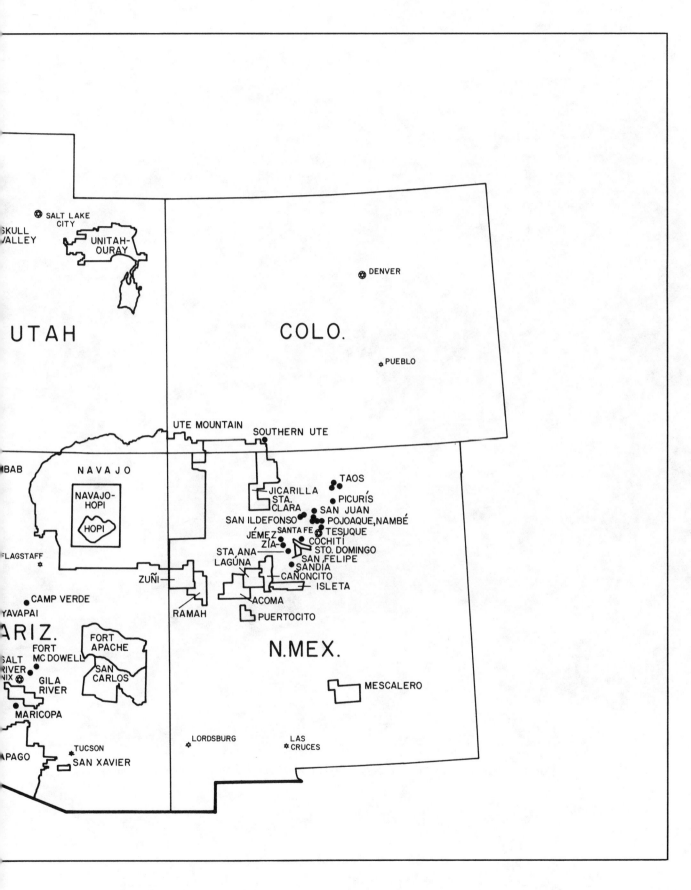

SALT LAKE
CITY

SKULL
VALLEY

UNITAH-
OURAY

DENVER

UTAH

COLO.

PUEBLO

UTE MOUNTAIN   SOUTHERN UTE

BAB

NAVAJO

NAVAJO-
HOPI

HOPI

TAOS

JICARILLA
STA.
CLARA   SAN JUAN
SAN ILDEFONSO   POJOAQUE, NAMBÉ
JÉMEZ   SANTA FE   TESUQUE
ZÍA   COCHITÍ
STA.ANA   STO. DOMINGO
LAGÚNA   SAN FELIPE
SANDIA
CAÑONCITO
ZUÑI   ISLETA

PICURÍS

FLAGSTAFF

CAMP VERDE

YAVAPAI

RAMAH

ACOMA

PUERTOCITO

ARIZ.

FORT
MC DOWELL

FORT
APACHE

SAN
CARLOS

N.MEX.

SALT
RIVER
NIX

GILA
RIVER

MESCALERO

MARICOPA

PAGO

TUCSON

SAN XAVIER

LORDSBURG

LAS
CRUCES

83

Matachines Dance at Santa Clara Pueblo, New Mexico. *New Mexico State Tourist Bureau.*

Exploring the Pueblo Country

New Mexico's nineteen pueblos are a living link with prehistoric America. Taos Pueblo has been inhabited continuously since long before America was "discovered" by the white man.

Not long ago some of the pueblos were almost inaccessible. Today all may be reached on good roads. There are nine living pueblos within fifty square miles around Taos and Santa Fe, possibly the oldest communities in the nation. All are tight clusters of adobe structures built around an open square. In most pueblos there are an adobe church with a cross and a bell, a kiva for ancient ceremonial rites, and a scattering of adobe beehive ovens that look like igloos.

Traditional Indian life is still carried on in the pueblos, but it is fading. What the white man's gunpowder could not accomplish the white man's technology is bringing to pass. But there is still time to observe the pueblo life in transition, a privilege made easier by a little understanding of the Indians themselves.

Some of the pueblos are liberal, some conservative. The liberal pueblos are more permissive and have a laissez-faire attitude about their traditions and the presence of visitors. The more conservative pueblos are stricter. They seek to protect their way of life, their rights, and the pueblo itself against the onslaught of white society. This is not easy, for they are beset with the pressures of the twentieth century. Radio, television, washing machines, freezers, refrigerators, jukeboxes, and automobiles are despoiling their traditions and eroding their languages.

The full bloods are vanishing. Indian males marry girls from other pueblos or bring back brides after military service from Germany, Japan, Korea, Turkey, the Philippines, and Vietnam. The Indian girls often marry outside their pueblos and go to live elsewhere. Intermarriage has brought an intermixture of blood and cultures.

Most of the Pueblo Indians are nominal Catholics. They have adapted the formal rites of the Church to their own ceremonials. Each pueblo has its own sacred Indian ceremonials. Some are performed in the secrecy of the kiva, a cellarlike ritual chamber entered from a tall ladder through a trapdoor in the roof. Some of the ceremonials are performed in the plaza. The latter are open to the public.

Indian ceremonials may be seen in New Mexico in any month of the year. In addition visitors may sometimes be pleasantly surprised with special ceremonials.

Once the Pueblo Indians were farmers, possibly the best dry-crop farmers in the world. In the beautiful and orderly fields surrounding their pueblos they raised corn, beans, squash, peas, pumpkins, grain, garden vegetables, and apples.

Pueblo Indians at Tesuque Pueblo, performing the Buffalo Dance, an ancient hunting ceremonial. *New Mexico Department of Development.*

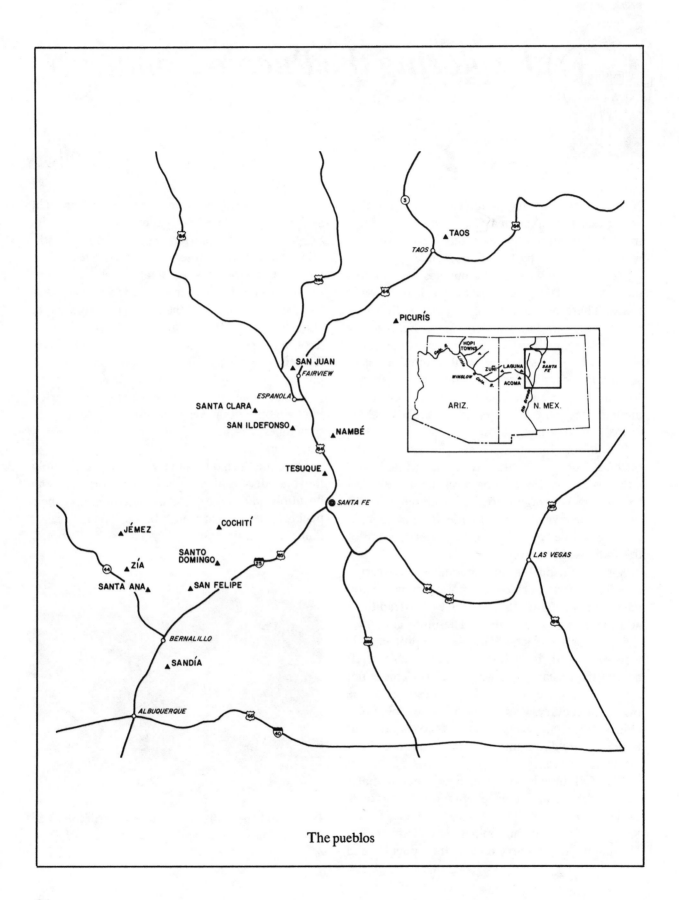

The pueblos

Taos Pueblo. *New Mexico Department of Development.*

Indians in ceremonial dress, Taos Pueblo. *New Mexico Department of Development.*

Wrapped in a white blanket, a Taos Indian stands beside the adobe communal house in Taos Pueblo. *New Mexico Department of Development.*

An Indian mending moccasins at San Ildefonso Pueblo. *New Mexico Department of Development.*

Today most of the men and many of the women work away from the pueblos, many in the atomic plant at Los Alamos. They commute to and from work, just as whites commute from their apartments, and the beautiful farmlands are now fields of weeds. The pueblos have become places to live, not to work.

Yet in striving to rescue or restore their crafts, many of the women are still expert weavers, potters, and basketmakers. In their spare time the men make colorful and delicate jewelry.

Each pueblo has a chief, or governor, whose term of office is one year. Some are re-elected for many terms. The visitor interested in making pictures should first look up the governor. He is usually found in his home near the plaza. In some pueblos, as in San Ildefonso, the governor has an office, where he collects parking or camping fees.

Here is where to go and what to see in the pueblos around Santa Fe and Taos, New Mexico:

From Black Canyon Campground (in the Santa Fe National Forest, seven miles northeast of Santa Fe) four pueblos, Tesuque, Nambé, San Ildefonso, and Santa Clara are within easy driving distance. About twenty campsites are available for trailers or campers in Black Canyon.

Tesuque is about ten miles north of Santa Fe. This pueblo is more than seven hundred years old. It has a population of about two hundred, who speak a mixture of Tewa, Spanish, and English. The pueblo is striving to restore its arts and crafts, which are almost lost. A growing number of the pueblo's young people participate in the ceremonial dances.

Nambé is five miles east of Pojoaque Creek, on the main highway. It has a population of nearly three hundred. Nambé was moved to this site in the seventeenth century, when the people retreated from the incursion of the Spaniards. A large bell is all that remains of the church, which had to be pulled down because it was unsafe. Several times each year the people stage colorful ceremonials. The most important event is the Nambé Waterfall Festival, held each year on July 4.

San Ildefonso has a population of about three hundred. It is one of the best-preserved pueblos, a storybook land. The pueblo is conservative, and no photographs can be made without payment of a fee. Here the famous María Martínez made her fine black matte and burnished pottery. The feast of San Ildefonso is celebrated on January 23, with spectacular Animal Dance dramatizations.

Santa Clara is just north of Española. It is the second-largest Tewa pueblo, with a population of more than seven hundred. It is a vital, liberal community, alive to the changing world. The people of Santa Clara permit photography of some of their dances, which are colorful and well performed. Santa Clara is also famous for its polished black pottery with strong designs, such as that of a bear paw.

When the tourist breaks camp at Black Canyon Campground, he should head northward to Taos and on the way stop off at San Juan. San Juan is about five miles north of Española. It is the largest of the Tewa pueblos, with a population of nearly twelve hundred. The rambling, old-fashioned general store dates back to Civil War days. Dance ceremonies are held several times a year. The San Juan Celebration is held on June 24. Arts and crafts are being revived, and the women make handsome pottery, skillfully decorated in red, brown, and black.

Continuing northward, the visitor reaches Taos, the most celebrated of the pueblos. Its fifteen hundred people speak Tiwa. It is famous for its five-story "apartment buildings," its beautiful skyline, its people, its arts, and its industries. Fees are charged for parking, taking photographs, and sketching or painting. A mountain stream, Taos Creek, tumbles through the plaza, which divides the pueblo into what is called the North House and the South House. The people of Taos are different from other Pueblo Indians, having been much influenced by the Kiowas and the Jicarilla Apaches. They hold many celebrations during the year.

From Taos, two other pueblos are of particular interest to the tourist. One is Cochití, halfway between Santa Fe and Albuquerque. The 650 people of Cochiti speak Keresan, a different language from Tewa and Tiwa. Cochití has a large kiva, a spacious plaza, and a fine church. The people are famed for their jewelry and drums. The drums are featured in their ceremonials.

Santo Domingo is seven miles south of Cochití. It is a thriving community, the largest of the Keres pueblos, with a population of about two thousand. It is also the most conservative. Huge signs warn that photography is strictly prohibited. The plaza is immense, with a trading post on one side. The big church has a façade of pure white, painted in many colors with Indian designs, including two horses. Most of the men wear red bands around their heads. Their hair is cut in bangs in front, and in back it is bound in a pug with colored yarn. The people make jewelry and pottery and sell it on the streets. With their total involvement in their own lives and their own ways, they are resisting the influence of the whites. Their pueblo is one of the last strongholds against the pressures of white civilization.

The Kiva, the Secret Place of the Most High

Few white visitors are privileged to see the inside of a kiva, the sacred ceremonial chamber of the Pueblo Indians. There, sheltered from the eyes of the curious, the Indian men celebrate their secret rituals.

Some of the kivas are circular, like giant drums. Other kivas, such as the Hopis', are rectangular, built on a straight north–south line. Probably the earliest kivas were circular, like those found today in Santo Domingo, Santa Clara, and Nambé.

The early kivas in Zuñi Pueblo were constructed in the plazas. After the coming of the Spaniards the kivas were hidden within the dwelling blocks, as they are to this day. The Zuñi kivas, like those of the Hopis, are rectangular but are not separate structures.

Hopi kivas. *Museum of Northern Arizona.*

Most of the kivas are halfway or more underground, like half-basements dug deep into the rock of the mesas or into the stony red clay of the valleys. The kivas have flat roofs, supported by log beams covered with adobe and entered through trap doors. Stout wooden ladders, some of them thirty feet or more tall, jut like giant spears through the trap doors from the floors of the kivas. In the middle of the floor of the kiva is a shallow fire pit. There is no chimney. The smoke curls up and out through the trap door.

The number of kivas in a pueblo varies, depending on the size of the pueblo and the number of religious groups. Each of the smaller pueblos has only one kiva. Old Oraibi (a Hopi pueblo in northeastern Arizona), possibly the oldest of the living pueblos, has thirteen kivas. In all, the Hopis have thirty-three.

Some of the kivas are small; some are huge. An early account described a kiva in Taos as large enough that a ball game could be played in it. The walls of the kivas are decorated with Indian symbols, painted in rich colors. Behind the ladder in most kivas is a low platform, and above it is a small, round hole, called the *si'papus*. The hole represents the beginning and the end, man's place of origin and his point of departure. Below the hole is the altar. In some kivas the altar setting is starkly simple; in others it is elaborate. Hopi altars have altar bowls and prayer sticks and are decorated with such items as pipes, feathers, rattles, and animal skins.

At stated times the males descend the ladders to perform their sacred rites. Some of the rituals are long, and in a few pueblos the women are permitted to bring food down to their menfolk. Sometimes the women are also permitted to see certain parts of the rituals, and on rare occasions they are permitted to conduct their own religious services in the kivas.

Different though the Pueblo Indians are, one community from another, they are united by their religion. They may speak different languages, belong to different tribes, and observe different traditions, but they have a common faith—that man must live in harmony with nature. This faith transcends all else. When they pray, whether in Taos, Zuñi, Acoma, or Old Oraibi, they pray for all people everywhere, not just for themselves.

For the most part these ceremonies are barred to the white man. He may observe some of the dances in the plazas, the rites in the fields before planting, and the fertility and harvest ceremonials. If he is fortunate, he may see the inside of a kiva, but the chances are that he will never be allowed to see the ceremonies held deep within these sacred chambers.

A replica of a Hopi kiva at the Museum of Northern Arizona. The fragments of paintings on the wall are from Awatovi Ruin, excavated by the Peabody Museum. *Museum of Northern Arizona.*

The Mystery
of the Indian Ruins

We think of the Indian country as "young," but in truth it is as old as many of the cities of the ancient world. While Babylon and Troy, Carthage and Ephesus, Nineveh and Corinth were flourishing on the shores of the Mediterranean Sea, Indians were founding communities in many parts of the Americas. Today little remains of the ancient cities of the Mediterranean, but in the Americas many remains of the prehistoric Indian communities can be seen.

The cliff dwellings of Canyon de Chelly in northeastern Arizona date back to the fourth century A.D. That was about the time of the fall of Rome and the beginning of the Dark Ages in Eu-

Square Tower House, Mesa Verde National Park. *Jack Boucher, National Park Service.*

A tourist photographs a section of Spruce Tree House, Mesa Verde National Park. Spruce Tree House is the third-largest and best-preserved classical cliff dwelling. *Troy Gruber, Bureau of Indian Affairs.*

The ladder in the foreground is the entrance to a kiva in Spruce Tree House. *Troy Gruber, Bureau of Indian Affairs.*

rope. Pueblo Bonito, the "Beautiful Village" of Chaco Canyon in northwestern New Mexico, was also founded during the Dark Ages. The cliff dwellings of Mesa Verde in southwestern Colorado and of Wupatki, northeast of Flagstaff, Arizona, were built during the time of the Crusades. And during that same period the Indian community with more than five hundred rooms, now called the Aztec Ruins, was built in northwestern New Mexico. Still more pueblos were built in America's Southwest as the Renaissance flowered in Europe.

Ruins of cliff dwellings and pueblos are to be found in many parts of the West, chiefly the Southwest. Though many of the pueblos are still "living" (that is, inhabited), the larger prehistoric communities are in ruins, abandoned many centuries ago. The ruins and their surrounding preserves range in size from a few acres to tens of thousands of acres. Aztec has 27 acres. Canyon de Chelly has 83,840 acres (its name is said to be a Spanish corruption of the Navajo word Tsegi, or Rock Canyon, and is pronounced "D'shay"). Like most of the larger ruins Canyon de Chelly is now a national monument.

Canyon de Chelly is about one hundred miles north and west of Gallup, near the Arizona–New Mexico line. Except for a small area the canyon is characterized by precipitous cliffs rising to about eight hundred feet. Six miles in from the mouth the canyon forks into two arms, the southern and the northern. In the latter, called Canyon del Muerto, are found most of the twelve hundred ruins of the area. The walls of Canyon del Muerto are high, and the gorge is narrow with sharp turns. On the floor of the canyon are groves of cottonwood trees and some Navajo hogans. The ruins for the most part are etched into the cliffs.

At one time there were probably hundreds of Indian villages in Canyon de Chelly. The Indians were farmers and hunters. They raised maize and squash and hunted with atlatls (spear throwers)

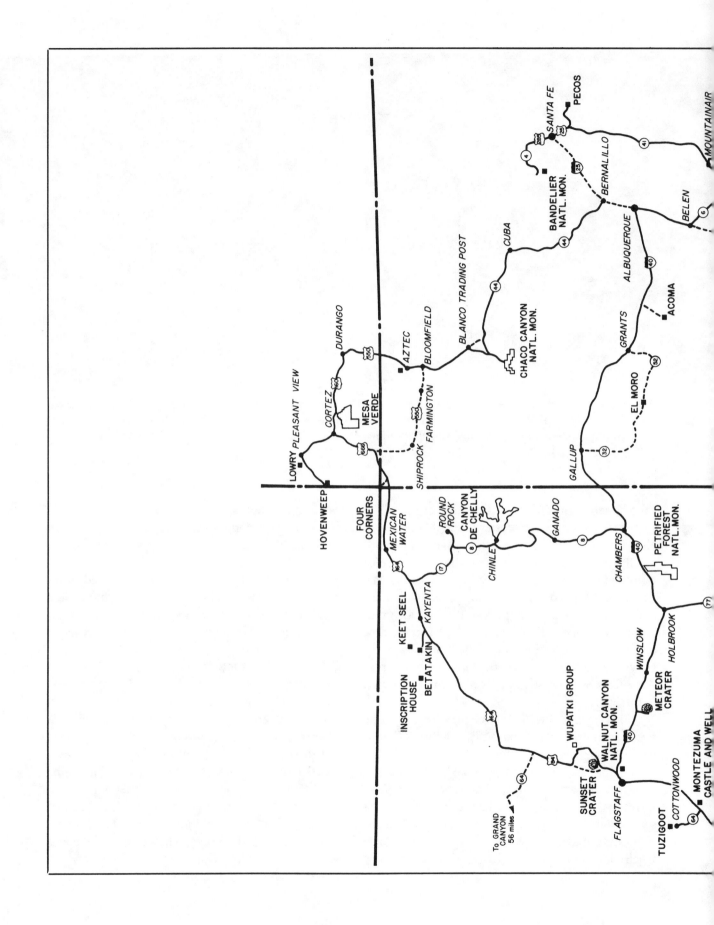

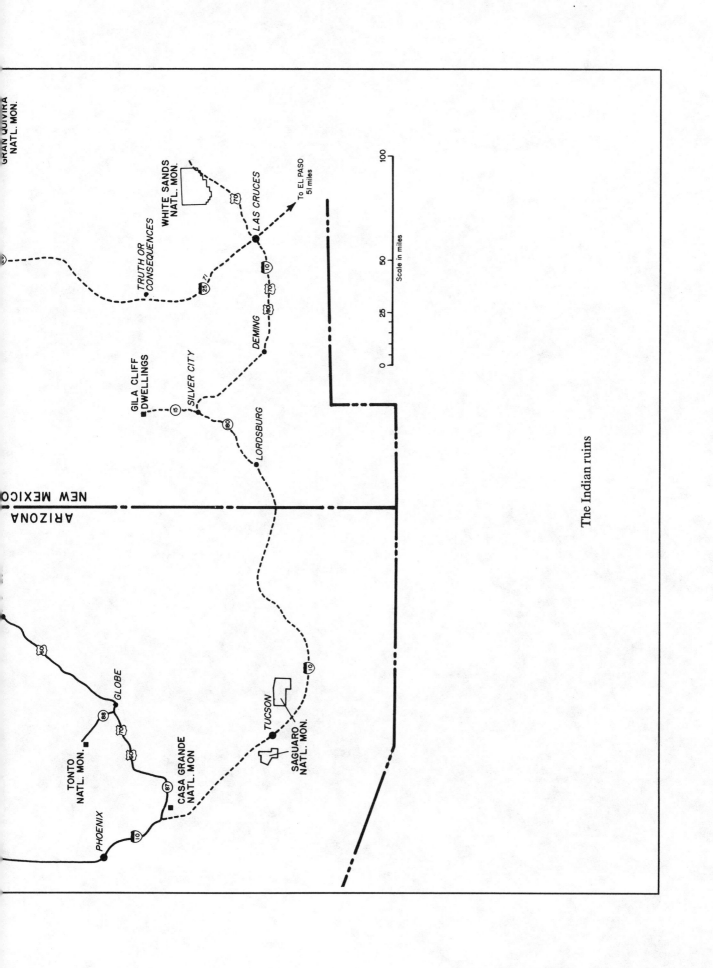

The Indian ruins

and bows and arrows. Their villages flourished for a time but then, for unknown reasons, were abandoned.

Centuries later the marauding Navajos filtered down from the north, took over the canyon, and made it their stronghold. In the meantime the Spaniards had arrived in the Southwest, and in 1805 one Lieutenant Antonio Narbona trapped and massacred a large number of Navajos in what is now called Massacre Cave in Canyon del Muerto.

The cliff dwellings called the White House are in the main canyon. Antelope House with its beautiful pictographs is in Canyon del Muerto. Here may be seen on the cliff face the Standing Cow Ruin and the Navajo painting of an attacking Spanish cavalry unit. In the same canyon is Mummy Cave with a large ruin and a three-story house.

A drive skirts the south rim, and there are a number of hiking trails in the region. Complete information can be obtained at the ranger station at the mouth of the canyon.

The Mesa Verde ruins and cliff dwellings are in the Four Corners country, ten miles east of Cortez, Colorado. This national park is large—51,334 acres—and worthy of several days' exploration. Here are three major cliff dwellings, of which the Cliff Palace is the most famous. Near the center of the park are the museum and Spruce Tree House, where the ancient rooms, 114 of them, extend almost one hundred feet back into a cave. The rooms are small, about six by eight feet, but possibly 250 persons lived in this cave at one time.

The third of the major attractions at Mesa Verde is Balcony House, named for its location and structure. On the mesa top is Cedar Tree Tower with its open kiva. An extensive picnic area was recently opened on Wetherill Mesa, part of the Mesa Verde National Park.

The White House, Canyon de Chelly National Monument, Arizona. *Fred E. Mang, Jr., National Park Service.*

The main ruin of Wupatki National Monument, Arizona. These red-sandstone pueblos were built by farming Indians. (Some authorities believe that the Hopi Indians are partly descended from these people.) Wupatki, which means Long House in the Hopi language, is the most important ruin in the San Francisco Mountains region. It was occupied longer than other pueblos, and the extreme dryness and excellent drainage have preserved wood, textiles, and other materials to an unusual extent. Rooms in this structure are dated between A.D. 1087 and 1197. It was abandoned about 1250. *George A. Grant, National Park Service.*

Wupatki, northeast of Flagstaff, Arizona, was in a sense a prehistoric boom town. Today it contains the ruins of some eight hundred homesites. Some are little more than pits enclosed in adobe foundations. Others are structures three stories high. Wupatki is a striking vista with its pueblos of red sandstone against the black of the basaltic cliffs. Today it is a national monument of 35,813 acres.

Sometime in the eleventh century a volcano erupted in the San Francisco Peaks near Wupatki, converting the region into a fertile farming area.

Tourists visiting Wupatki National Monument. *National Park Service Photo.*

The cinders and the ash, thirsty for water, seized and held the scarce moisture. The violent rupture also created a spring, and it, with the cinders and ash, created a fertile soil. A prehistoric land rush followed. Indians from many regions, with different customs, traditions, and legends, moved into the area. They intermixed and created a unique cultural pattern. Wupatki became a melting pot, and the new arrivals built one of the most spectacular pueblos in northern Arizona. Wupatki flourished for about a century and a half. Then, sometime in the thirteenth century, it was abandoned.

Among the best known of the prehistoric Indian ruins is Chaco Canyon—now also a national monument of 21,478 acres. In the canyon, forty miles north of Crown Point, New Mexico, is perhaps the greatest architectural development of the Pueblo Indians of the United States. Pueblo Bonito is the center of these ruins. In its heyday the community comprised about eight hundred rooms. It was the largest of the ancient apartment houses. At one time it housed twelve hundred persons. Some of its buildings were five stories high, a remarkable achievement for a people of the stone age.

At least two distinct groups of Indians pooled their skills to build the Chaco Canyon community. Archaeologists say that it is one of the most extraordinary pre-Columbian settlements north of Mexico. It flourished and was abandoned about five hundred years before the Pilgrims landed on the eastern shores of America.

The houses belonged to the women. They helped build them, took care of them, and enlarged and renovated them. The men built, owned, and maintained the kivas (there are thirty-two rectangular kivas in Chaco Canyon). The women also developed the arts and crafts. They devised the coil method of pottery making, distinguished for its form and decoration.

A dramatic hazard of the community was a towering, massive rock, later named Threatening Rock. It weighed about 100,000 tons and hovered over the canyon at a frightening angle. In an effort to protect themselves against it, the Indians braced it with poles and sticks. It teetered for years, and then one day, long after the Indians had abandoned the region, it crashed onto the ruins.

Among the smallest but most interesting ruins of the Southwest are the Aztec Ruins in northwestern New Mexico, near Farmington. Scientific research has been carried out there for years, and about three-quarters of the site has been excavated. What makes it additionally interesting is that Indians from other pueblos, after abandoning their own homes, went there.

The name Aztec has no connection with the Aztecs of Mexico. It was coined, or corrupted, by late-arriving Americans, centuries after the first Indians lived there.

The original pueblo was built in a U shape. It had about five hundred rooms. There were thirty-six small kivas and one large one. The great kiva, built for the whole community, was restored in 1934. It is circular and semisubterranean and has a stairway entrance at each end.

An interesting museum at this site contains ex-

The Standing Cow Ruin, Canyon de Chelly National Monument. This blue-and-white painting, Navajo in origin, gave the site its name. *Fred E. Mang, Jr., National Park Service.*

hibits of Indian tools and weapons, all made of stone, wood, or bone. The Indians at Aztec had no metal except a little copper that was used for bells.

There remains a question: Why did the Indians who built all these magnificent communities abandon them? Around A.D. 1200 the Indians of Mesa Verde left their farms on the mesas and moved down into the canyons. About a century later they abandoned the area altogether. Many of them drifted southward. They moved in and occupied the Aztec community, which had been abandoned by the Indians from Chaco Canyon. In like manner the Indians of Canyon de Chelly abandoned their clusters of apartment buildings.

Why? Was it a long period of drought? Was it disease? Was it the pressure of attacks by raiding and marauding peoples coming down from the north? Was it because the water supply failed? Or was it because they, as farmers who practiced irrigation, eventually leached out and sterilized the soil so that farming at those sites became hopeless?

Chaco Canyon National Monument, New Mexico. These ruins represent the highest point of prehistoric pueblo civilization in the United States. *Fred E. Mang, Jr., National Park Service.*

Pueblo Bonito, Chaco Canyon National Monument. *Fred E. Mang, Jr., National Park Service.*

Aztec Ruins National Monument, New Mexico, looking west from the highest point in the northeast corner. *Homer F. Hastings, National Park Service.*

Aztec Ruins National Monument. The ruins of a great prehistoric town built of masonry and timber in the twelfth century. *Fred E. Mang, Jr., National Park Service.*

After years of exploration the mystery of the ancient ruins still poses these questions, and the ruins are still to be found in many parts of the Southwest, each with its own dramatic story. Among them are the following:

Bandelier National Monument, New Mexico (27,103 acres)

El Morro National Monument, New Mexico (240 acres)

Gila Cliff Dwellings, New Mexico (583 acres)

Walnut Canyon, Arizona (1,879 acres)

Tonto National Monument, Arizona (1,120 acres)

Montezuma National Monument, Arizona (783 acres)

Hovenweep National Monument, Colorado and Utah (491 acres)

Casa Grande National Monument, Arizona (473 acres)

Navajo National Monument, Arizona (360 acres, including three of the best-known cliff dwellings, Keet Seel, Betatakin, and the Inscription House Ruins, as well as Tsegi Canyon)

Echo Cave Ruins and cliff dwellings, Monument Valley Navajo Tribal Park, Arizona

Kinishba Ruins, Apache Reservation, Arizona

Fortified Hills Ruins, Gila Bend Reservation, Arizona

Hopi Reservation, northeastern Arizona (ruins dating back to A.D. 1600 at Walpi and to A.D. 1100 at Old Oraibi)

Gila Cliff Dwellings, New Mexico. *Parker Hamilton, National Park Service.*

The Navajos

In the little more than one hundred years since the United States Army rounded up 8,500 Navajos and herded them on the "Long Walk" from northern Arizona to the detention camp at Fort Sumner in the Bosque Redondo in southeastern New Mexico, the Navajos have made a remarkable comeback. Today they are America's largest Indian group, numbering about 130,000. They have the largest reservation—nearly 16 million acres—larger than the combined states of Massachusetts, New Hampshire, and Vermont. The Navajo Reservation covers most of Arizona north and east of Flagstaff and overlaps into New Mexico and Utah.

The Navajos operate their own eleven-million-dollar sawmill at Navajo, New Mexico. They have electronic plants at Shiprock, New Mexico, and at Fort Defiance and at Page, Arizona. They have forty-six elementary schools, two boarding high schools, nine day schools, and eight school dormitories. In 1969 they established the Navajo Community College, the first college founded on an Indian reservation, operated by the Indians themselves.

The Navajos have 5 excellent hospitals, 3 health centers, and 115 public-health clinics. There are 130 trading posts on the reservation. They operate their own parks and recreation department. From their capital at Window Rock, Arizona, the Navajos govern their vast domain with a tribal council of seventy-two members, a chairman, and a vice-chairman.

They have managed to do what no other American tribe has done, hold onto their land. In fact, in the passing years they have expanded it and have become stronger rather than weaker.

The Navajos call themselves "the Dineh" ("the People"), and according to their lore they emerged from the underground in the Southwest. Anthropologists say that, like the other Indian groups, they came from Asia, across the Bering land bridge into Alaska. They are Athapascans, of the same linguistic stock as the Apaches. They drifted down through Canada, latecomers to the Western Hemisphere. When they arrived in what is now southwestern Colorado and northwestern New Mexico in the fourteenth century, they found Indians already there, established in pueblos. They raided the Pueblo Indians and overran their lands. From their victims they learned farming, weaving, certain arts and crafts, and some religious practices. In some of these activities they even surpassed the Pueblos.

They settled down and gradually changed from a nomadic to a sedentary life. They raised sheep, goats, and, after the Spaniards arrived, horses. They built permanent dwellings, circular one-room structures of logs and adobe, with the doorways facing the east. Unlike the Pueblos, they established no communities but scattered their hogans over the entire territory.

They claimed all the land between their four sacred mountains: Mount Blanco, east of Alamosa, Colorado; Mount Hesperus, west of Durango, Colorado; Humphrey's Peak, north of Flagstaff, and Mount Taylor, near Grants, New Mexico.

By the time the Spaniards arrived in the Southwest, the Navajos had become a powerful and aggressive people. They resisted the Spanish intrusion. When the Spaniards captured Navajo women and children and sold them into slavery, the Navajos retaliated by capturing Spaniards and selling them into slavery. They raided the Spanish settlements and drove off Spanish flocks and herds for their own use.

A Navajo hogan. *Bureau of Indian Affairs.*

They continued the practice against the Mexicans after Mexico won its independence from Spain and took over the Southwest. And they continued it against the white settlers after Mexico ceded the Southwest to the United States following the Mexican War. At length the white settlers appealed to the government for help against the raiding Navajos. This brought the Navajos into direct confrontation with the United States. It was a crucial turning point in the history of the tribe.

In 1846 the Navajo Nation and the United States government signed a treaty. Subsequently they signed six more treaties. All were violated by both sides. The government established Fort Defiance in the Navajo country, the first military post in the area. But the fighting went on. The Union government, by then engaged in the Civil War, determined to settle the "Navajo problem" once and for all. It adopted an all-out policy of subduing or annihilating the entire Navajo people. Columns of troops crisscrossed the Navajo country, hunting down and killing Navajos wherever they could find them. They killed sheep, cattle, and horses, burned the hogans, and destroyed the crops and orchards. About half of the Navajos eluded the troops and took refuge in the remote canyons and mountains. Those who were rounded up, about eighty-five hundred, were marched to Fort Sumner in the Bosque Redondo on the Pecos River. There, held as captives in a barren and forbidding country, they fell victims to raids by marauding Indian enemies. Disease killed them in horrifying numbers, their crops failed, the water was bad, there was a shortage of firewood, and they were helpless against infestations of insects.

For four years their pleas for relief fell on deaf

Navajo wagons parade at the Inter-Tribal Indian Ceremonial, Gallup, New Mexico. *Mullarky Studio.*

ears. In 1868, after their incarceration at Fort Sumner was an admitted failure, they were given the choice of being removed to Indian Territory (Oklahoma) or returning to a portion of their former country in the Southwest. They chose to return to the Southwest. The treaty providing for their return was the eighth and last treaty between the Navajos and the United States government.

Since then, in a little more than a century, the Navajos have become the leading tribe in the United States. Unlike other reservations the Navajo Reservation has grown in size. By executive order and congressional action at least a dozen additions have been made to the reservation. The Navajos are increasing in population at a rate five times as fast as the national average. In addition to the 125,000 Indians living on the main Navajo Reservation, another 3,500 live in the off-reservation communities of Ramah, Cañoncito, and Alamo, New Mexico.

Most of the Navajos are young; the median age is younger than eighteen. One in four Navajos is between eight and thirty-five years old.

Many other Indian tribes have lost their languages, but more than 97 per cent of the Navajos still speak their own tongue. Most of them also speak English to some extent.

Many Navajos still live in their traditional hogans, where the major ceremonies are held. The hogans continue to be tied to the secular and religious life of "the People." But more and more Navajos are now living in frame dwellings equipped with modern appliances.

World War II wrought the big change in Nava-

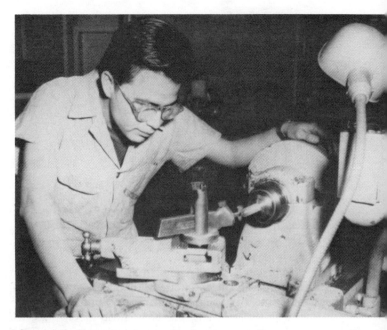

Navajo workers at the General Dynamics plant, Fort Defiance, Arizona. Rolls of electrical wire can be seen in the foreground. *Bureau of Indian Affairs.*

The Intermountain School machine shop. *Bureau of Indian Affairs, Department of the Interior.*

jo life. More than fifteen thousand Navajos were recruited for work in industries and on railroads. Another thirty-six hundred served in the armed forces. When the war ended, a good many did not return to the reservation. Those who did brought back new concepts, which were soon reflected in Navajo life. Dramatic changes began to take place on the reservation and in the tribe's dealings with outsiders and the government. The tribe developed industrial and commercial enterprises involving arts and crafts; timber, oil, and gas production; and power plants. They also established a first-rate parks and recreation department with their own corps of Navajo Rangers. Today they have an excellent system of tribal parks, campgrounds, and picnic grounds. At Monument Valley, twenty-six miles north of Kayenta, Arizona, they have established Monument Valley Navajo Tribal Park with a visitors' center and an arts-and-crafts shop. And at Window Rock, one of the scenic attractions of the area, they have established the modern seat of their tribal government, with a complex of buildings.

Nearby is the Navajo Museum and Zoo. Just south of Window Rock is Tse Bonito Tribal Park with several imposing sandstone monoliths called the Haystacks. The park was named for the spring

that was the first stopping place out of Fort Defiance in 1864, when the thousands of Navajos started their "Long Walk" to the Bosque Redondo.

On the Arizona-Utah border is Lake Powell Navajo Tribal Park, near splendid Lake Powell, created by Glen Canyon Dam on the San Juan River. This is a huge park of 2.25 million acres. Nearby is the sacred Navajo Mountain, 10,338 feet high, and the famous Rainbow Bridge.

Navajo National Monument near Tsegi is run by the National Park Service. It has three attractions in three separate locations: Inscription House, where an ancient inscription was found; the historic Keet Seel (Broken Pottery) Ruin, and Betatakin (Ledge House), the ruin of a pueblo community that was abandoned seven hundred years ago.

West and south, adjoining Grand Canyon National Park, is Grand Canyon Navajo Tribal Park, a spread of about 360,000 acres. The park straddles the breath-taking Little Colorado Gorge. There the roaring Little Colorado flows into the Colorado River, and near there, at Navajo Point, is the Desert View Campground, with Cedar Mountain standing by.

Not so many years ago few of these remote areas were accessible to the public. Now all of them are.

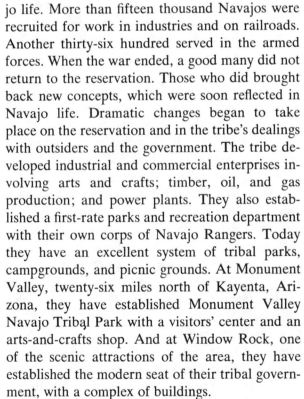

Turquoise

Indians of the Southwest cherish turquoise not only for its beauty but also for its meaning in their lore. The Navajos say:

When the Dineh came from the underworld, First Man brought turquoise with him. From their high places, the Dineh found much of the land covered with water. There was no sun, no moon. First Man directed shovels to be made of turquoise to dig the channels to drain the water. And it was done. With shovels of turquoise tipped with coral they drained the water.

From his high place First Man saw that at dawn the White Light rose in the east, and that the Yellow Light rose in the west. When they met in the sky, it was day. But even so it was not light enough. So First Man took a piece of the rich blue turquoise that he had brought from the underworld and chipped and chiseled it until it was round and flat and smooth. Then on its surface he etched a face. He gave the radiant disk to Johano-ai, the Sun Carrier.

Thus, when Johano-ai, mounted on his beautiful turquoise stallion, rides through the skies, the turquoise sun he carries banishes the storm clouds and brings pleasant blue skies.

The Zuñis also have their lore about turquoise. They say that turquoise was stolen from the blue of the heavens by the storm. To them it is the symbol of the vaulted sky and the restless sea, a gift of the sky and a protection from evil.

In Zuñi country the use of turquoise antedates the arrival of the Zuñis themselves. In the ruins of Hawikuh, a pre-Zuñi community, inlaid turquoise has been found in combs and amulets. Fray Marcos de Niza, a Francisan missionary, reported in 1539: "The people have Emralds (*sic*) and other jewels, although they esteem none so much as *turqueses*, wherewith they adorn the walls of the porches of their houses and their apparell and vessels. They use them instead of money."

In ancient Pueblo Bonito, in Chaco Canyon, more than fifty-thousand pieces of turquoise, all hand-worked, were found in a single chamber.

The ancients attributed many different powers to turquoise—victory, good fortune, steadfast friends. It was also revered as a potent love charm. The Navajos show their four rain gods wearing necklaces of turquoise, and they decorate their god of the whirlwind with pendants of turquoise. Apache medicine men wear turquoise, and the Pueblo Indians bury turquoise with their dead.

Yet, much as the Indians of the Southwest esteemed turquoise, they were late in adopting it in their jewelry making. The Zuñis did not begin using it in jewelry until about 1890. But once they started, they used it more extensively than the Navajos did.

The oldest Navajo jewelry utilizing turquoise also goes back only to about the turn of the century. The early jewelry of the Navajos had no stone settings at all. They tended to put more emphasis on silverwork, both hammered and cast, using turquoise mainly as decoration. Even today, though a good deal of their jewelry is decorated with turquoise, they use less of it than the Pueblos and the Zuñis do. The Zuñis also use turquoise in their carvings of spirits and animals.

It was natural that the Indians of the Southwest used turquoise, for it is found in rock deposits in the Indian country of Arizona, New Mexico, Colorado, and Nevada. It is also found today in the Cerrillo Peaks and the Burro Mountains of New Mexico, in Esmeralda and Nye counties of Nevada, and in the Mojave Desert.

The oldest turquoise mines are in far-distant reaches of the world—in India, Central America, Turkestan, and Iran and on the Sinai Peninsula. The Egyptians dug turquoise in the Sinai seven thousand years ago. It has probably been mined since the stone age. Today some of this "foreign" turquoise finds its way into the Indian jewelry of the Southwest. In its cruder form, as a mineral, turquoise is not particularly scarce, but turquoise *gems* are rare. Tons of minerals yield only a few gems.

Turquoise is only moderately hard, harder than glass but easily marred by harder materials. The ideal color of turquoise is a cool sky blue or a light cerulean blue. In most turquoise there is a tendency toward greenishness, ranging all the way from a pale green to a heavy solid green. Some regard greenishness in turquoise as lowering the value of the stone. Still, many Indians prefer the green stones. The Zuñis choose deep, clear colors and well-matched stones, and they are partial to spider-web turquoise, which has delicate tracings of black lines.

Ever since the ancients dug for turquoise in the Nishapur mines of Persia (now Iran), experts have been debating what is true quality in turquoise. The ancient Persians held that the charm of turquoise depends on a quality they called *zat*, a milky appearance that indicates a certain density. If the turquoise did not have *zat*, the Persians counted it as inferior.

The American Indians' evaluation is different. They have their own scale of quality. To them the intrinsic value of turquoise is incidental to its mystical qualities. It guards the wearer from harm, enables him to banish dark forebodings, and excites joyous emotions.

Today imitations abound. Synthetic stones are used in some Indian jewelry, and some are bathed in oil for temporary luster. But the true value of fine turquoise remains unchallenged, a jewel of rare beauty.

The woman is wearing silver and turquoise jewelry and a belt with large silver buckles. *Smithsonian Institution National Anthropological Archives, Bureau of American Ethnology Collection.*

Navajo Rugs

The Navajos have been weaving for about 250 years. The transition from weaving blankets to weaving rugs came between 1870 and 1890, when commercial blankets arrived in the Southwest. The weaving of Navajo blankets is a long-dead craft, and the weaving of Navajo rugs is a dying one. Today fewer and fewer Navajo women can afford to weave rugs. They do it in their spare time, when they are not working for a salary or when the wool from the sheep they raise cannot be sold at a fair profit. They then card and spin the wool and weave it into rugs. Otherwise they sell the wool by the pound. As with other Indian crafts, the scarcity of genuine Navajo rugs serves to enhance their value.

The Navajos had long been exposed to weaving in their contacts with the Pueblos, the Pimas, and the Papagos. But they did not learn to weave until the Spaniards brought in sheep. Then, plundering and marauding, the Navajos raided the Pueblos, captured and carried away the Pueblo women, and stole their sheep. From the captive women the Navajos learned to raise sheep. The Navajo women learned to spin the wool and to weave on upright, or vertical, looms. They created intricate designs and in time became so expert that they surpassed the Pueblos in the quality of their weaving.

The Navajo women developed the craft into a fine art and expanded it into an industry. They enlarged the flocks of sheep. They experimented with the natural colors they found in many plants and concocted durable dyes. They used white and black wool in natural colors, mixed them to produce gray, developed many shades of yellows and rich indigo blue, mixed blues and yellows to produce greens, and make various shades of red from earths and plants. The brilliant dark red found in many Navajo rugs is known as Ganado red (named for the site of Hubbell's Trading Post in Arizona).

The Navajos developed many different weaves, among them the diagonal and diamond twills. As their skills increased, their styles evolved from one pattern into another. The first patterns, those of the late 1700's, were simply stripes of many colors, some matched, some contrasting. These gradually evolved into broken stripes, or terraces. This style gradually gave way to the diamond pattern, and it was while this pattern was in vogue that the Indians made the transition from blanket to rug weaving. Less expensive, commercially made blankets (Pendletons) were at first issued to them by the government and were later purchased. With commercially made blankets available the traders would no longer buy hand-woven blankets from the Navajos. But they would buy rugs, and so the Navajos turned to weaving rugs.

Each area developed its own style. Around Ganado they wove rugs in red, black, gray, and white in geometric designs. The Indians of the Two Gray Hills area wove rugs in the natural colors of the wool, usually with black borders, in geometric designs.

The Tuba City region became known for its gray, white, red, and black rugs in what the weavers called "storm designs," with jagged symbols of lightning and a boxlike figure in the middle.

The weavers of the Shiprock area produced rugs with the familiar *yei* design, the tall, slender figures resembling those in Navajo sand paintings. The *yei* are symbols of supernatural beings.

Keams Canyon rugs are red, black, gray, and white in much the style of those of Ganado.

Other areas developed other styles, and in all there is a wide range of variations.

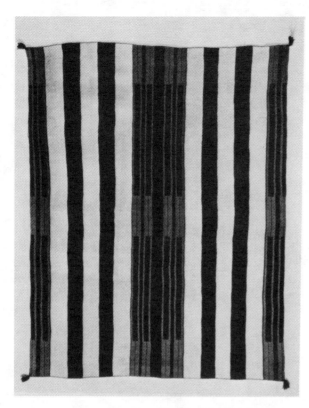

Navajo chief pattern blanket, ca. 1850–65. *Natural History Museum of Los Angeles County.*

Navajo serape-style blanket, ca. 1840–60. *Southwest Museum, Los Angeles.*

Navajo serape-style blanket, ca. 1860–70. *Natural History Museum of Los Angeles County.*

Navajo terraced child's blanket, ca. 1875–85. *Southwest Museum, Los Angeles.*

Navajo rugs may still be found in trading posts on the Navajo Reservation and in Indian stores, especially in the West, but most of the fine specimens—the antiques—are now in private collections or in museums.

Hubbell Trading Post, Ganado, Arizona. Navajo Indians have traded here since the post was founded by Don Lorenzo Hubbell in 1878. It is now a National Historic Site and is open daily. *Bob Petley, Petley Studios, Phoenix, Arizona.*

The Hopis

The name Hopi means "Peaceful People." The Hopis are deeply religious. They believe that everyone must live in peace and harmony with nature. Yet in early times they protected their faith with violence against their enemies, the Navajos and the Spaniards. Living on top of three mesas in northeastern Arizona, they withstood the onslaughts of their enemies for centuries.

Today the Hopi Reservation is an island within an island, completely surrounded by the Navajo Reservation. The inner island, some 631,000 acres, is totally Hopi. This is their stronghold. Around it is an area of 1,841,000 acres that is owned jointly by the Hopis and the Navajos. Each tribe has an undivided one-half interest in this area. The entire region lies within the huge Navajo Reservation. The Hopis and the Navajos fought for years over the lands that they now occupy. At last the issue was decided by the courts.

The Hopi villages are clustered on three mesas along Arizona State Highway 264. The mesas are numbered from east to west: First Mesa, Second Mesa, and Third Mesa.

The Hopis have lived on these mesas for more than a thousand years. As a people they are probably a mixture of Indian groups. Excellent farmers, they grow squash, beans, corn, cotton, and fruits on the desert lands below the mesas. The growing season is short, and the rainfall limited. Because of this they ask the gods for rain and good and bounteous crops, and at the same time they pray for the well-being of all peoples.

Just the same, the Hopis are strongly individualistic. They resisted the whites from the beginning. When the Spaniards tried to convert them to Catholicism, they killed the priests. They joined the Pueblo Indians in the revolt that temporarily drove out the Spaniards. All the Hopi villages except one joined in the revolt. The Hopis attacked and destroyed this village and then took in its refugees. Thirteen years later the Spaniards came back, but so formidable was the Hopi resistance that the Spaniards gave up trying to reconquer them.

The individualism of the Hopis is also reflected in their civil government. At first the Hopi villages tried to deal separately with the federal government, but the government insisted on dealing with the Hopis as a tribe. At length the Hopis reluctantly elected the Hopi Tribal Council to represent them. But to this day each village retains its political autonomy and runs its own affairs.

In social and religious affairs everything centers around the mother. The mother's clan is the ruling force of the family. The Hopis have many ceremonials. Most of them are held in their plazas. Some are closed to outsiders, but some are open, and these attract many hundreds of visitors, especially the Snake Dance, which is performed with live snakes. Each village has several kivas and a number of cults.

In their workaday lives in addition to farming many of the Hopi men are tradesmen, plumbers, carpenters, electricians, mechanics, and equipment operators. Both men and women are excellent craftsmen, and many of them are true artists. Hopi pottery and basketry are widely known, as are their silverwork, their weaving, and their imaginative carvings of kachina dolls. The Hopi Silvercraft Guild stores on the reservation market the finest of their work. Many visitors buy there, even Indians from other pueblos. Also a good deal is shipped off the reservation and sold elsewhere.

Perhaps as interesting as the crafts are the Hopi villages themselves. With changing fortunes, some of the villages have been moved, some abandoned,

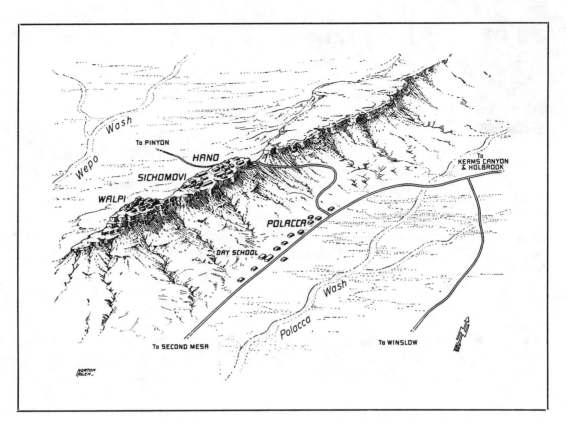

First Mesa

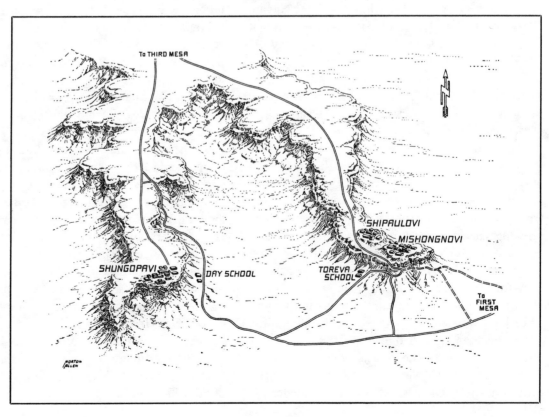

Second Mesa

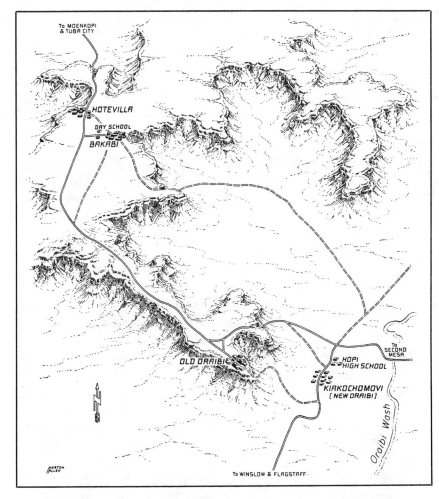

Third Mesa

Panoramic maps of the three mesas. *Walter Collins O'Kane, Sun in the Sky: The Hopi Indians of the Arizona Mesa Lands (Norman, University of Oklahoma Press, 1950).*

and some almost lost except in legend. The villages themselves are almost living artifacts.

There are three villages on each mesa. Walpi, on the First Mesa, was founded about 1680, the year of the Pueblo Rebellion. Sichomovi was founded about seventy years later, sixteen years before the American Revolution. Hano was founded by Tewa Pueblo Indians who fled from New Mexico at the time of the rebellion.

On Second Mesa, Shungopovi was rebuilt on the mesa top when the first village, at a lower level, was destroyed in the rebellion. Mishongnovi, a very old community, was re-established where it now stands just after the rebellion. Shipaulovi was built about the same time, possibly as an alternative refuge from the Spaniards.

On Third Mesa, the westernmost mesa, stands Old Oraibi. This village, dating back more than

eight hundred years, is perhaps the best known of all the Hopi villages. It has a colorful and strife-ridden history of dissidence and secession. In 1906 one faction moved out and started a new village, Hotevilla, also on Third Mesa. Another group, for different reasons, moved out and in 1890 formed New Oraibi. Still another group split off from the Hotevilla group and built the village of Bakabi on Third Mesa.

Forty miles west of Third Mesa is the Hopi farming community of Moenkopi, unique because of its irrigated fields. It is the westernmost of the Hopi villages.

Strong individualists though they are, the Hopis are held together by their religion. More than anything else it has helped them preserve their ancient way of life.

The Zuñis

Forty miles south of Gallup, on New Mexico State Highway 53, is Zuñi Pueblo, the only surviving pueblo of Coronado's fabled Seven Cities of Cíbola. Zuñi is the largest pueblo in New Mexico. More than five thousand Zuñis (the name is a Spanish corruption of Sünyítsi) live there, in the valley of the Zuñi River, in the shadow of Thunder Mountain. It is old—about a thousand years old.

Zuñi Pueblo, in Valencia County, was once the center of a large number of settlements in what is now New Mexico—among them Ojo Caliente, Nutria, Pescado, and Tekapo. Today the Zuñi Reservation covers about 440,000 acres, mostly in McKinley County. In times past the range of the Zuñis was much larger, extending from Gallup to St. Johns, in eastern Arizona. After the white man came, the Zuñis ranged eastward to the Río Grande and northward to the Gila River. In those years the region was the scene of pageantry and blazing drama rarely enacted in a comparable area anywhere. The Indians called this tribal range Shíwona. When the advance party of Spaniards arrived in 1539, the Zuñis had roamed the region for five hundred years.

The first messengers from the Spaniards were Indians sent ahead by a Barbary black named Estevanico, who had once been a slave. The Indians took with them Estevanico's magic token, a gourd painted scarlet and decorated with a white feather and a black feather. Inside the gourd were pebbles, and when they shook it, it rattled. The Zuñi chief hurled the gourd to the ground and warned that if Estevanico intruded he would be killed. Estevanico ignored the warning. Instead he donned his most elegant clothes and, leading his handful of armored soldiers, started for Zuñi Pueblo. Some distance behind his force was the main body of the Spanish expedition, headed by

Marcos de Niza, a Franciscan friar. The expedition had been sent from Mexico City by the Spanish viceroy Antonio de Mendoza. Their objective was to capture the remarkable multistoried pueblos of Shíwona for Charles V of Spain and at the same time to convert the Indians to Catholicism. The Spaniards, mispronouncing the name Shíwona, called the region Cíbola.

When Estevanico and his men entered the community, brandishing weapons, the Indians were waiting. They trapped Estevanico, seized and stripped him, locked him up, and the next morning killed him.

Fray Marcos prudently retreated. The next year Francisco Vásquez de Coronado showed up with seventy-five cavalrymen and thirty infantrymen and, in the Battle of Hawikuh, conquered the Zuñis.

But that was not the end of the bloodshed. The Zuñis were subdued but not subjugated. They ceased their hostility, but their will to be free was not dead. It was a hair-trigger peace.

Throughout the next century violence broke out sporadically. The Zuñis killed two friars and then fled to their stronghold on Thunder Mountain, the great rock mesa jutting one thousand feet above the valley.

When the pueblos rebelled in 1680, more than twenty-five hundred Zuñis joined in the rebellion and drove out the Spaniards. When the Spaniards, under Diego de Vargas, returned with an overwhelming force in 1692, the Zuñis again took refuge on Thunder Mountain. They stayed there several years. When it was apparent that resistance was hopeless, they straggled back and reluctantly accepted their fate under the Spaniards.

In the meantime, their natural life had changed. Coronado had brought along cattle, sheep, swine,

Zuñi Indian women balance decorated pots on their heads at the Inter-Tribal Indian Ceremonial, Gallup. *New Mexico Department of Development.*

work horses, mules, and fowls. The Zuñis, who had been successful farmers, had grown corn, hunted, and gathered wild foods. With the arrival of the Spaniards they became herders and stock-growers.

Before the conquest the Zuñis had a highly developed pottery craft handed down from the older women to the younger. The best of the early pottery was black painted over white clay. After the conquest the Zuñis lost interest in ceramics. Their skills, their inventiveness deteriorated. Some of the pueblos stopped making pottery altogether. Years later some undertook to revive the craft. They began using red, as well as black, and created some original and dramatic designs. But in time they became standardized, and the original freshness was lost. Today little pottery is made at Zuñi Pueblo.

In another craft, however, the Zuñis have become proficient: silver jewelry. Among the jewelry of the Pueblo Indians the Zuñis' is distinctive. They have mastered the use of shell beads—seashells, olivellas, clams, and oysters—and they have become noted for their beautiful turquoise and shell mosaics. Often their work is elaborate—clusters of brilliant stones on rings and pins, often distinctive by the use of jet.

Much as Zuñi life has changed since the coming of the white man, in one respect it has changed but little—that of religion. The life of the Zuñis is religion-oriented. The sun is the source of all life, representing the supreme deity. The most spectacular of the religious ceremonies—and perhaps one of the most impressive of all Indian rituals—is the Shalako Kachina Ceremony. Part of this ceremony, held in late November or early December of each year in Zuñi Pueblo, is open to the public. The giant Shalako figures are impersonations of the sacred kachinas (see the next section). The first of the ceremonies takes place in middle or late afternoon. This part is usually open to the public. Rituals are held at several locations. Later in the evening there are festivities in the Shalako houses. Various Indian religious characters perform ancient ceremonies. The next day there is a race between the Shalako figures on the south side of the Zuñi River. The Shalako figures, so tall that they are ungainly and almost top-heavy, run back and forth. The Zuñi Indians watch with anxiety, for, should a Shalako figure stumble and fall, it would be an omen of bad luck.

Few religious ceremonies have survived from such ancient times. The Shalako reflects the indomitable faith of the Zuñi people.

The Sacred Kachinas

Often the newcomer's first impression of the kachina statues is that they are Indian dolls. They are much more. To the Hopi, the Zuñi, and other Pueblo Indians, they are symbols of benevolent supernatural beings. Kachinas represent the life force of mankind.

In size they range from a few inches to more than a foot high. The Hopis carve them from the roots of cottonwood trees, paint them in vivid colors, and dress them in pelts, feathers, protruding eyes and ears, beaklike noses and mouths, sometimes horns or claws, and usually elaborate headdresses.

There are many Hopi kachinas; the number is almost limitless. Each kachina represents a different spirit, though the more formidable of the gods are never impersonated. The latter are, in the hierarchy of spirits, Sky Father and Mother Earth. They may be thought of as principles of life and beauty.

It is a Hopi principle that everyone must live in peace and harmony with nature. Also, since the Hopis have high regard for their ancestors, the kachina dances have elements of ancestor worship. All these spirits, some personified in kachinas, guide their lives.

The lore of the kachinas and the lives of the Hopis are interwoven. The gods taught them to farm, to dance, to hunt, to weave, and to make pottery, baskets, and jewelry. The spirits danced in their fields when rain was needed, and the rains came. They danced for them when the Indians were sad or lonely. They brought good times, happiness, prosperity, serenity, joy.

So it was until the evil times came. Then the good feelings, the joy, the prosperity vanished. The Hopis and the spirits fought. The spirits went away and refused to come back.

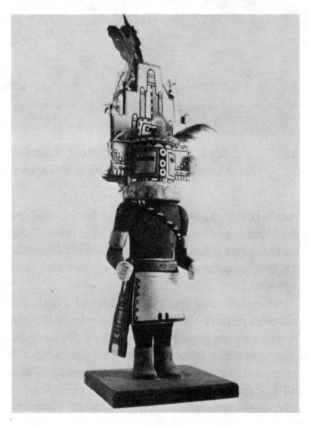

Niman Kachina. *Marc Gaede, Museum of Northern Arizona.*

The Hopis were in despair. They suffered. They pleaded. At last the kachinas agreed to compromise. They permitted the people to impersonate them. The men disguised themselves as kachinas with costumes, wigs, paint, feathers, wings, and claws. The kachinas taught them their ceremonies and rituals, and the menfolk danced and made ceremonies.

The kachinas were pleased. They rewarded the best dancers by endowing them with their own sacred spirits. Ever since then each year the Hopi

116

Patun Kachina (Squash Kachina). *Marc Gaede, Museum of Northern Arizona.*

Kachinas. Left: unidentified; right: Kweo (Wolf). *Heard Museum Collection.*

Old Mask Kachina (Tewa Clan). *Marc Gaede, Museum of Northern Arizona.*

men have impersonated the kachinas and performed their religious ceremonies. They dance to propitiate the kachinas for all mankind, not only for themselves.

The kachinas reflect the attitude of the Hopis toward their children. They are kind to them but often strict. Sometimes the kachinas are regarded as ogres that frighten and even eat children. When children are willful, the kachinas are said to impose severe punishment. The parents are then able to intercede and plead for leniency, which the kachinas always bestow.

In their midsummer ceremonial, the Niman (Home) Festival, the Hopis celebrate the summer solstice. The ceremony lasts for sixteen days. When it is finished, the Hopis bless the kachinas with a short ceremony and pray for the blessings of the kachinas on all peoples everywhere and on all plants and animals. Then the kachinas "depart" for their "home" in the San Francisco Mountains north of Flagstaff, Arizona.

All through these ceremonies the kachinas wear masks. Then, in the Bean Dance, the men take off

Kachina, Buffalo Mosairu. *Claude Bate, Heard Museum Collection.*

their false faces and dance throughout the night. The young look on and thus learn the meaning of the kachinas and are themselves prepared for their own eventual role as impersonators of the kachinas.

The men dominate the kachina ceremonies; they even impersonate the female kachinas. Occasionally women's groups take part in some of the dances and processions.

The term "kachina" is used by all Pueblo Indians. It does not, however, have precisely the same meaning for all the tribes. Consequently the figurines are different from tribe to tribe. Those of the Hopis are small, a few inches tall, and are carved to stand alone. Those of the Zuñis, and some of those of the Río Grande Pueblos, are usually taller and heavier, a foot or so tall. Often the taller ones cannot stand alone.

Figurines of the kachinas are sometimes given by Indians as gifts to remind the receiver of the Great Spirit.

There are magnificent collections of kachinas in a number of museums, notably in the Heard Museum in Phoenix, Arizona, and the Northern Arizona Museum in Flagstaff. There are also some fine private collections.

Today kachina dolls, like many other cherished crafts of the Indians, are being manufactured for the tourist trade. Some are carefully and imaginatively carved by the Indians, but many are made by non-Indians on what is virtually an assembly-line basis.

Butterfly Kachina Maiden (Polik Mana), a Hopi kachina. *Heard Museum Collection.*

The Pimas and the Papagos

The Pimas and the Papagos of southern Arizona are of the same stock. Both are probably descended from the ancient peoples of the Hohokam culture, who prospered in the area of the Salt River Valley about the time of Christ. Factionalism split the two tribes centuries ago—and has split them several times since. On the eve of the Civil War, Congress established the Gila River Reservation south of Phoenix with agency headquarters at Sacaton. About one hundred years later, in 1962, the administration of the Pimas was divided between this reservation and the Salt River Agency at Scottsdale.

Today the Pimas and the Papagos live on six reservations, including the Gila River and Salt River reservations and the extensive Papago Reservation west of Tucson and extending south to the Mexico border. Some of the reservations are shared with the Maricopa Indians.

The Pimas called themselves the "River People." They distinguished themselves by their ingenious use of river water. They engineered the flow of water for considerable distances to their fields and constructed irrigation ditches, dams, and reservoirs. At one time they maintained a network of nearly two hundred miles of irrigation ditches, all built by hand. They produced superior crops, and built solid, permanent houses of adobe.

Then came marauders, Indian raiders from the east. The peaceful Pimas were no match for them and fled. After the raiders had left, the Pimas drifted back, to find their homes and fields destroyed. They started anew. They re-established their fields and rebuilt their water systems and houses. Again the raiders returned, and again the Pimas fled, later returning once more to rebuild. After the third raid the Pimas did not rebuild. Instead they erected temporary lodges and tilled

San Xavier Cathedral, Papago Reservation, Arizona. *Photograph by Doris Morris.*

their fields tentatively, ready at all times to flee to the mountains. Spanish missionaries and military forces and, later, American explorers entered their lands, but for the most part the Pimas followed their own ways.

Then gold was discovered in California. In 1849 gold seekers streamed through the Pima country. The Pima helped them, and the gold seekers pushed on. But when the rush was over, the whites returned, this time to stay. They settled on the rich farmlands of the Gila River and diverted the water for their own use. To get more water, the Pimas moved to the Salt River valley. The controversy over water continued for years. To provide irrigation water and electric power the government built Coolidge Dam on the Gila River. But the Pimas' rights to the water were never resolved.

The Pimas are good farmers. Today they operate a community farm on the Gila River Reservation. There they grow the famous Pima cotton. But there is not enough work for all. Only about one-third of the Pimas live on their reservations the year around. The remainder are obliged to seek work elsewhere.

During World War II a Pima Indian, Private Ira H. Hayes, was one of the six famous Marines who raised the American flag under heavy fire on the summit of Mount Suribachi on Iwo Jima. Only three of the six survived the war. When Hayes returned to the reservation, one thousand Pima Indians met to honor him at his birthplace, Bapchule, Arizona.

Today the Pimas live on three reservations in Arizona: the Gila River Reservation, south of Phoenix; the Salt River Reservation (47,000 acres), north of Scottsdale; and the Ak-Chin Reservation (21,500 acres), near Maricopa.

Nearly all the Pimas speak English. They have a high regard for education. The Spaniards did not succeed in converting them to Catholicism. Today they are mainly Presbyterian. Their basketry and pottery are widely known. Unfortunately their arts and crafts are dying out. Each year they hold a tribal fair called Mul-Chu-Tha, which features an Indian rodeo and Indian games and dances.

When the Papagos split away from the Pimas, they drifted southward and settled in the desert. They call themselves the "Desert People." Others call them the "Bean People." The Papagos live on three reservations: the Papago Reservation (2,775,000 acres), on the Arizona-Mexico border with agency headquarters at Sells; the San Xavier Reservation (17,000 acres), west of Tucson; and the Gila Bend Reservation.

One legacy the Spaniards left the Papagos was stock raising. Today the Papagos are best known as cattlemen and to a lesser extent as farmers. They have a good-sized tribal herd, managed by a livestock board of eight members. Income from the herd is not enough to support them, however, and many Papagos live in want.

Like the Pimas, the Papagos are basketmakers. They fashion coiled baskets in many shapes, using beargrass, yucca, and devil's-claw. They make attractive willow baskets and small souvenirs of horsehair. They also make a limited amount of pottery and carve wooden bowls, but these crafts have little economic importance. The income from them is not large enough to support the tribe.

The Spanish missionaries were more successful with the Papagos than they were with the Pimas. They converted the Papagos to Catholicism. The beautiful San Xavier del Bac Mission southwest of Tucson was built by Papago labor under the supervision of the clergy.

The big public festival of the Papagos is the three-day All-Indian Tribal Fair and Rodeo at Sells. It is held early in November, and is a colorful celebration. In addition to the rodeo it features games, dances, and contests, a happy getting-together time for the Papagos and their friends.

The Apaches

The mere mention of the name Apache evokes images of ruthless raiders and fierce warriors. The Apaches resisted white incursion into their lands almost to the last man. They asked no quarter, and they gave none. Their name is Zuñi for "Enemy."

While the Civil War raged in the East and South, hostile Apaches terrorized Arizona Territory and had it at their mercy. During those years and later one formidable leader after another—Cochise, Mangas Coloradas, Victorio, Geronimo—led them with such boldness and ferocity that it took more than thirty years to "pacify" them.

The Apaches are of the same linguistic stock as the Navajos—Athapascan. They drifted down from the north about the tenth century A.D. In the limitless expanse of the Southwest they moved apart. One group went its way and eventually became the Navajos. The other went its way and became the Apaches. The early Spaniards distinguished between the two groups by calling one group Apaches de Navajo and the other Apaches de Jicarilla (Jicarilla is Spanish for "Little Basket"). A characteristic of the Apaches has been their lack of tribal solidarity, as reflected in the many subtribes, bands, and families.

Today there are four major Apache reservations in the Southwest, and on each live several groups. The Jicarilla Apaches, whose reservation is in north-central New Mexico, are divided into two groups, the Olleros ("Mountain People") and the Llaneros ("Plains People"). The Mescalero Apaches, whose reservation is in southeastern New Mexico, are closely related to the Apaches of Texas and the eastern Chiricahuas. The western Apaches live on the adjoining Fort Apache and San Carlos reservations in eastern Arizona. There are found Chiricahua, White Mountain, San Carlos, Tonto, and Mohave Apaches. Still another Apache group lives at Camp Verde in central Arizona.

There are probably about fifteen thousand Apaches in the Southwest. About twelve thousand live in Arizona. About fifteen hundred live on the Jicarilla Reservation and about the same number on the Mescalero Reservation in New Mexico.

San Carlos is the largest of the Apache reservations, encompassing almost 1,900,000 acres. It is cattle and timber country. Fort Apache Reservation is almost as large, with nearly 1,700,000 acres. The Indians of Fort Apache call themselves the White Mountain Tribe. They have a forest of 720,000 acres and a tribal sawmill on the White River. They also have the largest privately owned recreation area in the western United States, with 300 miles of trout streams and several fine lakes. At Fort Apache is the site of the last cavalry post disbanded in Indian country. Nearby are the Kinishba Pueblo ruins.

The Jicarilla Apache Reservation is large, too, with more than 740,000 acres. Once the Jicarilla Apaches ranged over what is now Colorado, across New Mexico, and into Oklahoma. Although the Jicarillas, like the rest of the Apaches, are not Pueblo people, they are a link between the Pueblo Indians and the Indians of the Plains. In fact, they adopted many of the characteristics of the Plains Indians—beaded buckskin, braided hair, and even tipis. They were the sworn enemies of the Comanches, and their warfare with them was long and bitter. Eventually the Jicarillas took refuge in the mountainous area between Taos and Picurís Pueblo.

The Mescalero Apaches were influenced by the Indians east of them, those from Texas. The Mescaleros got their name from their practice of eating parts of the mescal cactus. Their reservation,

122

The puberty ceremony (also called the Sunrise Ceremony) for an Apache girl, conducted by the elders of the tribe on the Fort Apache Reservation, Arizona. *Bureau of Indian Affairs.*

northeast of Alamogordo in the Sacramento Mountains, is about 460,000 acres.

Today the Apaches are successful in many fields. They raise cattle and sheep, farm, are active in most of the trades, and are artists and business and professional men. Along with the Zuñis and other Indians of the Southwest, many of them are experts in fighting forest fires.

These pursuits are a far cry indeed from their early role as defenders of their territories against the whites. Raiding and using guerrilla tactics, the Chiricahua chief Cochise fought off the American army for ten years. At last, in 1871, when the

noted Indian fighter General George Crook was sent to run him down, Cochise surrendered. In 1873 the Apaches were rounded up and marched to the San Carlos Reservation. But Geronimo refused to give up. He struck again and again with raiding parties, fleeing across the Mexican border, hiding, and returning to strike again. In 1883, General Crook persuaded him to surrender, but in 1885, Geronimo fled again. The next year he surrendered once more and then escaped again. When he surrendered the last time, in 1886, he and his handful of warriors were sent to Fort Marion, Florida. Later he was moved to Alabama and then to Fort Sill, Oklahoma, where he died in 1909. Outnumbered and outgunned, the Apaches learned that bravery was not enough. The white tide rolled over them.

With their old way of life went many of their skills. Once Apache women were excellent basketmakers. No longer. For this reason the true, early Apache baskets are rare and expensive. Yet many of the old Apache ways—their ceremonials—survive. The Apache Mountain Spirits Dance is one of the best known of all Indian ceremonial dances. In July the Mescaleros celebrate the girls' puberty ceremony, and each season they perform the historic Bear Dance. Early in July the Jicarillas hold their annual feast, and in September near Horse Lake they commemorate the friendship of the two Apache branches, the Olleros and the Llaneros, with a reunion ceremony. In early fall they and the Taos Indians honor their great friendship by participating in each other's events.

The Apaches remain one of the most colorful and most remarkable of all the Indian peoples.

The mission church on the Mescalero Apache Reservation in southern New Mexico. It was built by Albert Braun, a Franciscan priest, with the aid of a handful of Apache Indians. As far as possible native materials were used: limestone was quarried from nearby hills, and timber was cut from the forests. The project was begun in the 1920's and was completed in the late 1930's. *New Mexico Department of Development.*

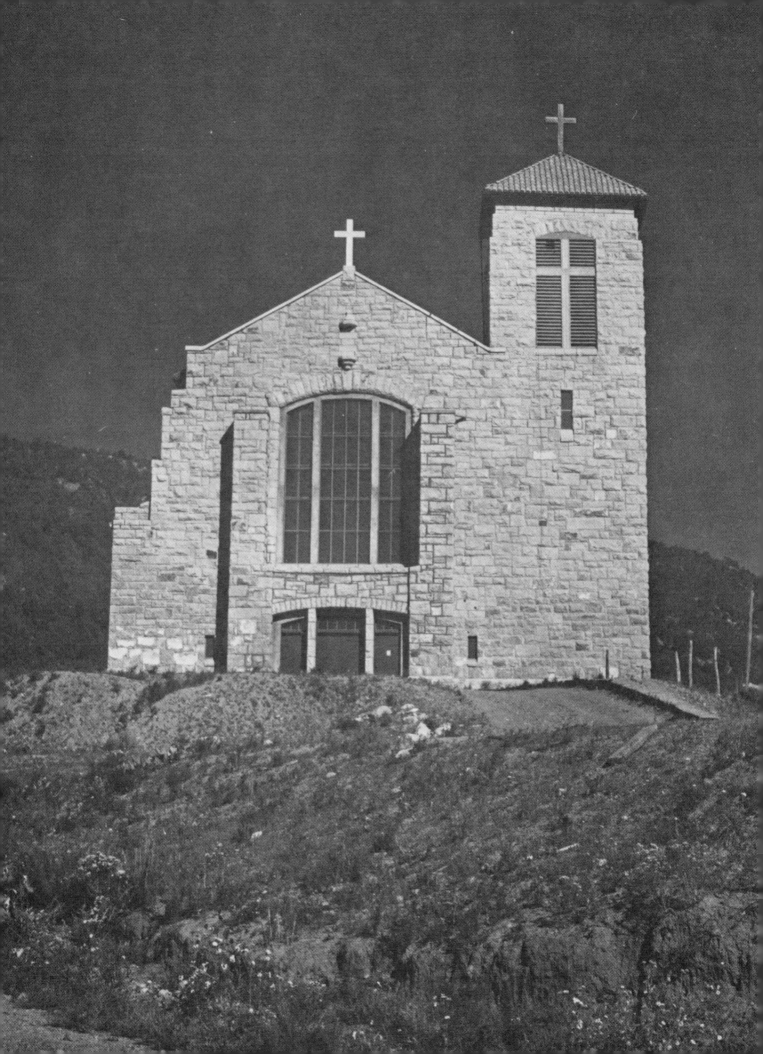

Mohave Indians parade at the Inter-Tribal Indian Ceremonial, Gallup. *Mullarky Studio*.

TRIBES AND RESERVATIONS

Tribe	Reservation or Location	Acres	Population	Address
		Arizona		
Apache				
Mohave-Apache	Fort McDowell	575	550	Rt. 1, Box 510 Scottsdale 85257
San Carlos	San Carlos	1,900,000	4,500	Box 0 San Carlos 85550
White Mountain	Fort Apache	1,665,000	6,000	Box 708 Whiteriver 85941
Yavapai-Apache	Camp Verde	500	500	Rt. 2, Box 615 Camp Verde 86322
Yavapai-Apache	Yavapai-Prescott	1,500	100	Box 1390 Prescott 86301

Colorado River
  Chemehuevi
  Cocopah
  Mohave
  Quechan
  Yuma
	Colorado River
	  (Arizona and
	  California)
		326,000	1,700	Rt. 1, Box 23-B
				Parker 85344

Havasupai	Havasupai	3,050	300	Supai 86435
Hopi	Hopi	2,473,000	5,000	Box 123 Oraibi 86099
Hualapai	Hualapai	995,000	680	Box 168 Peach Springs 86434
Navajo	Navajo	16,000,000	130,000	Window Rock 86515
Paiute	Kaibab-Paiute	120,000	60	Box 302 Fredonia 86022
Papago	Papago	2,775,000	5,500	Box 277 Sells 85634
Papago	Gila Bend	10,337	342	Gila Bend 85337
Papago	San Xavier	71,000	928	San Xavier 85640
Papago-Pima	Ak-Chin	21,500	250	Box 12 Sells 85634

Tribe	Reservation or Location	Acres	Population	Address
Pima-Maricopa	Salt River	46,000	2,300	Rt. 1, Box 120 Scottsdale 85256
Pima-Maricopa	Gila River	371,000	5,250	Box 97 Sacaton 85247

California

Tribe	Reservation or Location	Acres	Population	Address
Cahto	Laytonville	200	65	Laytonville 95454
Cahuilla	Agua Caliente	2,600	74	Palm Springs 92262
	Augustine	500	0	Thermal 92274
	Cabazon	1,700	5	Indio 92201
	Cahuilla	18,270	23	Anza 92306
	Santa Rosa	11,000	7	Hemet 92343
	Soboba	5,000	180	San Jacinto 92383
	Torres Martinez	25,330	65	Thermal 92274
Chukchansi	Table Mountain	. . .	. . .	Friant 93626
Chumash	Santa Ynez	100	42	Santa Ynez 93460
Diegueno	Barona	5,000	111	Alpine 92001
	Campo	15,000	30	Campo 92206
	Cuyapaipe	4,100	. . .	Pine Valley 92062
	Inaja-Cosmit	880	. . .	Julian 92036
	Manzanita	3,600	7	Pine Valley 92062
	Sycuan	640	31	El Cajon 92020
	Viejas	1,610	100	Lakeside 92040
	Santa Ysabel	15,500	144	Santa Ysabel 92070
Hoopa	Hoopa Valley	86,000	1,000	Hoopa 95546
Kashia-Pomo	Stewarts Point	40	75	Stewarts Point 95480
Luiseño	La Jolla	8,200	40	Valley Center 92082
	La Posta	3,600	0	Boulevard 92005
	Los Coyotes	25,000	42	Warner Springs 92086
	Mesa Grande	120	0	Santa Ysabel 92070
	Pala	7,700	255	Pala 92059
	Pauma Yuima	250	60	Valley Center 92082
	Pechanga	4,100	25	Temecula 92390
	Rincón	. . .	. . .	Valley Center 92082
	San Pasqual	1,380	20	Valley Center 92082
Maidu	Enterprise	40	4	Oroville 95965
Miwok	Jackson	330	7	Jackson 95642
	Shingle Springs	160	0	El Dorado 95623
	Sheep Ranch	1	1	Sheepranch 95250
	Tuolumne	323	50	Tuolumne 95379
Mixed (Wailaki-Yuki-Nomelacki-Mono-Pomo)	Round Valley	18,500	340	Covelo 95428
Paiute	Bishop	875	500	Bishop 93514
	Cedarville	17	13	Cedarville 96104

Tribe	Reservation or Location	Acres	Population	Address
Mono	Big Sandy	8	38	Auberry 93602
	Cold Springs	100	27	Tollhouse 93667
Paiute-Shoshone	Big Pine	280	50	Big Pine 93513
	Fort Bidwell	3,300	54	Fort Bidwell 92112
	Fort Independence	353	62	Box 67 Independence 93526
Paiute-Shoshone	Lone Pine	237	115	Lone Pine 93545
Paiute-Maidu	Susanville	30	45	Susanville 96130
Pit River	Alturas	20	12	Alturas 96101
	Big Bend	40	10	Big Bend 96011
	Lookout	40	2	Lookout 96054
	Montgomery Creek	72	4	Montgomery Creek 96065
	Roaring Creek	80	5	Montgomery Creek 96065
	X-L Ranch	9,200	30	Alturas 96101
Pomo	Dry Creek	75	14	Geyserville 95441
	Hopland	. . .	. . .	Hopland 95449
	Manchester, Point Arena	364	65	Point Arena 95468
	Middletown	108	21	Middletown 95461
	Sulphur Bank	50	30	Clearlake Oaks 95423
	Upper Lake	. . .	. . .	Upper Lake 95485
Serrano	Morongo	32,250	242	Banning 92220
	San Manuel	650	20	San Bernardino 92402
	Twentynine Palms	160	. . .	Twentynine Palms 92277
Tachi	Santa Rosa	170	82	Lemoore 93245
Tule River	Tule River	55,000	300	Box 589 Porterville 93257
Washoe	Woodfords Colony	80	250	Woodfords 95546
Wintun	Cortina	640	0	Williams 95987
	Colusa	270	17	Colusa 95932
	Grindstone	80	25	Orland 95963
	Rumsey	66	3	Rumsey 95679
Yurok	Hoopa Extension	6,800	150	Weitchpec 95546
	Resighini	230	0	Klamath 95548
	Trinidad	55	26	Trinidad 95570
	Berry Creek	33	2	Berry Creek 95916
	Big Lagoon	5	50	Orick 95555
	Colorado			
Ute	Southern Ute	307,000	760	Tribal Affairs Bldg. Ignacio 81137
	Ute Mountain	590,000	1,140	Towoac 81334
	Nevada			
Paiute	Pyramid Lake	1,195,086	400	Box 256 Nixon 89424

Tribe	Reservation or Location	Acres	Population	Address
	Summit Lake'	10,500	70	Box 284 Stewart 89437
	Winnemucca	340	130	Winnemucca 89445
	Fort McDermitt	16,400	360	McDermitt 89421
	Lovelock	20	140	Lovelock 89419
	Las Vegas	10	90	800 W. Paiute Dr. Las Vegas 89101
	Moapa	1,200	75	Moapa 89025
	Yerington (Campbell Ranch)	12	40	Yerington 89447
	Yerington	10	130	Yerington 89447
	Walker River	320,000	375	Schurz 89427
Paiute-Shoshone	Fallon Council	5,500	200	Fallon 89406
Paiute-Washoe	Reno-Sparks	30	500	78 Reservation Rd. Reno 89502
Shoshone	Battle Mountain	700	60	Battle Mountain 89820
	Shoshone-Temoak	200	250	Elko 89801
	Ruby Valley–Temoak	15,000	180	Elko 89801
	Elko Colony	200	150	Elko 89801
	Duckwater	800	70	Duckwater 89314
	Ely Colony	10	35	Ely 89301
	South Fork Colony	15,000	110	Lee 89829
	Yomba	4,700	60	Austin 89310
Shoshone-Paiute	Duck Valley	145,000	820	Owyhee 89832
Washoe	Washoe	900	1,200	Stewart 89437
	Washoe-Carson Colony	150	130	Carson City 89701
	Dresslerville Colony	40	160	Gardnerville 89401

New Mexico

Tribe	Reservation or Location	Acres	Population	Address
Apache-Jicarilla	Jicarilla	750,000	1,600	Dulce 87528
Apache-Mescalero	Mescalero	460,000	1,500	Mescalero 88340
Navajo	Ramah	. . .	1,060	United Pueblo Agency Box 1667 Albuquerque 87103
	Cañoncito	. . .	850	United Pueblo Agency Albuquerque 87103
	Puertocito (Alamo)	. . .	800	United Pueblo Agency Albuquerque 87103
	Checkerboard Area	. . .	15,000	Window Rock, Ariz. 86515
Pueblo	Acoma	25,000	2,500	Tribal Governor Box 64 via San Fidel Acomita 87049

Tribe	Reservation or Location	Acres	Population	Address
	Cochití	28,000	650	Box 1667 Albuquerque 87103
	Isleta	211,000	2,300	Isleta 87022
	Jémez	88,500	1,600	Rural Route San Ysidro 87053
	Laguna	420,000	2,500	Laguna 87026
	Nambé	19,000	225	Nambé Rt. J Santa Fe 87501
	Picurís	1,500	150	Penasco 87553
	Sandía	23,000	175	Box 1667 Albuquerque 87103
	Santa Ana	4,200	400	Box 1667 Albuquerque 87103
	Santa Clara	46,000	725	Española 87532
	Santo Domingo	70,000	2,000	Santo Domingo 87052
	San Felipe	49,000	1,000	Box 1667 Albuquerque 87103
	San Ildefonso	26,000	200	Rt. J, Box 315A Santa Fe 87501
	San Juan	12,000	650	Española 87532
	Taos	75,000	900	Box 258 Taos 87571
	Tesuque	17,000	200	Tesuque 87574
	Zía	112,000	425	San Ysidro 87053

A Pueblo woman baking bread in a beehive adobe oven at San Ildefonso. *New Mexico Department of Development.*

Tribe	Reservation or Location	Acres	Population	Address
	Zuñi	407,000	5,000	Box 338
				Zuñi 87327
Ute	Ute	. . .	few	Towoac, Colo. 81334
	Utah			
Ute	Allen Canyon	2,000	200	Blanding 84511
	Uintah-Luray	852,400	1,565	Fort Duchesne 84026
Shoshone	Goshute	76,500	110	Ibapah 84034

The mission church at Isleta, south of Albuquerque, New Mexico. The mission was built by Franciscan friars around 1630. *New Mexico Department of Development.*

Laguna (named for a lake formed by a nearby river) is the only pueblo founded since the arrival of Europeans in New Mexico. The mission was erected in 1699, and, unlike many of the old churches, it was constructed of stone rather than adobe. *New Mexico Department of Development.*

CAMPGROUNDS

Arizona

Colorado River Reservation (5 mi. N. of Parker, on both sides of river)

    Bluewater Marina (2 mi. N. of Parker): 80 units, water, toilet, fee
    La Mars Park (1 mi. W. of Parker): 50 units, water, toilets, fee
    Lost Lake (30 mi. N. of Blythe, Calif.): 200 units, water, toilets, fee
    Write: Chairman, Tribal Council, Rt. 1, Box 23-B, Parker, Ariz.   85344

Fort Apache Reservation (165 mi. E. of Phoenix)

    White Mountain: 18 campgrounds, 700 units, water, toilets, fee
    Write: White Mountain Recreation Enterprise, Box 218, White River, Ariz.   85941

Fort McDowell Reservation (20 mi. N.E. of Phoenix on State 87)

    Fort McDowell: 10 units, water, toilets, fee
    Write: Fort McDowell Reservation, Route 1, Box 907, Scottsdale, Ariz.   85251

Havasupai Reservation (floor of Grand Canyon)

    Havasupai Canyon (S. of Supai Village): water, toilets, fee
    Navajo Falls (S. of Supai Village): water, toilets, fee
    Write: Havasupai Enterprise, Supai, Ariz.   86435

Hopi Reservation (N.W. Ariz., within Navajo Reservation)

    Pumpkin Hill (W. of New Oraibi): no water, no toilets, no fee
    New Oraibi (1 mi. E. of New Oraibi): no water, no toilets, no fee
    Second Mesa: picnic area only, no water, no toilets, no fee
    Keams Canyon: public park, 12 units, water, toilets, fee
    Hopi Trailer Park (Keams Canyon): water, toilets, fee
    Write: Hopi Tribal Council, Box 123, Oraibi, Ariz.   86039

Hualapai Reservation (S. rim of Grand Canyon, near Kingman)

    Camping at all levels along Colorado River, fee
    Write: Hualapai Recreation Dept., Box 216, Peach Springs, Ariz.   86434

Navajo Reservation (N.E. Ariz. extending into N.Mex. and Utah)[1]

---

[1] The Navajo National Monument at Tsegi Canyon, operated by the National Park Service, also has an excellent campground.

Monument Valley (Monument Valley Station): 16 units, water, toilets, fee
Four Corners (Four Corners Monument): 10 units, water, toilets, fee
Tsaile South Shore (S. of Lukachukai): 11 units, no water, toilets, fee
Little Colorado River (State 64, Navajo Peak, Gorge Overlook): 7 units, water, toilets, fee; also 28 picnic areas, including remote areas, and 40 rest areas, including remote areas
Write: Supervisor, Research Section, Navajo Parks and Recreation Dept., Window Rock, Navajo Nation, Ariz. 86515

Papago Reservation (S. Ariz. on Mexico border)

Camping anywhere on reservation except where posted; obtain camping permits from tribal office, Sells
Write: Papago Tribal Office, Sells, Ariz. 85634

Salt River Reservation (E. of Scottsdale)

Verde River Area: 10 units, no water, toilets, fee, also picnic areas

San Carlos Reservation (120 mi. E. of Phoenix)[2]

Cassadore Springs: 10 units, water, toilets, no fee
Cienega Park: 60 units, water, toilets, fee
Point of Pines: 20 units, water, toilets, fee
San Carlos Marina: 18 units, water, toilets, fee
Write: San Carlos Apache Tribe, Box 0, San Carlos, Ariz. 85550

California

Chemehuevi Reservation (Lake Havasu, San Bernardino County)
Campgrounds under construction

Fort Independence Indian Reservation (Fort Independence)
Fort Independence (State 395): 100 units, water, toilets, fee

Hoopa Indian Reservation (35 mi. N.E. of Eureka)
Hoopa (11 mi. N. of Willow Creek): 100 units, water, toilets, fee

Los Coyotes Reservation (Warner Hot Springs)
Los Coyotes (12 mi. E. of Warner Springs): 100 units, water, toilets, fee

Manzanita Reservation (off State 8)
Manzanita (between San Diego and El Centro): 75 units, water, toilets, fee

Tule River Indian Reservation (Tulare County)
Tule River (17 mi. E. of Porterville): 150 units, water, toilets, fee
Write: Indian Campgrounds, Inc., 2991 Fulton, Sacramento, Calif. 95821

Colorado

Southern Ute Reservation (S.W. Colo.)
Lake Capote Area (14 mi. W. of Pagosa Springs): 19 units, water, toilets, fee
Write: Southern Ute Agency, Ignacio, Colo. 81137

---

[2] There are smaller camping places and picnic grounds, as well as trout streams and fishing reservoirs.

Nevada

Pyramid Lake Reservation (28 mi. N. of Reno)[3]
    Warriors Point (W. beach of lake): water, toilets, fee
    Sutcliff (below Warriors Point): water, toilets, fee
    Write: Pyramid Lake Paiute Tribal Council, Box 256, Nixon, Nev.   89424

New Mexico[4]

Jicarilla Apache Reservation (Dulce)
    Stone Lake (27 mi. from Dulce): 36 units, water, toilets, fee (also lodge)
    Lower Mundo Lake (6 mi. from Dulce): 50 units, water, toilets, fee
    Dulce Lake (4 mi. from Dulce): 16 units, water (lake), toilets, fee
    Navajo River (2 mi. from Dulce): open sites, water (river), toilets (pit), fee
    Embom Lake (14 mi. from Dulce): 5 units, water (lake), toilets (pit), fee
    Write: Department of Tourism, Box 384, Dulce, N.Mex.   87528

Mescalero Apache Reservation (S.C. N.Mex.)[5]
    Cienegita Lakes (Ruidoso): 20 units, water, toilets, fee
    Eagle Creek Lakes (Ruidoso): 100 units, water, toilets, fee
    Ruidoso Creek (Ruidoso): 100 units, water, toilets, fee
    Silver Springs (Cloudcroft): 45 units, water, toilets, fee
    Write: Recreation Area Manager, Box 176, Mescalero, N.Mex.   88340

Navajo Reservation (N.W. N.Mex.)[6]

    Morgan Lake (S. of Fruitland): 5 units, no water, toilets, fee
    Shiprock (Shiprock): 3 units, water, toilets, fee
    Wheatfields Lake (N. of Navajo): 26 units, water, toilets, fee
    Write: Navajo Parks and Recreation Dept., Window Rock, Ariz.   86515

Acoma Pueblo (50 mi. W. of Albuquerque)

    Acomita Lake (5 mi. W. of Acoma Pueblo): few units, no water, toilets, fee
    San Jose River (5 mi. N. of Acoma Pueblo): few units, no water, toilets, fee
    Write: Acoma Pueblo, Box 64, San Fidel, N.Mex.   87049

Isleta Pueblo (8 mi. S.W. of Albuquerque)

    Picnic area (no camping): water, toilets, fee

Jémez Pueblo (44 mi. N. of Albuquerque)

    Holy Ghost Spring (40 mi. N. of Bernalillo): 8 units, water, toilets, fee
    Sheep Lake (near Isleta Pueblo): water, toilets, fee
    Thompson Springs (near Isleta Pueblo): water, toilets, fee
    Write: Jémez Pueblo, Rural Rt. via San Ysidro, N.Mex.   87053

Laguna Pueblo (45 mi. W. of Albuquerque)

    Paguate Reservoir: water, toilets, fee

---

[3] Camping permitted anywhere on reservation except where posted; some picnic areas.
[4] The following pueblos permit visitors between 8 A.M. and 5 P.M. but have no camping facilities: Sandía, Zía, Santa Ana, Santo Domingo, Cochití, San Felipe, Tesuque, Nambé, Pojoaque, San Ildefonso, San Juan, Picurís, Taos. For information about fishing and hunting licenses inquire at tribal headquarters at each pueblo.
[5] There are also lodges at Apache Summit and Sierra Blanca Ski Resort.
[6] Navajo National Monument at Tsegi Canyon also has an excellent campground.

Santa Clara Pueblo (5 mi. S. of Espanola)[7]

> No. 7, No. 8, No. 11: water, toilets, fee
> No. 12 (Tsee-Ee-Wade): water, toilets, fee
> No. 13 (Puganini) (Santa Clara Canyon): water, toilets, fee
> No. 15 (Ka Aa Nea) (Santa Clara Canyon): water, toilets, fee
> No. 16 (Ka Wa Pon) (Santa Clara Canyon): water, toilets, fee
> Write: Chairman, Santa Clara Pueblo, Espanola, N.Mex.   87532

Zuñi Pueblo (40 mi. S. of Gallup)

> Blackrock (36 mi. S. of Gallup): 10 units, water, toilets, fee
> Eustace (38 mi. S. of Gallup): 6 units, water, toilets, fee
> Nutria (49 mi. S. of Gallup): 10 units, water, toilets, fee
> Ojo Caliente (55 mi. S. of Gallup): 5 units, water, toilets, fee
> El Morro (15 mi. S. of Zuñi): 5 units, water, toilets, fee
> Write: Chairman, Zuñi Council, Box 338, Zuñi, N.Mex.   87327

Utah

Uintah and Ouray Reservation (N.E. Utah)[8]

> Big Spring: 10 units, no water, toilets, no fee
> Cedarview: 15 units, no water, toilets, no fee
> Upper Yellowstone River: 9 units, no water, toilets, no fee
> Yellowstone River: 9 units, no water, toilets, no fee
> Weaver Reservoir: 10 units, no water, toilets, no fee
> Write: Uintah and Ouray Reservation Agency, Fort Duchesne, Utah   84026

[7] All the campsites (more than 300) and trailer sites (25) are in the Santa Clara Canyon, west of the pueblo. Camping facilities are also available at Frijoles Mesa.

[8] There are also 12 smaller campgrounds and lodging at Vernal, Roosevelt, and Duchesne.

CALENDAR OF INDIAN EVENTS

Date	Place	Event
	January	
New Year's Day	Most pueblos, N.Mex., Ariz.	Corn, Turtle, and Other Dances
6	Most pueblos, N.Mex., Ariz.	King's Day Inauguration
23	San Ildefonso, N.Mex.	Buffalo and Comanche Dances, Feast
Late	Hopi villages, Ariz.	Kiva and Buffalo Dances
Late or early Feb.	Acoma Pueblo, N.Mex.	Governor's Fiesta
	February	
2	Cochití, Santo Domingo, San Felipe pueblos, N.Mex.	Buffalo Dances and Candlemas Celebration
1st week	Taos Pueblo, N.Mex.	Los Comanches
Mid-month	San Juan Pueblo, N.Mex.	Special Dances
Late	San Juan Pueblo, N.Mex.	Clan Dances
Late	Isleta Pueblo, N.Mex.	Evergreen Dances
Late	Hopi villages, Ariz.	Bean Dances in Kivas
	March	
Early	St. John's Mission, Gila River Reservation, Ariz.	Indian Dance Festival
2d weekend	Sacaton, Ariz.	Mul-Chu-Tha Fair and Rodeo
19	Old Laguna Pueblo, N.Mex.	St. Joseph's Feast Day
27	Cochití Pueblo, N.Mex.	Keresan Dances
Easter week	Pascua, Tucson, Ariz.	Yaqui Dances and Pageant
	Most pueblos, N.Mex.	Celebration of Opening of Irrigation Ditches
Easter	Most pueblos, N.Mex.	Easter Ceremonies, Footraces
After Easter	Most pueblos	Spring Ceremonies
Late	Ignacio and Towoac, Colo.	Bear Dance, Spring Welcome
Last week	Salt River Reservation, Ariz.	Pima Trade Fair and Dances
Last week	Fort Yuma Reservation, Calif.	Yuma (Quechan) Tribal Powwow

Date	Place	Events
	April	
1–4	All pueblos, N.Mex., Ariz.	Spring Corn Dances
Easter week	Yaqui Village, Tucson, Ariz.	Festival of St. Francis
Early	Northern Ute, Fort Duchesne, Utah	Bear Dance
Late	University of New Mexico, Albuquerque, N.Mex.	Intertribal Dances
	San Xavier Reservation, Tucson, Ariz.	Powwow
	May	
1	San Felipe Pueblo, N.Mex.	Feast Day and Corn Dance
3	Taos Pueblo, N.Mex.	Corn Dance and Ceremonial Dances
3	Cochití Pueblo, N.Mex.	Corn Dance
14–16	Taos Pueblo, N.Mex.	San Ysidro Fiesta
Late	Tesuque Pueblo, N.Mex.	Spring Dances
	Southern Ute Reservation, Colo.	Bear Dance
	Pala Reservation, Calif.	Corpus Christi Festival
Memorial Day	Morongo Reservation, Calif.	Malki Spring Festival
	Havasupai Reservation, Ariz.	Indian Dances
	Flagstaff, Ariz.	Indian Fair
	June	
Early	Sacaton, Ariz.	Yaqui Pageant
Early	Ute Mountain, Towaoc, Colo.	Bear Dance
8	Santa Clara Pueblo, N. Mex.	Buffalo Dance
13	Sandía Pueblo, N.Mex.	Feast and Corn Dance
13	Taos, Santa Clara, San Juan pueblos, N.Mex.	San Antonio Day
13	Cochití, San Ildefonso pueblos, N.Mex.	San Antonio Day
2d week	Leavitt Reservation, Janesville, Calif.	Bear Dance
Mid-month	San Carlos Reservation, Peridot, Ariz.	Apache Ceremonials
24	San Juan, Taos, Isleta, Cochití, Laguna and Acoma pueblos, N.Mex.; and Papago Reservation, Ariz.	San Juan's Day
24	Tule River Reservation, Calif.	San Juan's Day
24	Jémez Pueblo, N.Mex.	Rooster Pull
29	Acoma, Isleta, Laguna, Santa Ana, San Juan, and Taos pueblos, N.Mex.	San Pedro's Day

Date	Place	Events
	July	
1–4	Window Rock, Ariz.	Indian Rodeo
3–6	Mescalero Apache Reservation, N.Mex.	Mountain Spirits Ceremony
4	Nambé Pueblo, N.Mex.	Waterfall Ceremony
4	Most pueblos, N.Mex., Ariz.	Feasts, games, races
4	Walker River Reservation, Schurz, Nev.	Fiesta
1st week	Duck Valley Reservation, Owyhee, Nev.	Feast and games
2d weekend	Jaynesville, Calif.	Bear Dance
14	Cochití Pueblo, N.Mex.	Feast, Green Corn Dance
18	Mission San Diego de Alcala, San Diego, Calif.	Festival of Bells
3d week	Fallon, Nev.	All-Indian Celebration
25–27	Taos Pueblo, N.Mex.	Corn Dance
25	Santa Ana and Laguna pueblos, N.Mex.	Santiago's Day Dances
25	Cochití Pueblo, N.Mex.	Corn Dance
25	Acoma and Santo Domingo pueblos, N.Mex.	Rooster Pull
26	Santa Ana and Acoma pueblos	Feast Day and Corn Dance
Late	Santa Clara Pueblo, N.Mex.	Puye Ceremonial
Late	Hopi villages, Ariz.	Niman Kachina
Late	Southern Ute Reservation, Colo.	Sun Dance
Late	Ute Mountain Reservation, Colo.	Sun Dance
Late	Uintah and Ouray Reservation, Duchesne, Utah	Sun Dance
Late	Papago Reservation, Ariz.	Sajuaro Festival
	August	
4	Jémez Pueblo, N.Mex.	Old Pecos Bull Dance
4	Santo Domingo Pueblo, N.Mex.	Fiesta, Ripe Corn Dance
10	Picurís Pueblo, N.Mex.	Feast Day
10	Acoma and Laguna pueblos, N.Mex.	San Lorenzo Day, Corn Dance
12	Santa Clara Pueblo, N.Mex.	Santa Clara Day
15	Mesita Village, Laguna Pueblo, N.Mex.	Feast of St. Anthony, Dances
15	Zía Pueblo, N.Mex.	Assumption Day, Corn Dances
3d week	Supai, Ariz.	Havasupai Peach Festival
3d Sat. and Sun.	Santa Fe, N.Mex.	Annual Indian Market
28	Isleta Pueblo, N.Mex.	Spanish Fiesta
Late	All Hopi pueblos, Ariz.	Snake Dance

Date	Place	Events
4th weekend	Peach Springs, Ariz.	Hualapai Powwow
Weekend before Labor Day	Whiteriver, Ariz.	Apache Fair, Crown Dance

September

Date	Place	Events
2	Acoma Pueblo, N.Mex.	St. Stephen's Day, Corn Dance
3–6	Whiteriver, Ariz.	Apache Fair
4	Isleta Pueblo, N.Mex.	St. Augustine's Day, Dances
Early	Window Rock, Ariz.	Navajo Tribal Fair
8	San Ildefonso Pueblo, N.Mex.	Pinnhut Festival
11–13	Southern Ute Reservation, Colo.	Tribal Fair, Dances
14–16	Jicarilla Apache Reservation, N.Mex.	Ghost Dance, Fiesta
15	Tuolumne, Calif.	Acorn Festival
19	Laguna Pueblo, Old and New, N.Mex.	Fiesta and Harvest Dances
25	Laguna Pueblo, Old and New, N.Mex.	Fiesta and Social Dances
28–30	Taos Pueblo, N.Mex.	Sundown Dance
30	Taos Pueblo, N.Mex.	San Geronimo Feast Day
Late	San Juan Pueblo	Fiesta and Harvest Dance
Late	Isleta Pueblo, N.Mex.	Evergreen Dance
Late	Tuba City, Ariz.	Indian Fair
Late	Shiprock, N.Mex.	Navajo Fair

October

Date	Place	Events
4	Papago Reservation, Ariz.	Feast of St. Francis
4	Nambé Pueblo, N.Mex.	Elk Dance, Fiesta
17	Laguna Pueblo, N.Mex.	Harvest Dances Celebration
Late	Most pueblos, N.Mex., Ariz.	Ceremonial Dances

November

Date	Place	Events
Early	Papago Reservation, Ariz.	All-Indian Tribal Fair and Rodeo
12	Jémez Pueblo, N.Mex.	Harvest Fiesta, Corn Dances
12	Tesuque Pueblo, N.Mex.	Feast Day, Buffalo Dances
Mid-month	Peridot, Ariz.	Apache Memorial for Veterans
Last week	Parker, Ariz.	Tribal Thanksgiving

December

Date	Place	Events
2–4	San Xavier, Ariz.	St. Francis Feast
Early	Zuñi Pueblo, N.Mex.	Shalako Kachina Ceremony
10–12	Las Cruces, N.Mex.	Celebration, Tortugas Indians
12	Jémez Pueblo, N.Mex.	Matachines Dance
Week before Christmas	Colorado River Reservation, Parker, Ariz.	Indian Water Festival
24	All Río Grande pueblos	Night Bonfires, Processions

Date	Place	Events
25	All pueblos, N.Mex., Ariz.	Midnight Mass, Dancing in Churches
25	Most pueblos, N.Mex., Ariz.	Deer and Matachines Dances
25	Colorado River Reservation, Parker, Ariz.	Christmas Tree for Tribes
26	San Juan Pueblo, N.Mex.	Turtle Dance
31	Sandía Pueblo, N.Mex.	Deer Dance

THE CENTRAL REGION

A dancer at the American Indian Exposition, Anadarko, Oklahoma. *Fred W. Marvel, Oklahoma Tourism and Recreation Department.*

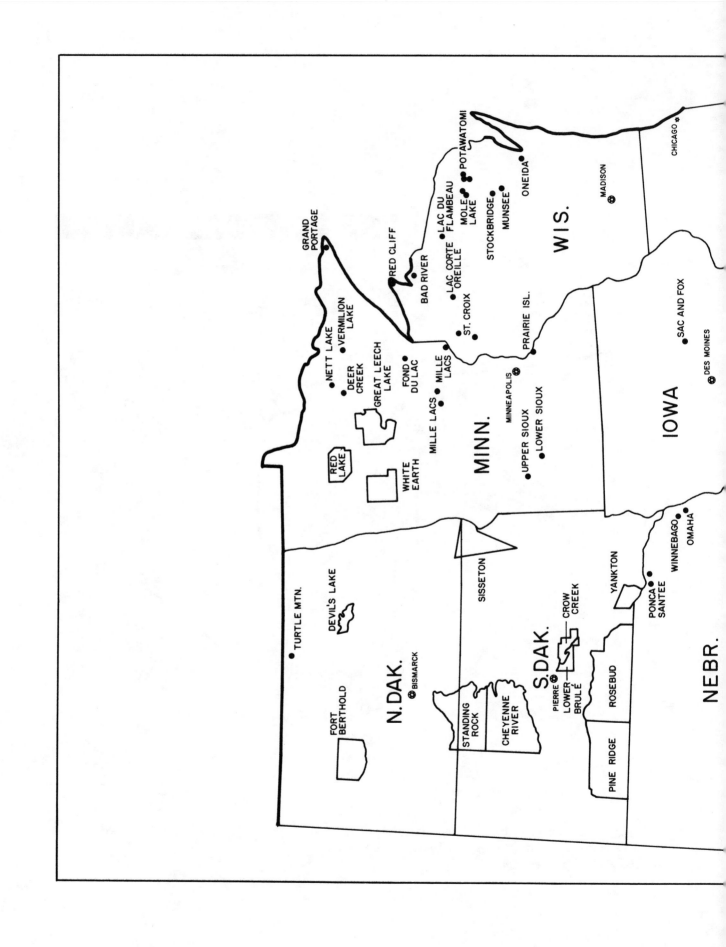

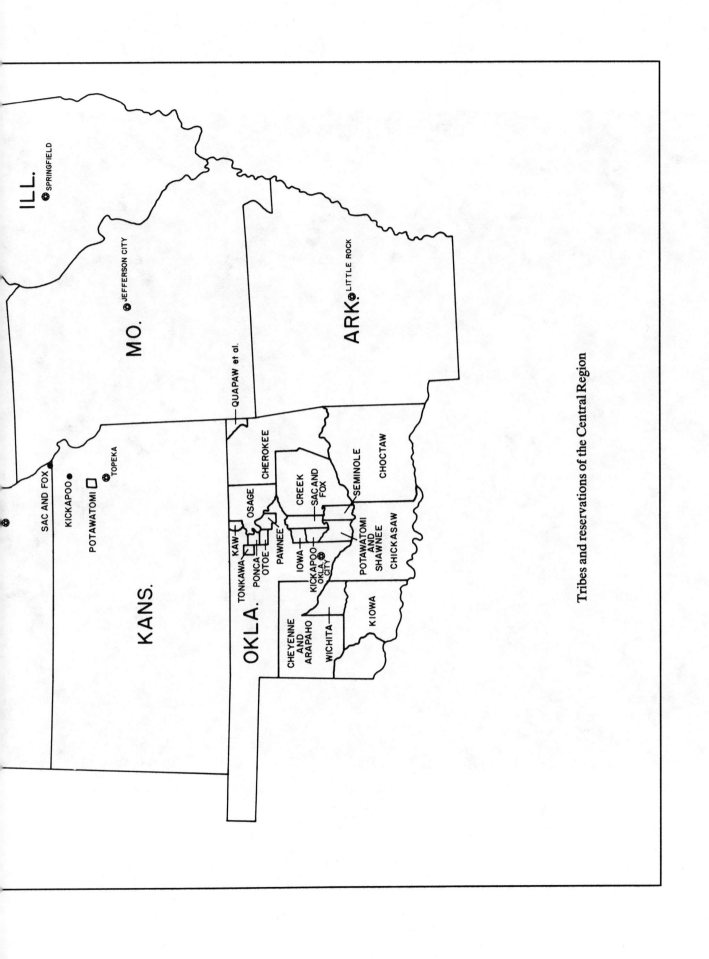

Tribes and reservations of the Central Region

Sisseton Sioux Indians. *Travel Division, South Dakota Department of Highways, Pierre, South Dakota.*

The Sioux

In the northern woodlands of the Great Lakes a party of Iroquois venturing westward ran into a band of Sioux. Face to face, the Iroquois demanded, "Who are you?"

"We are Sioux. Who are you?"

"We are Iroquois. What do you do?"

"We hunt buffalo." the Sioux warrior replied. "And what do you do?"

"We hunt men."

"You need hunt no further!" the Sioux shouted. "We are men!"

An Iroquois sprang at him. The Sioux warrior leaped to meet him, struck him with his quirt, and counted coup.

Instantly fighting exploded between the two groups. The Sioux band killed or captured all the Iroquois. Then they subjected the captives to the degrading indignity of slitting their noses, the Sioux punishment for unfaithful wives.

"Now go," the Sioux leader ordered, "and tell your chiefs to send no more women to look for men."

The Sioux are the prototype of the fighting American Indians. Audacious, bold, arrogant warriors, they believed themselves superior to all other men. They fought their Indian enemies for two hundred years and then took on the whites for another fifty years.

They have become prototypes of the American Indians: tall, lithe, well proportioned, with noble features, high-bridged noses, and broad cheekbones, garbed in fringed and beaded buckskins, wearing war bonnets of eagle feathers.

When they acquired horses, they became masterful horsemen, incomparable buffalo hunters, deadly cavalry in warfare. Mounted, they were ruthless, overwhelming adversaries, courageous almost to the point of folly. They were also deeply

A Cheyenne River Sioux tipi, Eagle Butte, South Dakota.

religious and had a rigid moral code. They instilled and supported these values with rituals. One of the ties that held the many Sioux tribes together was their communal rituals.

The name Sioux is a French corruption of what their enemies, the Chippewas, called them, a name meaning "Adders." The Sioux called themselves Dakotas, meaning "Allies," or Oteeti Cakowin, meaning "Seven Council Fires." One of the Seven Council Fires, or tribes, is the Teton Sioux.

The Tetons, the best known and most militant of the Sioux divisions, consisted of seven tribes: the Brulés, the Hunkpapas, the Miniconjous, the Oglalas, the Two Kettles, the Sans Arcs, and the Blackfeet. The image of the Sioux Indians was

A young Cheyenne River Sioux dancer, Eagle Butte.

generated almost entirely by these tribes. On the Northern Plains they were formidable. The names of their leaders—Sitting Bull, Crazy Horse, Red Cloud—have become immortal.

The Plains were not the original home of the Sioux. The Siouan group of tribes once occupied more territory than any other Indians within the present borders of the United States. Early in their history they ranged from Florida to Virginia and the Carolinas. They were a restive, dynamic people. Around 1500 they started on their great migrations. Some pushed westward across the wilderness until they reached the Pacific. Others moved northwest. In 1673, Père Marquette and Louis Jolliet found them near the confluence of the Arkansas and Mississippi rivers. White men encountered them later in Kentucky and Ohio, and, still later, in southern Minnesota, northeast Iowa, and Wisconsin.

The Sioux tribes in Wisconsin were almost surrounded by Algonquian tribes—the Chippewas and the Sacs and Foxes. The powerful Chippewas, armed with guns provided by the French, drove them out of Wisconsin.

By the early 1700's the Sioux had crossed the Missouri River. In the Dakota country they consolidated their bands and became virtually unconquerable. While they were entrenching themselves, the whites on their peripheries were warring with each other. The Sioux were aware of the struggle between the British and the French but paid little attention to it. Nor did the American Revolution have much effect on them. To them these were white men's wars on the other side of the continent.

By 1800 the western Sioux had halted the westward push of the Algonquians and the Iroquois. They controlled the west bank of the Mississippi River and dominated the vast area stretching from the Platte River to Canada, from Minnesota to the Yellowstone. In time the Sioux pushed to the Powder River country of Montana.

But in 1840 the curtain went up on a new phase of their history. The white man was coming.

It started without fanfare. The white settlers pushing into the upper Mississippi area had come to take the land and to usurp the Indians' rights. The whites were coming to stay.

At first the Sioux only remonstrated. In 1851 the Santees, the eastern division of the Sioux, surrendered most of their lands in Minnesota, thinking that this concession would satisfy the whites. It did not. The whites kept pushing westward. The first serious bloodshed occurred in 1856, when Sioux attacked whites, killing and scalping them.

In 1862 the Minnesota frontier again erupted. The infuriated Sioux attacked white settlements and killed the settlers or took them captive and held them as hostages.

The United States Army struck back with quick and heavy reprisals, causing many Sioux who had taken no part in the attacks to rally to the Santees. They retaliated with more raids and destruction of outposts, telegraph lines, wagons, and livestock. The government responded with more troops and artillery.

When the uprising was over, some eight hundred settlers and soldiers and an unknown number

Cheyenne River Sioux Powwow (spring), Eagle Butte. *Travel Division, South Dakota Department of Highways, Pierre, South Dakota.*

of Santees had died. The surviving Minnesota Sioux were rounded up and removed to reservations in the Dakotas. The state of Minnesota posted a bounty of twenty-five dollars for each Sioux scalp. White bounty hunters organized parties to hunt down and kill the Indians who had not been rounded up.

Bloody though it was, the Minnesota uprising was only a prologue. The Tetons, the western Sioux on the Northern Plains, were still free. Relations between them and the whites worsened. The government sent its most seasoned Indian fighters into the Sioux country. Crazy Horse, the Oglala chief, defeated General George Crook in the Battle

of the Rosebud. Then he and Chief Gall joined Sitting Bull, the Hunkpapa leader, with his force of Sioux and Cheyennes. The stage was set for the Little Big Horn. There they destroyed Lieutenant Colonel George A. Custer and his command.

But the end of Sioux domination was in sight. The final curtain fell on December 29, 1890, at Wounded Knee, on what is now the Pine Ridge Reservation. There the Seventh Cavalry surrounded a body of Sioux under Chief Big Foot and opened fire. About three hundred Sioux and thirty-one soldiers were killed. It had taken the whites about fifty years to dispossess the Sioux.

Today most of the Sioux are on reservations in

Cheyenne River Sioux Powwow, Eagle Butte. *Travel Division, South Dakota Department of Highways, Pierre, South Dakota.*

The Sun Dance, Pine Ridge Reservation, South Dakota. *Publicity Division, South Dakota Department of Highways.*

The Sun Dance, Pine Ridge Reservation, South Dakota. *Publicity Division, South Dakota Department of Highways, Pierre, South Dakota.*

Arikara gospel singers from South Dakota.

the Dakotas. They still speak and write the Dakota language. But remnants of the great Siouan family are scattered. The Osage, Iowa, Missouri, Quapaw, Ponca, Oto, Kansa (Kaw), and Omaha tribes are in Oklahoma. The Crows are in Montana. The Winnebagos are in Wisconsin and Nebraska. The Catawbas are in South Carolina, and the Biloxi live on the Gulf Coast.

There are nine Sioux Reservations in South Dakota: Standing Rock (part of which is also in North Dakota); Cheyenne River, south of Standing Rock; Sisseton, in the northeast; Lower Brulé and Crow Creek, in the south-central area; Pine Ridge, Rosebud, and Yankton, on the southern edge; and Flandreau, in the eastern part.

The Devils Lake Reservation in North Dakota is a Sioux reservation, and two Sioux tribes, the Hidatsas and the Mandans, live on the Fort Berthold Reservation (the third tribe on the reservation is the Arikaras, a Caddoan group).

The reservations of the two Dakotas together comprise about 6,000,000 acres. Only about 2,000,000 acres are tribally owned. About 3,500,000 acres are owned by individuals, and the federal government owns about 127,000 acres. Except for the Turtle Mountain Chippewa Reservation, of about 75,000 acres, all the rest are Sioux lands. Yet what the Dakota Sioux retain is a small fraction of the vast territories that the far-flung Siouan family once claimed as its own.

The Chippewas

Among the most formidable of the American Indians were the Iroquois and the Sioux. The Iroquois dominated the Northeast. The Sioux dominated the Northern Plains. Between them were the Chippewas (also called the Ojibways). The Iroquois crushed the Algonquians and drove them from the upper New York and Ontario areas. But when the Iroquois pushed westward, they met the Chippewas, and the Chippewas stopped them cold.

The Chippewas lived in the area northeast of Lake Superior and the vicinity of Lake Huron. They ranged as far east as what is now New England and from Sault Sainte Marie around both sides of Lake Superior. Those who lived north of the Sault were called the Saulteurs by the French. About the time of the American Revolution War they occupied the northern timber country of what is now Minnesota.

West of the Chippewas were the Sioux, the overwhelming force of the Northern Plains, their blood enemies. The showdown came in Minnesota. The Chippewas drove the Sioux from the Mille Lacs area across northern Minnesota to the Turtle Mountains in northernmost North Dakota. They pushed westward all the way to Montana and penetrated into Saskatchewan.

The Chippewas fought the Sioux for nearly two centuries. In the process they underwent a profound change. In the northern woodlands, around the Great Lakes, they had been canoe Indians, fishermen, nomadic hunters, fur traders, and sometimes farmers. When they pushed westward into the Northern Plains, they forsook the canoe for the horse. They adopted the ways of the Plains Indians. They became horse Indians and buffalo hunters.

The Chippewas are of Algonquian stock. They are related to the Indians of New England and of the North Atlantic coast. Once they were the largest tribe north of Mexico, and today they are the second-largest group in the United States. About 1640 they numbered around thirty-five thousand. Longfellow immortalized them by mistake in his "Hiawatha." He dramatized the legends of the Chippewas, believing that they were the legends of the Iroquois.

A good part of the Chippewas' power lay in their ingenious use of the forests and waterways around them. The woodlands were heavily forested with birch trees. The Chippewas early learned to use birch bark to make utensils, baskets, and food containers and to cover their houses. They used it as paper, on which they drew pictures and inscribed messages. Most important, they used it to make canoes.

They made strong, swift canoes, each light enough to be carried by one man. Thus the network of waterways, streams, rivers, lakes, became a ready system of transportation and communications. The Chippewas could portage their canoes overland from one stream or lake to another. Thus they had access to thousands of square miles of territory. From Detroit they could go by canoe to Hudson Bay, and from Lake Michigan they had several water routes to the Mississippi. From Green Bay they paddled down the Fox River to Lake Winnebago, and from there down the Fox to Portage, in south-central Wisconsin. There they portaged their canoes to the Wisconsin River and paddled down to the Mississippi, near Prairie du Chien. They did the same from the region of present-day Chicago to the Mississippi.

Because they could get around with such facility, they were able to dominate vast territories. By controlling the waterways, they controlled the

A young Chippewa of the White Earth Reservation, Minnesota. The costume, of velvet and beadwork, is worn by an employee of the Cass Lake Agency. *Bureau of Indian Affairs.*

means of communication and travel in the area. In this regard no other Indians could compete with them.

Living among the waterways, they became expert fishermen and trappers; living in the forest, expert hunters. Maize, necessary to many other tribes, was not important to the Chippewas. They gathered the wild rice that grew in the shallow waters. They gather it to this day, and for some Chippewas it has become a profitable commercial crop.

Like the Iroquois and the Sioux, the Chippewas were warriors. They were quick to fight and were dangerous adversaries. They joined the Hurons, Senecas, and Ottowas in Pontiac's war against the British. When this effort failed and Pontiac was killed, they joined Tecumseh and his Shawnees and a confederation of other tribes against the Americans. This effort also failed. In the meantime, they were at war with other tribes, notably the Foxes. When Black Hawk, the Sauk chief, tried to organize an alliance of tribes, the Chippewas stayed out. They rarely fought the whites, not because they did not oppose them but because they were usually out of the mainstream of the western expansion of the whites. Their last battle, in 1898, eight years after the last Sioux encounter at Wounded Knee, was at Leech Lake, Minnesota, where a band of Chippewas took on units of the United States infantry and lost.

Today there are nineteen Chippewa reservations, scattered from Michigan to North Dakota. The westernmost reservation is the Turtle Mountain Reservation, on the Canadian line in North Dakota. Some ten thousand Chippewas live on this reservation. Most of the remaining Chippewas, possibly fifteen thousand, live in Minnesota. The three major Chippewa reservations in Minnesota are Red Lake, Greater Leech Lake, and the largest, White Earth.

Wisconsin has six Chippewa reservations. The two largest, Lac du Flambeau and Lac Courte Oreilles, lie in tourist country. In season the tourist business is brisk at Lac du Flambeau, where the Chippewas stage powwows and performances. The Lac Courte Oreilles Chippewas also perform each summer at Hayward. They do a thriving tour-

Chippewa dancers at the Gathering of the Tribes Powwow, Hayward, Wisconsin. *Historyland, Hayward, Wisconsin.*

ist business and run a cranberry-growing enterprise on the side.

The picture is less bright on the other Chippewa reservations of Wisconsin. The St. Croix Chippewas depend on seasonal work. Late in summer they and the Chippewas of Sokaogan Community harvest wild rice. In winter they trap muskrats and minks.

Many Chippewas have left the reservations and little of their culture is left. Their arts and crafts consist mainly of beadwork, and a little bric-a-brac. Their traits and language and customs are just about gone. Most Chippewas have adopted the white man's ways, his dress, his music, his foods, his jobs, and even his hobbies and his sports.

There is probably no longer a full-blood Chippewa on the reservation.

The Indians of Oklahoma

About 10 to 12 per cent of all the Indians of the United States, representing about thirty-five tribes, live in Oklahoma, a state that has no reservations. In addition to full-blood Indians, there are many citizens of mixed Indian and white blood. Only a small fraction of Oklahoma's Indians are indigenous to the region. The overwhelming majority either migrated there or were moved there by the federal government.

Long before the first whites came, the ancestors of the Pawnees, the Wichitas and the Caddoes, lived in the region. Then the Indians of the Plains filtered in. Farmer Indians settled in the fertile valleys of the Arkansas, Canadian and Red rivers. By the time of George Washington's first inaugural, events taking place along the eastern seaboard had crystallized into the "Indian problem." The problem haunted the new nation—and has haunted it ever since.

What was to be done with the Indians? There seemed to be three choices:

1. Establish a separate domain for each tribe.

2. Move the Indians to the West, out of the way of the whites.

3. Educate the Indians for citizenship and integrate and assimilate them into the white man's world.

Some of the eastern tribes voluntarily moved westward to get out of the way of the whites. Several tribes in the Middle West, the Delawares, Sacs, Foxes, Potawatomis, and Kaskaskias, ceded their lands in Indiana, Wisconsin, and Illinois and moved across the Mississippi River. About 1817, under pressure from the whites, the Five Civilized Tribes—the Cherokees, Choctaws, Chickasaws, Creeks, and Seminoles—began moving from the Southeast to the West. The Cherokees ceded about one-third of their lands in the Southeast for equal acreage in "the Arkansas Land." But not all the Cherokees agreed to this arrangement. Many opposed the move and resisted it.

President Andrew Jackson minced no words. He gave the Indians a choice: conform or get out. With the Indian Removal Act of 1830 displacement of the Indians to the Trans-Mississippi West became national policy. The massive trek was on.

By force, most of the Cherokees were transplanted to the Oklahoma Territory. The Five Civilized Tribes were given all of Oklahoma Territory except the Panhandle and the Northeast, which was already occupied by Senecas, Pawnees, and Quapaws.

The Cherokees readily adapted themselves and formulated a written constitution. They talked of colonizing the territory, forming a totally Indian state, and naming it Sequoyah. In 1843 the Cherokees called a great council of eighteen tribes at Tahlequah to adopt a code of tribal laws.

Each of the Five Civilized Tribes established its own nation and its own capital: the Cherokees at Tahlequah, the Choctaws at Tuskahoma, the Creeks at Okmulgee, the Chickasaws at Tishomingo, and the Seminoles at Wewoka. Each had its own tribal government. The chiefs were elected by the members of the tribes. The governments were patterned much after that of the United States, with executive, legislative, and judicial branches. The federal government recognized the Indian nations as legitimate political entities. They were actually nations within a nation.

As "nations" they were similar. In nearly all other respects they were different. Each tribe has its own history, its own culture, its own legends and lore, its own scale of values, its own economic base. The Cherokees, a particularly energetic and enterprising people, prospered. By the time of the

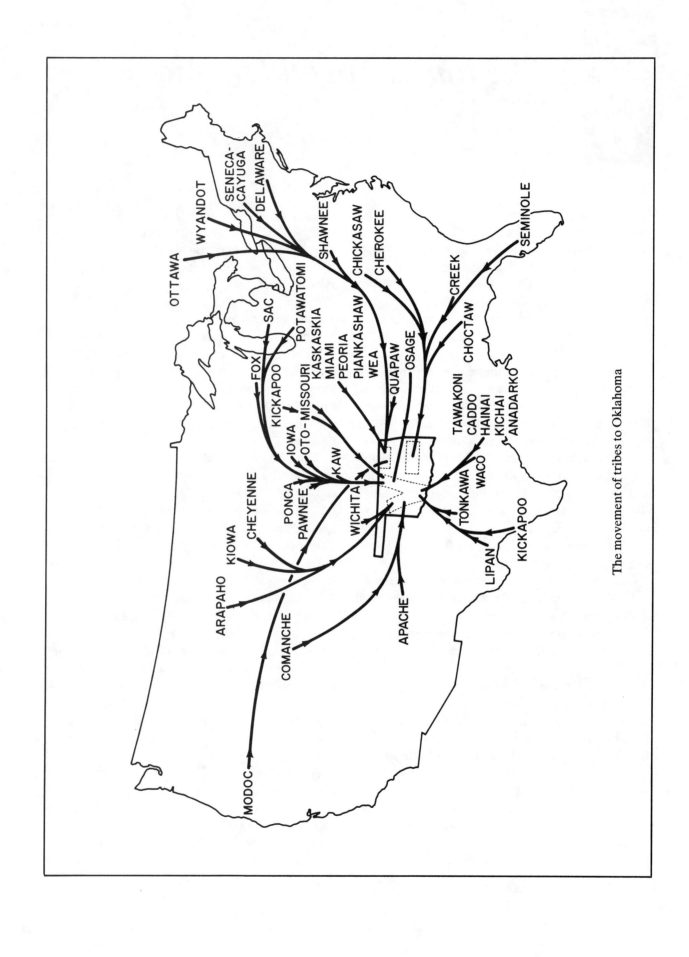

The movement of tribes to Oklahoma

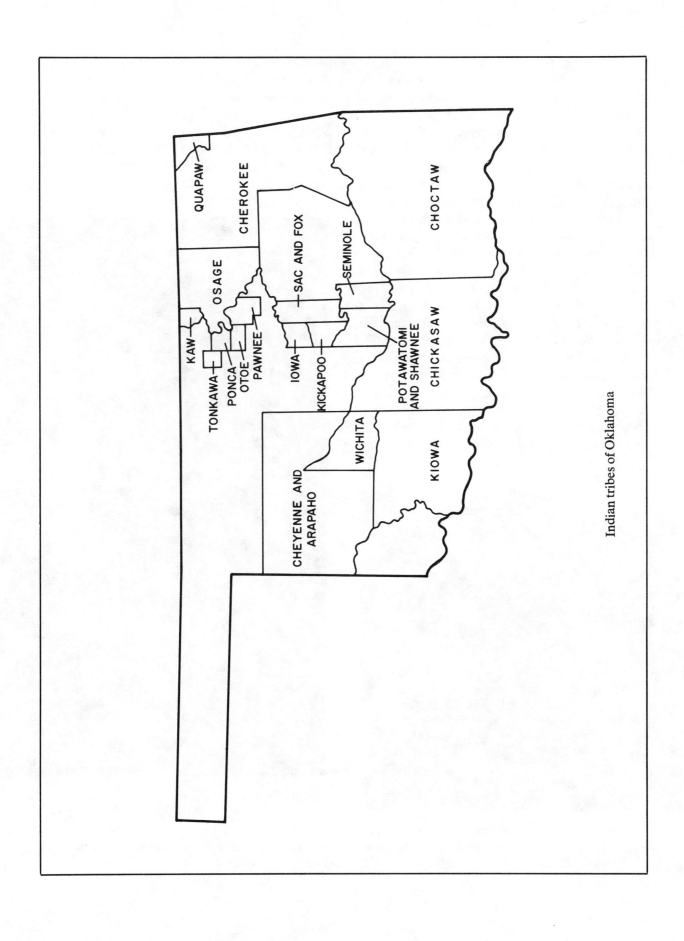

Indian tribes of Oklahoma

Civil War they had made the most of decades of peace and learning to live the white man's way. The Civil War changed all that. Most of the Indians of the Five Civilized Tribes sided with the South. They recruited contingents to fight for the Confederacy. Those who sided with the North fled to Kansas. When the war was over, the Confederate Indians surrendered. As part of the punishment for their "treason" the western part of their territory was taken from them. Other Indians were moved in—Osages, Arapahoes, Cheyennes, Wichitas, Kiowas, and Comanches.

This was only the beginning. Dozens more tribes, strangers to each other, even blood enemies, were put together cheek by jowl. Kiowas, Comanches, and Apaches, all of different linguistic families, were placed together on one reservation. The Comanches spoke a Shoshonean tongue, the Apaches spoke Athapascan dialects, and the Kiowas spoke a Kiowan tongue. Iowa Indians, a Siouan tribe, were placed with five Algonquian tribes: Kickapoos, Potawatomis, Shawnees, Sacs, and Foxes. Indian Territory thus became the "depository" of tribes from the Northeast, the Northwest, the Gulf Coast, California, and scores of regions between.

Added to all this was another, even more menacing problem. White pressure to enter the Territory was building. In 1887 the Dawes Act broke up the reservations into individual allotments and

A Cherokee housewife, in the authentic historical village at Tsa-La-Gi, Tahlequah, Oklahoma, cleans house just as her forebears did three hundred years ago. The village is open to tourists from early May to early September.

Children at the Greyhorse Osage War Dances, near Pawhuska, Oklahoma. *Fred W. Marvel, Oklahoma Tourism and Recreation Department.*

A Cherokee basketmaker works at Tsa-La-Gi.

opened the "surplus lands." The whites started maneuvering to get these lands. It was the "Indian Problem" all over again.

The halls of the Congress rang with debates on the question. The wrangling spilled over into the press and echoed throughout the nation. The Indians remonstrated, but to no avail. Divided by tribalism, they were unable to prevail.

When the tribal governments were abolished, the Five Civilized Tribes lost their right to elect their own chiefs. The chiefs were appointed by the President of the United States. Not until 1970, by act of Congress, were the Five Civilized Tribes again authorized to elect their own chiefs. Each tribe now has a principal chief and elected council members. They act officially for the tribe.

The great majority of the Indians of Oklahoma are now intermingled with the general population.

The Osage Nation still has a government at Pawhuska, although the Osage Reservation no longer exists. It is now Osage County.

Some of the tribal groups have adopted written constitutions and bylaws and operate faithfully under them. Most tribal groups do not have written constitutions. While they manage their own affairs, the federal government still has a hand in them by way of service. For this purpose the state of Oklahoma is divided into two areas, the Eastern, headquartered at Muskogee, and the Western, at Anadarko. The Eastern Area Office serves fourteen tribes: the Five Civilized Tribes, the Osages, the Wyandots, the Eastern Shawnees, the Miamis, the Seneca-Cayugas, the Quapaws, the Modocs, the Ottawas, and the Peorias. The Western Area Offices serves eighteen tribes: the Kiowas, the Comanches, the Kiowa-Apaches, the Fort Sill

Dancers perform the Green Corn Dance in the drama *Trail of Tears* at Tahlequah. The revered Sequoyah, inventor of the Cherokee syllabary, is at the top center.

Cherokee women cool their feet as they make baskets at Tsa-La-Gi.

The Victory Dance, performed in *Trail of Tears*.

The Phoenix Dance, performed in *Trail of Tears*.

An Indian dancer performing at the State Fair of Oklahoma. *State Fair of Oklahoma.*

American Indian Ceremonial Dance Competition at the annual State Fair of Oklahoma. *State Fair of Oklahoma.*

A powwow in Tulsa, Oklahoma. *Fred W. Marvel, Oklahoma Tourism and Recreation Department.*

Apaches, the Wichitas, the Caddoes, the Delawares, the Cheyenne-Arapahoes, the Pawnees, the Poncas, the Oto-Missouris, the Kaws, the Tonkawas, the Absentee Shawnees, the Iowas of Oklahoma, the Kickapoos of Oklahoma, the Sac and Foxes of Oklahoma, and the Citizen Potawatomis.

Today Oklahoma is a melting pot of Indian blood. There are more different kinds of Indians in Oklahoma than in any other state. They are descendants of Indians from the Eastern Seaboard to the Gulf Coast, from the Pacific to the Great Lakes, from the mountains, the plains, the prairies, the plateaus, the deserts, the hilly wilderness, and the swamps. They have intermixed with each other and with the whites to the extent that their Indianness is almost submerged. Because of this there is no accurate way to count the number of Indians in the state. Any guess is an approximation, beyond the tribal censuses, which are taken from tribal rolls.

Yet vestiges of tribal life still exist, especially among the stronger tribes that strive to preserve their tribal identity.

Today, more than a century after their resettlement in Oklahoma, most Indians manifest the same individuality as whites. They cannot be grouped as a race, nor scarcely even as tribes.

The Indians of Oklahoma embrace different religions. Some are Protestants, some Catholics, some profess no religion, and some still cling to their tribal faiths.

The lands that had been set aside exclusively for their use were breeched. The two million acres of "unassigned lands" were cut up into 160-acre homesteads, and, in 1889, Indian Territory experienced the first of its five sensational "land runs." It was a winners-take-all white man's scramble for Indian lands.

It did not end there. The pressure continued. Only about half of what is now the state of Oklahoma was occupied by Indians. Voices in Congress clamored for opening the remaining area for white settlement. In 1890, Congress lopped off that portion of Indian Territory and named it Oklahoma Territory. Three years later the Dawes Commission wiped out all the tribal holdings. All Indian lands in the Territory passed from tribal to individual ownership.

At the turn of the century the two territories had a population of about four hundred thousand persons, of whom only about 14 to 15 per cent were Indians. The Indian Territory had become predominantly white. In 1906, Congress terminated both Indian Territory and Oklahoma Territory. The next year the state of Oklahoma was ad-

Cheyenne Sun Dance pledgers. *American Museum of Natural History.*

mitted to the union. It became the only state in the Union with five recognized capitals in addition to its own state capital.

The Indian capitol buildings still stand (except for the Seminole capitol at Wewoka, which burned), but in the state of Oklahoma the tribal governments have only limited autonomy.

Individual as they are, there are ties that bind them. The Oklahoma Inter-Tribal Council has been organized to represent all the Indian tribes of Oklahoma, wherever they came from and wherever they live in the state.

Oglala Sioux Sun Dance. *Travel Division, South Dakota Department of Highways.*

TRIBES AND RESERVATIONS

Tribe	Reservation or Location	Acres	Population	Address

Illinois

Note: There are no reservations in Illinois. Most of the Indians of Illinois live in urban centers in Alexandria, Cook, and Peoria counties.

Tribe	Reservation or Location	Acres	Population	Address
		Iowa		
Mesquakie	Sac and Fox Settlement	3,600	850	Tama 52339
		Kansas		
Iowa	Iowa-Kansas	. . .	1,520	BIA Office, Horton 66439
Kickapoo	Kickapoo	. . .	1,000	Same
Potawatomi	Potawatomi	. . .	2,150	Same
Sac and Fox	Sac and Fox	. . .	230	Same
		Minnesota		
Chippewa	Grand Portage	44,700	250	Box 489 Bemidji 56601
	Leech Lake	27,760	2,800	Same
	White Earth	27,560	2,100	Same
	Fond du Lac	21,366	700	Same
	Bois Forte (Nett Lake)	41,750	680	Same
	Mille Lacs	3,600	800	Same
Santee Sioux	Upper Sioux, Granite Falls	750	70	Same
	Lower Sioux	1,750	100	Same
	Prairie Island	530	. . .	Same
	Prior Lake	. . .	260	Same
Chippewa	Red Lake	636,964	4,000	Red Lake 56671
		Nebraska		
Omaha	Omaha	27,700	1,300	Winnebago 68071
Winnebago	Winnebago	27,000	650	Same
Santee-Sioux	Santee-Sioux	3,600	250	Same

Tribe	Reservation or Location	Acres	Population	Address
		North Dakota		

Sioux
  Arikara
  Hidatsa
  Mandan
	Fort Berthold	1,000,000	7,350	Affiliated Tribes
				New Town 58763

Santee Sioux	Devil's Lake	. . .	. . .	Fort Totten 58335
Yankton Sioux	Standing Rock	306,333	2,050	Fort Yates 58538
Chippewa	Turtle Mountain	69,810	7,340	Turtle Mountain Agency Belcourt 58316

Oklahoma
Eastern Oklahoma Tribes
(Area Office, Muskogee   74401)

Tribe	Address
Cherokee	Bartlesville 74003
Chickasaw	6033 Glencove Place Oklahoma City 73132
Choctaw	302 W. Willow Durant 74701
Creek	605 N. Alabama Okmulgee 74447
Seminole	Box 632 Wewoka 74884
Osage	Box 2 Pawhuska 74056
Wyandotte	Box 15 Wyandotte 74370
Eastern Shawnee	Box 754 Quapaw 74363
Miami	Rt. 2 Miami 74354
Seneca-Cayuga	1621 "D" St. N.E. Miami 74354
Quapaw	Rt. 1 Quapaw 74363
Modoc	111 "C" St. S.E. Miami 74354
Ottawa	Box 110 Miami 74354
Peoria	820 "C" St. N.W. Miami 74354

South Dakota

Tribe	Reservation or Location	Acres	Population	Address
Teton Sioux	Cheyenne River	1,413,000	4,300	Eagle Butte 57625
Yankton Sioux	Crow Creek	127,500	1,800	Fort Thompson 57339

Tribe	Reservation or Location	Acres	Population	Address
Santee Sioux	Flandreau	2,180	. . .	Flandreau 57028
Teton Sioux	Lower Brulé	114,500	. . .	Lower Brulé 57548
Oglala Sioux	Pine Ridge	1,650,000	8,780	Pine Ridge 57770
Teton Sioux	Rosebud	977,000	7,201	Rosebud 57570
Sisseton Sioux	Sisseton	105,912	2,400	Sisseton 57262
Teton Sioux	Standing Rock	848,600	5,000	Fort Yates 58538
Yankton Sioux	Yankton	35,000	. . .	Wagner 57380

Wisconsin

Tribe	Reservation or Location	Acres	Population	Address
Chippewa	Bad River	55,044	440	Great Lakes Agency Ashland 54806
Potawatomi	Forest County	11,660	229	Same
Chippewa	Lac Courte Oreilles	43,000	760	Same
	Lac du Flambeau	44,400	900	Same
	Mole Lake	1,700	130	Same
Oneida	Oneida	2,600	1,700	Same
Stockbridge- Munsee	Stockbridge-Munsee	15,000	450	Same
Winnebago	Winnebago Communities	4,100	1,350	Same
Chippewa	Red Cliff	7,350	435	Same
	St. Croix	2,230	300	Same
Menominee	Menominee	233,800	3,270	Same

Western Oklahoma Tribes
(Area Office, Box 368, Anadarko   73005)

Tribe	Tribal Roll	Agency Address
Kiowa	6,250	Anadarko 73005
Comanche	6,250	Same
Kiowa-Apache	1,000	Same
Fort Sill Apache	150	Same
Wichita	580	Same
Caddo	1,760	Same
Delaware	800	Same
Cheyenne-Arapaho	6,674	Concho 73022
Pawnee	2,110	Pawnee 73022
Ponca	1,910	Anadarko 73005
Oto-Missouri	1,410	Same
Kaw	250	Same
Tonkawa	90	Same
Absentee Shawnee	1,540	Shawnee 74801
Iowa of Oklahoma	276	Anadarko 73005
Kickapoo of Oklahoma	1,100	Same
Sac and Fox of Oklahoma	1,980	Same
Citizen Potawatomi	10,968	Same

A member of the Stockbridge-Munsee Reservation in Wisconsin at work in the Stockbridge Arts and Crafts Shop. *Bureau of Indian Affairs.*

Winnebago contest dancer, Stand Rock Indian Ceremonial.

Winnebago War Dance, Stand Rock Indian Ceremonial, Lac du Flambeau, Wisconsin.

Climax of Winnebago War Dance, Stand Rock Indian Ceremonial.

CAMPGROUNDS

Iowa

Sac and Fox Settlement (3 mi. W. of Tama on U.S. 30)

> Powwow (on Iowa River): few units, water, toilets, no fee; three miles of river fishing
> Write: Tribal Council, Area Field Office, Tama, Iowa   52339

Minnesota

Grand Portage Reservation (on Pigeon River)

> Three primitive areas on Lake Superior: few units, water, toilets, no fee; also marina-trailer complex
> Write: Agency, Box 489, Bemidji, Minn.   56601

Red Lake Reservation (30 mi. N. of Bemidji)

> Sandy Beach (12 mi. W. of Red Lake): many units, water, toilets, fee; also 45 picnic sites; firewood free
> Write: Red Lake Reservation, Red Lake, Minn.   56671

Nebraska

Omaha Reservation (N.E. Nebr., 20 mi. S. of Sioux City)

> Big Elk Park (28 mi. S. of Sioux City): 8 units, water, toilets, no fee; also 32 trailer hookups

Winnebago Park (7 mi. E. of Winnebago): 6 units, no water, toilets, no fee
> Write: Tribal Agency, Winnebago, Nebr.   68071

North Dakota

Fort Berthold Reservation (W.Cen. N.Dak.)[1]

> Bear Den (153 mi. N.W. of Bismarck): 150 units, no water, toilets, no fee
> Deep Water: 50 units, water, toilets, no fee
> Four Bears: (156 mi. N.W. of Bismarck): 100 units, water, toilets, no fee
> Lost Bridge (135 mi. N.W. of Bismarck): 20 units, no water, toilets, no fee
> Lucky Mound (125 mi. N.W. of Bismarck): 50 units, water, toilets, no fee
> Mosset Resort: 150 units, water, toilets, fee
> Shell Creek (167 mi. N.W. of Bismarck): 100 units, no water, toilets, no fee
> Twin Buttes (125 mi. N.W. of Bismarck): 100 units, water, toilets, no fee

[1] Firewood available at all campsites; 25 picnic areas. Lake Saka-Ka-Wea has 600 mi. of shoreline.

White Shield (98 mi. N.W. of Bismarck): 200 units, water, toilets, no fee
Write: Three Affiliated Tribes, New Town, N.Dak.   58763

Standing Rock Reservation (60 mi. S. of Bismarck)[2]

Fort Yates (Fort Yates): 70 units, water, toilets (pit), no fee
Froelich Dam (8 mi. N. of Selfridge): no water, toilets, no fee
Coulee Park (1 mi. N. of Fort Yates): no water, toilets, no fee
Write: Recreational Development Director, Standing Rock Reservation, Fort Yates, N.Dak.   58538

Turtle Mountain Reservation (W. of Rolla, near Canadian border)[3]
Broken Arrow: 10 units, water, toilets, fee
Sundown Park: 10 units, water, toilets, fee
Camp Waupun: 15 units, water, toilets, fee
Wheaton Lake: 5 units, water, toilets, fee
Red Bear Picnic Area: 5 units, water, toilets, fee
Belcourt Lake (4 mi. N. of Belcourt): 5 units, water, toilets, fee
Gordon Lake (4 mi. N. of Belcourt): 5 units, water, toilets, fee
Write: Tribal Secretary, Turtle Mountain Band, Belcourt, N.Dak.   58316

Oklahoma

There are no Indian campgrounds as such in Oklahoma because there are no Indian reservations in the state. There are, however, many public campgrounds throughout the state.
Write: Tourism and Information Division, Industrial Development and Parks Department, Will Rogers Memorial Building, Oklahoma City, Okla.   73105

South Dakota

Cheyenne River Reservation (93 mi. N.W. of Pierre)[4]
Write: Tribal Chairman, Cheyenne River Sioux Tribe, Eagle Butte, S.Dak.   57625

Crow Creek Reservation (Fort Thompson)

Old Fort Thompson (Fort Thompson): 30 units, water, toilets, no fee
West Bend (30 mi. from Fort Thompson): 30 units, water, toilets, no fee
De Grey (45 mi. from Fort Thompson): 30 units, water, toilets, no fee
Good Soldier Creek (Big Bend): 20 units, water, toilets, no fee
Crow Creek Complex (Fort Thompson): 25 units, water, toilets, fee; also trailer hookups
Write: Crow Creek Agency, Box 616, Fort Thompson, S.Dak.   57501

Lower Brulé Reservation (S.Cen. S.Dak., adjoining Crow Creek Reservation)[5]

Lake Sharpe (Big Bend Dam): 12 units, water, toilets, no fee
Counselor Creek (Lower Brulé): 6 units, no water, no toilets, no fee
Good Soldier Creek (Big Bend Dam area): 10 units, water, toilets, no fee
Narrows (Lower Brulé): 6 units, no water, toilets, no fee
Community Park (Lower Brulé): 6 units, water, toilets, no fee
Iron Nation (W. of Lower Brulé): water, toilets, no fee

[2] Some trailer sites are available at Froelich Dam; picnic sites at all campgrounds. Extensive campground development is planned.
[3] All areas may be used for picnics.
[4] There are no developed campgrounds on the reservation. A few free campsites are available in each community park and in areas of access to Oahe Reservoir.
[5] There are 20 picnic areas and 25 rest areas on the reservation.

Cedar Creek and La Roche (W. of Lower Brulé): no water, toilets, no fee
Write: U.S. Army Engineers, District Corps of Engineers, Omaha, Nebr.   68102

Pine Ridge Reservation (110 mi. S.E. of Rapid City)[6]

Sun Dance Grounds (Pine Ridge): 300 units, water, toilet, fee
Big Foot Area (Porcupine): many units, water, toilets, fee
Crazy Horse Park (Manderson): many units, water, toilets, fee
Three Moccasins (Pine Ridge): 100 units, water, toilets, fee
Write: Director, Oglala Sioux Ranger Corps, Pine Ridge, S.Dak.   57770

Rosebud Reservation (S.Cen. S.Dak. on Nebraska line)

Crazy Horse Canyon Park (Rosebud Reservation): few units, water, toilets, fee
Ghost Hawk Park (18 mi. S.W. of Mission): 220 units, water, toilets, fee
Write: Rosebud Agency, Rosebud, S.Dak.   57570

Sisseton Reservation (N.E. S.Dak., S.E. N.Dak.)[7]

Sica Hollow: 125 units, water, toilets, fee (use sticker)
Clear Lake: open grounds, water, toilets, fee (use sticker)
Pickerel Lake: open grounds, water, toilets, fee (use sticker)
Write: Tribal Planner, Sisseton, S.Dak.   57262

Standing Rock Reservation (N.Dak. and S.Dak. state line)[8]

Celebration Grounds (18 mi. S.W. of McLaughlin): 200 units, no water, toilets, no fee
Indian Creek (3 mi. E. of Mobridge): many units, water, toilets, fee
Wakpala (15 mi. N. of Mobridge): many units, water, toilets (pit), no fee
Write: Recreation Development Director, Standing Rock Reservation, Fort Yates, N.Dak.   58538

Wisconsin

Bad River Reservation (S.E. of Duluth on Lake Superior)

Marble Beach (14 mi. E. of Ashland): 58 units, water, toilets, fee; also 58 trailer sites, 40 picnic areas
Write: Great Lakes Agency, Ashland, Wis.   54806

Red Cliff Reservation (3 mi. N. of Bayfield)

Red Cliff: 34 units, water, toilets, fee; also 32 trailer sites, hookups, fee
Write: Red Cliff Reservation, Rt. 1, Bayfield, Wis.   54814

[6] The Oglala Sioux Game Range is now in operation.
[7] All campgrounds are operated by the State Game and Fish Department in conjunction with the tribe. There are 44 lakes in the area.
[8] Extensive campground development is planned.

CALENDAR OF INDIAN EVENTS

Date	Place	Event
	May	
1	Tahlequah, Okla.	Cherokee Village
6–Aug. 6 (Saturdays)	Lower Brulé, S.Dak.	Calf Roping
7	Tahlequah, Okla.	Cherokee Homecoming
7	Encampments at Wounded Knee, Kyle, Oglala, Allen, Porcupine, and Manderson, S.Dak.	Powwows and Dances
Memorial Day weekend	Black River Falls, Wis.	Winnebago Powwow
Memorial Day weekend	Devil's Lake Reservation Fort Totten, N.Dak.	Powwow and Dances
	June	
Evenings, all summer	Chicago Indian Center, Chicago, Ill.	Intertribal Ceremonies
Evenings, June–Aug.	Red Lake Reservation, Minn.	Powwow, Fish Fry
June	White Earth Reservation, Minn.	Centennial Celebration and Occupancy
June	Turtle Mountain Reservation, N.Dak.	Sun Dance
Early	Belcourt, N.Dak.	Sun Dance, Grass Dance
Mid-month	White Cloud, Kans.	Iowa Tribe Powwow
Mid-month	Fort Yates, N.Dak.	Powwow
11–14	Pawhuska, Okla.	Osage Dances
14–15	Kyle, S.Dak.	Powwow
Mid-June–late Aug.	Hot Springs, S.Dak.	Crazy Horse Pageant
18	Grass Mountain, S.Dak.	Powwow
18–21	Clinton, Okla.	Intertribal Powwow
24–27	Hominy, Okla.	Osage Ceremonial Dances
26–28	El Reno, Okla.	Intertribal Exposition
27–Aug.	Tahlequah, Okla.	"Trail of Tears"—Cherokee Drama
Late	Rosebud, S.Dak.	Spotted Tail Memorial Celebration

Date	Place	Event
June–Labor Day, daily	Wisconsin Dells, Wis.	Chippewa Powwow
June–Labor Day, Tues. and Thurs.	Lac du Flambeau, Wis.	Stand Rock Indian Powwow
Last weekend	8 mi. W. of Horton, Kans.	Kickapoo Powwow
Late	Murrow Dance Grounds, Binger, Okla.	Caddo Tribal Dance
Sat., June–Labor Day	Fort Thompson, S.Dak.	Powwow

July

Date	Place	Event
1–4	Sisseton, S.Dak.	Sioux Ceremonial
2–4	La Creek, S.Dak.	Powwow
2–5	Cannon Ball, N.Dak.	All-Indian Powwow
2–5	Pawnee, Okla.	Pawnee Powwow
2–5	Parmelee (Rosebud Reservation), S.Dak.	Sun Dance
3–5	Spring Creek (Rosebud Reservation), S.Dak.	Sioux Powwow
3–5	Carnegie, Okla.	Kiowa Gourd-Clan Dance
3–5	Greenwood, S.Dak.	Struck-by-the-Ree Powwow
3–5	Fort Thompson, S.Dak.	Powwow Dances
4	Hayward, Wis.	Gathering of Tribes
4	Redlake, Minn.	Indian Dancing Contest
Every Sat.	Anadarko, Okla.	Indian Ceremonials
4–5	Binger, Okla.	Caddo Indian Dance
4–6	Cannon Ball, N.Dak.	Powwow
1–Labor Day	Hayward, Wis.	Indian Dance
1st weekend	Ft. Cobb, Okla.	Indian Ceremonials
Summer season	Indian Centers Milwaukee, Wis.	Oneida Indian Club Powwow
9–11	Jim Thorpe Park, near Stroud, Okla.	Sac and Fox Powwow
14–16	Mission, S.Dak.	Antelope Powwow
15–16	Flandreau, S.Dak.	Santee Sioux Powwow
17	Stomp Grounds, Gore, Okla.	Red Bird Smith Birthday Celebration
17–19	New Town, N.Dak.	Mandan Powwow
3d weekend	Ball Club, Minn.	Chippewa Thanks for Wild Rice
21–23	Cherry Creek, S.Dak.	Powwow
Last weekend	Mayetta, Kans.	Potawatomi Powwow
23–25	Fort Totten, N.Dak.	Fort Totten Days Festival
Last weekend	Winnebago, Nebr.	Annual Powwow
Late	Stomp Grounds, Red Rock, Okla.	Oto-Missouri Powwow
28–30	Little Eagle, Standing Rock Reservation, S.Dak.	Powwow
Last weekend	Belcourt, N.Dak.	Powwow

Date	Place	Event
Late	N. of Red Rock (Noble County), Okla.	Oto-Missouri Powwow
31–Aug. 2	Ed Mack Farm, Shawnee, Okla.	Sac and Fox Powwow
30–Aug. 2	Pine Ridge, S.Dak.	Oglala Sioux Sun Dance

August

Date	Place	Event
1–17 (weekends)	Lake Andes, S.Dak.	Powwow
Early	Fond du Lac, Minn.	Chippewa Fair
3–5	Pine Ridge, S.Dak.	Sun Dance
1st weekend	Tokio, N.Dak.	Buffalo Dance
1st week	Fort Cobb, Okla.	Indian Ceremonials
4–6	Fort Yates, N.Dak.	Powwow
4–7	Talihina, Okla.	Choctaw Fair
7–9	Lower Brulé, S.Dak.	Indian Fair and Powwow
2nd weekend	Tama, Iowa	Mesquakie Powwow
11–13	Rosebud, S.Dak.	Spotted Tail Powwow
13–15	Bull Head, S.Dak.	Powwow
15	Macy, Nebr.	Omaha Indian Homecoming
14	Parshall (Mountrail County), N.Dak.	Reservation Fair
Mid-August	White Eagle, Okla.	Ponca Indian Fair
18–20	Rosebud, S.Dak.	Powwow
21–23	Rosebud, S.Dak.	Tribal Fair, Powwow
Late	Vineland, Minn.	Mille Lacs Chippewa Powwow
Last weekend	Belcourt, N.Dak.	Annual Powwow
19–22	Canton, Okla.	Arapaho Powwow
27–29	Fort Thompson, S.Dak.	Powwow
27–29	Eagle Butte, S.Dak.	Cheyenne River Fair

September

Date	Place	Event
2–4	Bull Creek, S.Dak.	Powwow
2–4	Soldier Creek, S.Dak.	Powwow
Labor Day	Sisseton, S.Dak.	Sioux Powwow
Labor Day	Nett Lake, Minn.	Wild Rice Harvest
Labor Day	Devils Lake, Fort Totten, N.Dak.	Sioux Fair and Powwow
Labor Day	Colony, Okla.	Cheyenne-Arapaho Powwow
Sept.–May	YMCA, St. Paul, Minn.	Indian Center Powwow
Labor Day	Fort Totten, N.Dak.	Fair, Sioux Powwow
3–6	Carnegie, Okla.	Kiowa Powwow
Early	Anadarko, Okla.	Mopope Powwow
1st Saturday	Tahlequah, Okla.	Cherokee National Holiday
Labor Day weekend	Colony, Okla.	Tribal Powwows
5–7	Eagle Butte, S.Dak.	Sioux Fair
17–19	New Town, N.Dak.	Tribal Arts and Crafts Fair
Fourth weekend after Labor Day	Oklahoma City, Okla.	Annual American Indian Ceremonial Dance

Date	Place	Event
Late	Hominy, Okla.	Tribal Dances
Last week	Wamblee, S.Dak.	Powwow
Labor Day	Lawton, Okla.	Gourd Dance Celebration
Labor Day	Black River Falls, Wis.	Winnebago Powwow

October

Weekends	Danbury, Wis.	Mille Lac Powwow
Weekends	Eastlake, Wis.	Chippewa Dances
Weekends	Vineland, Minn.	Ceremonial Dances
Early	Fort Totten, N.Dak.	Sioux Coronation
Early	Pawnee, Okla.	Pawnee Bill Art Show

November

9–11	Carnegie, Okla.	Kiowa Powwow
9–11	Indian City, Anadarko, Okla.	Veterans Day Powwow
11	Pawhuska, Okla.	Osage Indian Veterans Day
11	Greenwood, S.Dak.	Struck-by-the-Ree Powwow
11	Carnegie, Okla.	Kiowa Veterans Celebration

THE NORTHWEST

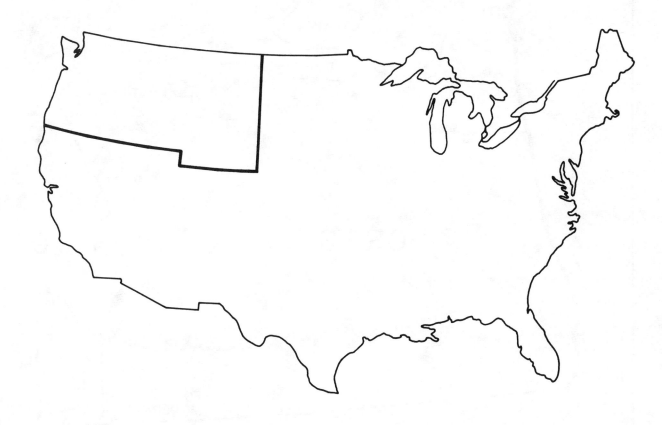

Louise Sheryl Edmo, a member of the Bannock-Shoshone tribes, Miss Indian America, 1972. *Archie Nash, Sheridan, Wyoming.*

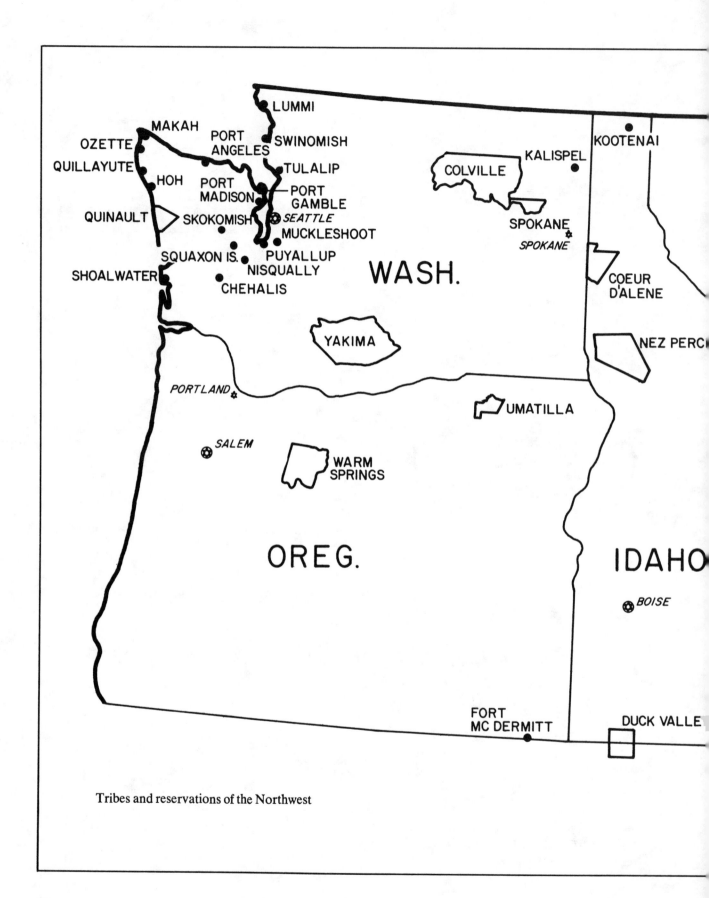

Tribes and reservations of the Northwest

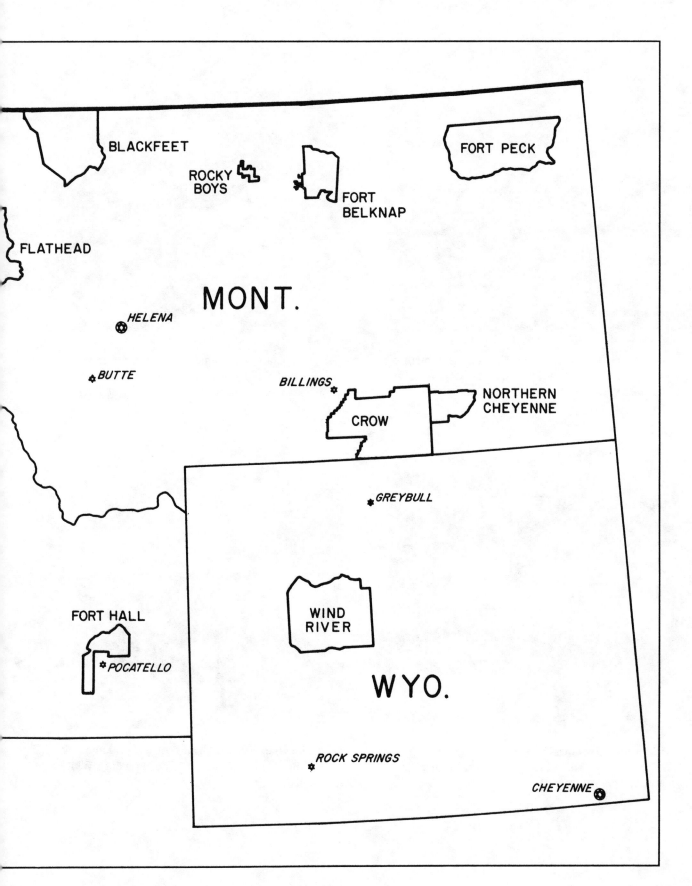

BLACKFEET

ROCKY
BOYS

FORT PECK

FLATHEAD

FORT
BELKNAP

MONT.

⊕ *HELENA*

✦ *BUTTE*

BILLINGS ✦

CROW

NORTHERN
CHEYENNE

✦ *GREYBULL*

FORT HALL

WIND
RIVER

✦ *POCATELLO*

WYO.

ROCK SPRINGS ✦

CHEYENNE ⊕

179

A Yakima Nation Summer Encampment memorial parade at White Swan, Washington. *Arlene Olney, Yakima Nation Review.*

A Yakima Nation Summer Encampment, White Swan. Wilfred Yallup (center) is one of the Yakimas' leading war-dance singers. *Arlene Olney, Yakima Nation Review.*

A Yakima Nation Summer Encampment, White Swan. The girl is riding in memory of her grandfather. *Arlene Olney, Yakima Nation Review.*

Robert Jim, the tribal chairman of the Yakimas, at the Yakima Nation Summer Encampment, White Swan. *Arlene Olney, Yakima Nation Review.*

The Indians of the Pacific Northwest

Draw a line north and south through Washington and Oregon where the Cascade Mountains bisect the states. East of the line is plateau country. West of it lies the humid coastal strip.

Because of the barrier of the Cascades two different Indian cultures evolved. Tribes on the eastern uplands, among them the Cayuses, Umatillas, and Paiutes, became horse Indians, influenced by the Indians of the Northern Plains. Those west of the barrier, such as the Tlingits of Alaska, were water Indians, fishermen and trappers, and with the great plenty of timber around them, fine woodworkers. They built oceangoing whaleboats and ventured far to sea on whaling expeditions.

Life was easy for the water Indians. There was plenty of food. They mastered ways of taking the plentiful salmon with nets and traps, spearing them, shooting them with bow and arrow, and sometimes simply clubbing them.

They were surrounded by forests of evergreens, especially red cedar. They learned to work the wood for many purposes. They built shelters, gabled lodges, and dugout canoes. The inside bark they used for weaving. They used red cedar for tools and utensils. They learned to steam and bend it, and with these skills they fashioned many devices. They became expert carvers and used the wood extensively in their arts and crafts. They made excellent baskets, some of them waterproof, and also wove fine blankets of dog hair. They became experts in inlaying bone, copper, and shells from the abundant waters around them. They decorated everything with elaborate designs.

Unlike other American Indians, they evolved an aristocracy. At the top were the chiefs, of royal blood. Under them were the members of the nobility, the privileged class. Below them were the common people, the workers. There was also a slave class, captives and their offspring. The rulers had hereditary prerogatives. They controlled wealth and social rank. Wealth was equated with the right to rule. They claimed the best fishing places and the exclusive right to practice certain crafts.

A ritual of this society was the potlatch, a feasting and gift-giving ceremonial. The potlatch took many forms, but its purpose and its nature were always the same. It was a display of wealth and status, and the well-to-do made the potlatches lavish and prestigious affairs. Potlatches were given on state occasions, as when a new chief honored the chief he succeeded. They were given to mark birthdays, adoptions, and marriages and were sometimes held simply to impress the right people, to demonstrate beyond question the hosts' wealth or station in life. Sometimes they were held to save face after embarrassing failures or disappointments.

The Indians east of the Cascades, on the High Plateau, lived a different kind of life. Through contact with the Indians of the Northern Plains they had become horse Indians. They fished the Snake and the Columbia, the two great rivers that sliced through the plateau, but, with the horse, they became buffalo hunters. They counted their wealth in horses. Except when they were actually hunting, their life had little formal organization. Their ceremonials became almost perfunctory. Only those related to replenishing their food supply were celebrated with dedication.

By the time the first white explorers arrived on the Pacific Northwest Coast, about a century after Columbus arrived in the Caribbean, about fifty tribes were living along the bays and rivers. They became used to seeing the great-winged ships and, from time to time, white men.

Tlingit totem pole on Prince of Wales Island. *E. E. Dale Collection in the Western History Collections, University of Oklahoma Library.*

By 1700, Yankee clippers were visiting the area. Fifty years later white traders arrived. Before the century was over, Captain Robert Grey sailed up the river and named it after his ship, the *Columbia*.

While the attention of the coastal Indians was drawn to the west, a party of whites was approaching overland from the opposite direction. Down the river from the great mountains came the Lewis and Clark Expedition.

This was the opening wedge from the east. The trickle of adventurers turned into a surging tide. From the whites the Indians learned to trap and to hunt for profit, but with the whites came trouble, disease, suffering, war, and death. By 1830 the Columbia River had become the main artery of travel in the Pacific Northwest. The newcomers brought smallpox. Some tribes, like the Chinooks, were almost wiped out.

In 1842 the Oregon Trail was opened to the Willamette Valley, bringing still more immigrants. By 1850 the friendliness of the tribes had turned to hostility. They were determined to drive out the whites. The situation was aggravated when gold was discovered in Washington and in British Columbia. Miners and fortune hunters flocked in, swelling the numbers of settlers. There was no stopping the westward push. Less than seventy-five years after the expedition of Lewis and Clark, the whites possessed the land, and most of the Indians were on reservations.

Today there are twenty-two reservations in the state of Washington. The three largest, Yakima, Colville, and Spokane, are in the plateau country east of the Cascades. The others are scattered along the coastal strip. About fifteen thousand Indians live on reservations in Washington.

The Yakima Reservation is in south-central Washington. Like the other plateau Indians, the Yakimas were hunters, fishers, and food gatherers before they became horse Indians. In season they fished for salmon and hunted deer, elk, and small game. They dug root plants, camas and bitterroot, and in the fall went on long huckleberry-harvesting expeditions.

As with so many Indians, the horse changed their lives. They became expert horsemen and raised large herds of horses. After their wars with the white man, they turned to the soil. Today most of their income is from timber.

The Yakimas, along with the other tribes living in Washington, Oregon, and Idaho, own about two million acres of forest lands. Each year the tribes jointly harvest about $8 million worth of timber, mostly giant evergreens.

Today some five thousand Indians live on the Yakima Reservation. They cling to their traditions and customs. The longhouses that once served as shelters are now community centers. There the Yakimas observe their tribal ceremonies.

The Colville and Spokane reservations have opened a number of campgrounds to the public, but there are no campground facilities on the Yakima Reservation.

Oregon has two reservations, Warm Springs and Umatilla, both east of the Cascades. Their combined Indian population is about thirty-six hundred.

There are probably more different kinds of Indians in the Pacific Northwest than anywhere else in the United States. They represent at least fourteen different linguistic stocks. The population of Warm Springs Reservation is a case in point. When the reservation was established in 1855, two groups, the Wasco and the Warm Springs tribes were settled on it. The Wascos were composed of three groups, the Dalles, Ki-gal-twal-la, and Dog River bands. The Warm Springs tribe was composed of four groups, the Taih, Wyam, Tenino, and Dock-spus bands. After the reservation was established, a band of Paiutes was assigned to it. Today the eight groups are called the Confederated Tribes.

Warm Springs Reservation has a population of about two thousand, of whom approximately 60 per cent are under the age of twenty-one.

The Confederated Tribes run several well-organized enterprises, including a sawmill and a plywood plant. They also operate the modern Kah-Nee-Ta Vacation Resort, complete with tourist facilities, including an Olympic-size swimming pool.

The Blackfeet

Until the whites crossed the Rocky Mountains, the Blackfeet had never heard of firearms. They already had horses, however, and with the combination of horses and firearms they became the most formidable power on the Northwest Plains.

The Blackfeet consisted of three tribes, the Piegans, the Bloods, and the Blackfeet proper. They were called Blackfeet because of the color of their moccasins, blackened with paint or by the burned prairies.

Facing them on the east were their enemies the Western Crees, the Crows, the Arapahoes, and the Chippewas. Threatening them also were the Shoshones, the Sioux, the Flatheads, and the Kutenais. But with the almost impregnable wall of the Rockies behind them, their position was strong. They called the mountains "the backbone of this land."

Superior horsemen, they became master raiders. Sometimes they raided their enemies to avenge wrongs. More often they raided to steal horses.

Even before the white traders and trappers appeared in their country, the Blackfeet were fierce and ruthless warriors. They raised no food. They depended mainly on hunting, especially buffalo. Even before they obtained guns, they devised ways to kill the buffalo by stampeding them over cliffs. Buffalo hunting became a communal adventure. With fast, well-trained horses it was no longer necessary to stampede the buffalo over cliffs. The Blackfeet hunted them on horseback.

With horses and guns guaranteeing their food supply, they had more time for leisure. They turned to crafts and made beautiful buckskin clothing decorated with fringes and glass beads. They carved tobacco bowls and stems, painted buffalo robes, and fashioned elaborate feather headdresses.

White travelers visiting among them called them the most self-sufficient and contented Indians of the Northern Plains. They pursued their own tribal life in their own way, fighting their enemies either for pride or satisfaction, taking scalps if it pleased them, and going on horse-stealing forays for excitement and pleasure.

Polygamy was a principle of their lives. Nearly all the males had several wives, and the stronger and abler had as many as seven. All the Blackfoot camps rang with the laughter of many children.

After Lewis and Clark growing numbers of whites went through the Blackfoot country. The whites were willing to trade guns and ammunition for furs. The Blackfeet traded but quickly discovered that the whites came prepared to do their own trapping. This deprived the Blackfeet of their commodities for trading. The Blackfeet retaliated first by trading their furs to the Big Knives (their term for the whites), and then by ambushing them, hijacking their furs, and selling them to Canadian traders across the border.

When the whites frustrated this practice, the Blackfeet determined to keep the whites out of their territory altogether. In the end this failed, too, for the overwhelming firepower of the whites was simply too much for them. The whites asserted their wants with gunpowder, which also, in the end, put a stop to the Blackfoot practice of horse stealing. The horse raids ended in the 1880's.

But in the meantime the Blackfeet had been devastated by a foe even more deadly, disease. The Blackfeet prospered in their strategic fortress area until 1836. That year they were hit by smallpox. Epidemics ravaged their camps for the next thirty years. By about 1870 about two-thirds of the Blackfeet had been wiped out.

A year later another blow fell. A tanning

process was developed to make buffalo hides useful as leather for industrial purposes. The demand for buffalo hides skyrocketed, and the systematic extermination of the buffalo herds began. In the next twelve years the buffaloes became almost extinct, and the main food supply of the Blackfeet was destroyed. In the winter of 1883–84, about six hundred Piegans starved to death in Montana. That time of tragedy became known as Starvation Winter. The six hundred were buried on a ridge south of the agency, today called Ghost Ridge.

By this time the great westward push of the whites was on. Indians everywhere were being rounded up and placed on reservations. The Blackfeet, once so formidable, were too weak to resist. They surrendered.

Today the main body of the surviving Blackfeet, about fifty-six hundred, live on the Blackfeet Reservation of 1.5 million acres in north-central Montana, on the Canadian line. Another five thousand live off the reservation. Few full bloods are left, but about 25 per cent of the enrolled members of the tribe are at least three-quarters Indian. Enrolled membership in the tribe requires one-half or more Blackfoot blood.

Most of the Blackfoot Indians are Catholic, but each year they take part in their own Indian cere-monials, the most widely known of which is the Sun Dance, the Medicine Lodge Ceremony.

Some of the older Blackfeet still speak the language, but among the young the language is fading out. The mixed bloods have some knowledge of the language; the younger ones speak mostly English with some words or phrases of the native tongue. Even to them the language is almost foreign.

In recent years the Blackfeet have made progress in agriculture and have done well with their cattle enterprise. At one point cattle were issued by the government to the Blackfeet. They have pursued cattle raising ever since. They also promote their crafts. Today the Blackfoot Crafts Organization maintains a store at St. Marys, near Glacier National Park, where arts and crafts may be purchased. The Blackfeet Reservation is the eastern gateway to Glacier National Park. The park lands were once part of the reservation. Today the park is one of the points of interest to those visiting the reservation. Another is the Blackfoot Historic Site, a four-hour, seventy-mile self-guided scenic tour. The tour is clearly charted for the motorist, and each of the historic sites is marked with an information panel.

Bridger Bowl Ski Area, Blackfeet Agency, Billings, Montana. *Bureau of Indian Affairs.*

185

The Crows

The white fur trappers and traders found the Crow Indians an extraordinary people, tall, lean, handsome, strong, fierce warriors. And fierce they were, particularly to their relatives, the Sioux, and also to the Blackfeet, the Cheyennes, and the Arapahoes. But to the whites they were friendly. They welcomed Lewis and Clark and in 1825 signed a treaty of friendship with the federal government. In turn the government rewarded them with a reservation of about 38.5 million acres in Montana and Wyoming. Today the Crow Reservation, consisting of only about 1.5 million acres, is the largest reservation in Montana.

The Crows are the second-largest tribe in Montana, numbering about 5,500. Of these, 4,350 live on the reservation. The remainder live in the vicinity.

The Crows belong to the Siouan linguistic family. They called themselves the Absarokas, "Children of the Large-beaked Bird." Others called them "Bird People," and from this the whites called them Crows.

In the course of several centuries they changed from a sedentary agricultural people situated on the other side of the continent, twenty-five hundred miles on the east, to warrior nomads and hunters of the Northern Plains country. Forced out of the northeast woodlands by the belligerent Iroquois, they pushed westward to the Great Lakes and on into what is now the Dakotas. There they settled along the Missouri River. The long migration changed their way of life. They almost abandoned agriculture. They raised only corn and squash. Their neighbors called them the "People Who Live in Earthen Lodges." With horses they became hunters and nomads; forced to fight other tribes for hunting grounds, they became warriors.

The momentous changes taking place in their way of life split them into factions. The group now known as the Absarokas quit agriculture altogether and pushed toward the Rockies. They traveled in two main bands and became thoroughgoing nomads. The River Crows lived along the Missouri, the Milk, and the Yellowstone rivers. The Mountain Crows lived in the high hills of northern Wyoming and southern Montana. A splinter group, known as the "Kicked-in-the-Bellies Band," wandered free.

The two major bands, the River Crows and the Mountain Crows, became increasingly militaristic. They were led by war chieftains who made the major decisions. Young warriors, aspiring to be chiefs, had to prove their daring and courage and cunning in battle. To become a chief, a warrior had to accomplish four deeds of war at the risk of his life. Most never made it, but the system perpetuated the leadership of the ablest warriors. When they grew too old to be effective in battle, they became counselors.

As warriors and hunters and nomads, they cultivated only one crop, tobacco. Tobacco and smoking were deeply related to their spiritual life. They raised "medicine" tobacco for use in their ceremonials and "ordinary" tobacco for smoking for pleasure. Their Tobacco Society Ceremonials were manifestations of their religion. They identified the Supreme Being as "First Maker," although (in white terms), they did not worship First Maker.

After Lewis and Clark passed through their country, fur companies and trappers began moving in. Trading posts sprang up, and when the Bozeman Trail brought wagon trains of immigrants, the government built three forts to protect them. The Sioux and their allies forced the government to shut them down.

Ethel Big Medicine, a Crow woman, controls the machine on which yarn is tufted on a jute backing to form a scroll-patterned carpet at Big Horn Carpet Mills, Inc., Montana. *Lyle C. Axthelm, Bureau of Reclamation.*

But the huge Crow Reservation began to shrink. In 1868 the Fort Laramie Treaty cut the reservation acreage from 38.5 million acres to about 9 million acres. The federal government claimed that in the 1825 treaty it had been "overly generous."

Eight years later Custer's command was wiped out at the Little Big Horn, on the Crow Reservation (today the site of the Custer National Monument, one of the main points of interest on the reservation). Nonetheless, two years after "Cus-ter's Last Stand," the Crows and most other tribes had been rounded up on reservations.

In 1882 the size of the Crow Reservation was reduced again. In exchange for cession of Crow lands to the government, the government erected a number of houses for the Crows. Eight years later the government bought another portion outright for $946,000, and in 1905 the reservation was cut to about 3 million acres, about 8 per cent of its original size. The Crows received less than five cents an acre for their land.

The tribal enemies of the Crows looked on with satisfaction. The Crows, who, they said, had gone out of their way to befriend the whites, had fared no better than they, who had fought the inexorable western movement.

But the Crows had learned to tolerate the whites and had made it a point to avoid fighting them. In this manner, at least, they had suffered smaller losses.

As they had for centuries, the Crows went their own way, independent. They practiced their ceremonials. They continued their Tobacco Society and held their Sun Dance.

As with other tribes, the Crow economy was traditionally linked with hunting and gathering edible plants. Today the basis of the Crow economy is their land. Some of it—not much—is used for farming. On some livestock is raised. Some of it is utilized to encourage commercial enterprises, among them the Arts and Crafts Guild. An industrial park has been set up on the reservation, and efforts are being made to establish enterprises that will provide employment. This is no easy task. Unemployment on the reservation has sometimes reached 65 per cent in winter, and the average annual unemployment rate is 28 per cent.

In 1948 the Crow tribe adopted a written constitution providing for a general-council form of government. Every enrolled member of the tribe present at a council meeting has a vote. Elections are held every two years for chairman, vice-chairman, secretary, and treasurer.

Today the Crows continue performing their ceremonials. The most important annual event is the re-enactment of Custer's Last Stand on the site of the battle at the Little Big Horn.

The Nez Percés

When Lewis and Clark reached the Nez Percé country in the early 1800's, the Nez Percés welcomed them. They gave them shelter, supplied them with smoked and dried salmon and roasted camas roots, and helped them build their dugout canoes for the journey down the Snake River to the Columbia.

The Nez Percés then numbered about six thousand. They lived in what are now central and western Idaho, northeast Oregon, and southeast Washington. They roamed the territory from the Blue Mountains of Oregon to the Bitterroot Range of Idaho and Montana. On hunting trips they crossed the Continental Divide and penetrated as far east as the Missouri River.

Lewis and Clark left their horses with the Nez Percés and then pushed on to the distant sea. A Nez Percé guided them to The Dalles. There he left them and made his way back to the Wallowa Valley of his people. The white explorers spent the winter on the Pacific Coast. In the spring they returned and reclaimed their horses from the Nez Percés.

For more than half a century the Nez Percés were friends of the whites. Old Chief Joseph, father of the hero of the Nez Percé War that was to come, was a devout Christian. He treasured his New Testament and often quoted from it.

The Nez Percés are the largest group of the Shahaptian linguistic family. They are related to the Yakima, Umatilla, Walla Walla, Cayuse, and Palouse Indians. They called themselves the "People of the Mountains."

They were a skilled and resourceful people. In their deerskin shirts and breechcloths, tailored moccasins and leggings, they bore themselves with pride and dignity. Many of them wore blankets and feathers.

By the time Lewis and Clark arrived in their country, the Nez Percés had been "horse Indians" for more than a century. Before that they had been fishermen and food gatherers. Their staples were salmon, roots, and berries. They did not practice agriculture, but they husbanded the camas prairies, relished camas roots, and prepared them in many ways.

Before they obtained horses, they lived in about seventy small communities or villages. Each village had its own chief and operated independently. There was no leadership above the village level and little tribal identity. They spoke dialects of the same language but had few other ties.

With horses, they became hunters. Buffalo hunting required "team effort," cooperation among the villages, particularly when the Indians crossed the Rockies on their seasonal buffalo hunts on the Northern Plains. Hunting chiefs were selected for the expeditions, and the young hunters from several villages joined in. This led to the formation of larger bands and the evolution of primitive tribal government.

These were the bands who confronted the white intruders of the mid-nineteenth century. In early years the Nez Percés readily traded with the trappers and fur traders who came their way. Even when the immigrants began arriving over the Oregon Trail, they traded with them. By this time the Nez Percés had become expert breeders of horses, had developed the famous Appaloosas, and were raising cattle. They traded horses, cattle, dried salmon, and camas roots, and became known among the whites as hard-driving traders.

Beginning in 1855 agents of the government made a series of treaties with the bands that were willing to deal with them. These bands ceded portions of the Nez Percé lands. But the Nez Percés of the Wallowa Valley in Oregon refused to cede any of their lands. They also refused to acknowledge that the other bands could cede any of the Nez Percé lands. The treaty making went on, however, and by 1869 the Nez Percés' lands had been cut to a fraction of their original size. Old Chief Joseph, disillusioned and heartbroken, died. The old friendliness between the whites and the Nez Percés turned sour. Within the ranks of the young Nez Percés resistance was growing.

Then gold was discovered on the Nez Percé lands, and a new wave of white invaders pushed in. The Nez Percés who had already ceded their land sold food and horses to the gold seekers. The prospectors built a mining camp at Lewiston, ravaged the countryside, and robbed and murdered the Nez Percés.

After gold seekers came land seekers, flooding through their country. The pressure split the Nez Percés into three factions. One was for making a deal with the whites. The second group was for compromise. The third group wanted no part of the whites. They demanded that the whites leave and that no more be permitted to enter. They appealed to the government, pointing to their years of peace and friendship. It availed them nothing. The Valley of the Winding Waters was opened to homesteaders, and the government repudiated its treaties.

Young Chief Joseph, called by his people "Thunder-Rolling-Over-the-Mountains," rallied his people, called the Non-Treaty Nez Percés. He counseled prudence. But the actions of the whites had stirred the young men, led by his brother Alokut (or Ollicut), who formed a war party.

In 1877, General Oliver O. Howard, the "One-Armed-Soldier-Chief," summoned Joseph and his chieftains to Fort Lapwai (built in 1862 for the protection of the whites and to prevent clashes between them and the Indians). Joseph and his chieftains came to the fort. With him were Chief Looking Glass, Chief White Bird, Alokut, and a small party of braves.

General Howard demanded that Joseph and his band give up their lands and move to Fort Lapwai. Joseph and his chieftains listened, parleyed, and left.

While he tried to accommodate to the demands of the government, his people were gathered on the Camas Prairies. Suddenly the word came. Some militant young Nez Percés had killed several settlers. The war exploded, thundering through the mountain passes, the valleys, and the canyons.

In the first battle, at White Bird Canyon, Chief Joseph ambushed and destroyed the troops sent after him. In the seventy-eight-day campaign that followed, Joseph fought off forces that outnumbered him ten to one. But in the end he was overwhelmed. It was the end of the line for the Nez Percés. They lost their Valley of the Winding Waters forever. Chief Joseph was never again permitted to live in the valley. He was a prisoner most of the rest of his life. He died on the Colville Reservation in Washington State in 1904.

Ever since the close of the war most of the Nez Percés have lived on reservations. Today there are about twenty-four hundred on the official tribal rolls. About fifteen hundred of these live on the Nez Percé Reservation area in Idaho.

Once they were expert basketmakers. They wove beautiful cups, food bowls, and fine, soft storage bags. Today they do beadwork and make leather goods. With several guilds they are encouraging their young in the Nez Percé arts and crafts.

One of the interesting attractions of the reservation is the Nez Percé Historical Park, commemorating the services of the Nez Percés to the Lewis and Clark Expedition. Many of the historical sites of the Nez Percés, such as the White Bird Battlefield, may be visited in the park.

Fort Lapwai is now the headquarters of the Nez Percé Indian Agency. There are no campground facilities on the reservation. However, the Nez Percés are making plans for a recreation complex in the Orofino-Dworshak Dam area.

The Shoshones

The Shoshones at one time had a vast territory. As a reward for their friendship, in 1863 the United States government "gave" them title to more than 44.6 million acres in the present states of Colorado, Montana, Idaho, Utah, and Wyoming. Today they own only a small fraction of that area. About two thousand Shoshones share with the Arapahoes the 1.9 million acres of the Wind River Reservation in Wyoming. Another twenty-six hundred share with the Bannocks the Fort Hall Reservation in Idaho. Other Shoshones are scattered in Nevada, Utah, and California.

The Shoshones are of the Uto-Aztecan linguistic family. They are related to the Comanches, the Kiowas, the Paiutes, and the Hopis. In early times, before their dispersal, they lived in the Great Basin, the vast dry saucer between the Wasatch Mountains and the Sierra Nevada. There, where the waters rush down out of the mountains and perish in the sands, they clawed a living out of the desert.

In time the migrant Plains Indians, the Sioux, the Cheyennes, and other tribes, ventured into the basin. They came mounted, and from them the Shoshones learned about horses. They too became horse Indians and hunters and migrants.

Some of the Shoshones moved north and east into the Wyoming country and became known as the Northern or Eastern Shoshones. Those who remained in the Great Basin area became known as the Western Shoshones. The horse gave them mobility, but the Western Shoshones remained poor. They also suffered raids at the hands of the Plains Indians. The Utes raided them, captured and carried them off, and sold them into slavery in the Spanish markets of what is now New Mexico.

In about 1800 raiding Crows captured a twelve-year-old Shoshone girl named Sacagawea. They took her eastward and sold her to the Mandans in a village on the Missouri River. There she remained a captive. When Lewis and Clark came through on their way to the Pacific, Sacagawea, then about eighteen, had married a French trapper, Toussaint Charbonneau, and had just had a baby.

Lewis and Clark were in need of a guide and interpreter who could lead them to the distant sea. Charbonneau made a deal to guide them, but it fell to his young Shoshone wife to do most of the work. Sacagawea, with her six-weeks-old baby strapped to her back, led the way.

As they pushed westward, Sacagawea recalled the country where she had spent her childhood. She recognized the landmarks that she had not seen since she had been captured six years before. When they reached the Shoshone country, she danced with joy. There she was reunited with her people. But when the question rose whether she should go to the Pacific with Lewis and Clark or remain with her people, she chose to go on.

Sacagawea guided Lewis and Clark through the Rockies and down to the coast. There they spent the winter. When they returned in the spring, Sacagawea came back with them.

The Shoshones were not yet aware of the existence of a ten-year-old boy, born into a different tribe, who would become their greatest leader. The boy was of Umatilla and Flathead blood. When he was thirty-two, he joined the Shoshone tribe. He quickly rose to power among the Shoshones and became Chief Washakie. His adopted tribe called him "White-Haired Chief with Scarred Face." Shoshone lore today is rich with the deeds and the exploits of Chief Washakie. Crowheart Butte, in the northwestern part of the

Chief Washakie (1804–1900), "wise ruler" of the Shoshones, and admired and respected by the whites. *Wyoming State Archives and Historical Department.*

Wind River Reservation, is revered as the place where Chief Washakie fought hand to hand with a Crow chief for the hunting rights in the Wind River Valley.

In the vigor of his younger days he led the Shoshones against the Crows, the Sioux, the Cheyennes and the Arapahoes. More than that, he protected the whites against his enemies, the Sioux and the Cheyennes. When peace finally came, the Shoshones were rewarded with the vast expanse of territory and were assured that it would be theirs forever. Fifteen years later, in 1878, that era ended. The government announced that the Arapahoes, the bitter foes of the Shoshones, would be moved onto the reservation with the Shoshones.

Chief Washakie spoke out against the move. He spoke for all Indians who had signed treaties with the government. He was proud, he said, that he had never spilled the blood of a white man. His pleas were classics of eloquence. His fame spread across the country into the halls of Congress. The government insisted that moving the Arapahoes onto the Shoshone Reservation was only a temporary measure. On this promise the matter stood. The Arapahoes were moved in. They are still there.

Chief Washakie lived to be about one hundred years old. He is buried at Fort Washakie, now the headquarters of the Wind River Agency. (One tradition has it that Sacagawea is also buried there.) But long before his death Chief Washakie had witnessed the loss of most of the Shoshone lands. In the early 1870's gold was discovered at South Pass. This led to loss of lands to the government in the Brunot Cession of 1874.

Today the Wind River Reservation is seventy miles wide, east to west, and fifty-five miles north to south. It lies between Thermopolis on the northeast, Shoshoni on the east, Lander on the south, and Dubois on the west.

With the passing years relations mellowed between the Shoshones and the Arapahoes. The Shoshones generally live in the western part; the Arapahoes in the eastern. They co-operate in many areas but are not integrated. Each tribe has its own enterprises. The Arapahoes raise most of the cattle, but both tribes encourage livestock enterprises.

There is plenty of water on the reservation, enabling the tribes to carry on big irrigation projects. There are many minerals and oil and gas, which produce income.

Directions for a self-guided tour of the reservation are available at the agency headquarters. The tour charts the many natural attractions, Crowheart Butte, the historic sites, the abandoned mining camps, the ghost towns, and the blockhouse in Fort Washakie. Looking toward more tourism, the tribes are projecting a recreation complex at Bull Lake.

A highlight of the summer season is the Sun Dance. This ritual is conducted for healing, thanksgiving, repentence, forgiveness, and resurrection. The ceremonies usually begin in the evening or in the early morning, and they last for seventy-two hours. During that time the dancers neither eat nor drink. They chant prayers which are carried to the Supreme Being on the rays of the sun.

An aerial view of Kah-Nee-Ta Lodge, Warm Springs Reservation, Oregon.

TRIBES AND RESERVATIONS

Tribe	Reservation or Location	Acres	Population	Address
		Idaho		
Blackfoot Fort Hall Bannock Shoshone	Fort Hall	524,000	2,700	Fort Hall 83203
Coeur d'Alene	Coeur d'Alene	68,000	900	Northern Idaho Agency Lapwai 83540
Kootenai	Kootenai	2,680	70	Sandpoint 83840
Nez Percé	Nez Percé	760,000	2,400	Nezperce 83543
		Montana		
Blackfoot	Blackfeet	901,939	5,800	Browning 59417
Crow	Crow	1,567,348	3,500	Crow Agency 59022
Kootenai Salish	Flathead	617,553	2,900	Dixon 59831
Assiniboin Gros Ventre	Fort Belknap	595,660	2,100	Harlem 59526
Assiniboin Sioux	Fort Peck	889,255	3,100	Poplar 59255
Northern Cheyenne	Northern Cheyenne	433,273	2,100	Lame Deer 59043
Chippewa Cree	Rocky Boys	107,612	900	Box Elder 59521
		Oregon		
Cayuse Umatilla Walla Walla	Umatilla	. . .	1,600	Warm Springs 97761
Wasco Warm Springs[1] Paiute	Warm Springs	651,000	2,000	Warm Springs 97761

[1] The Warm Springs acreage includes that of the Umatilla Reservation. The Klamath Reservation was terminated in 1963.

Tribe	Reservation or Location	Acres	Population	Address
		Washington		
Columbia	Colville	. . .	. . .	Coulee Dam 99116
Colville				
Lakes				
Nespelem				
Nez Percé				
Yakima	Yakima	. . .	5,500	Toppenish 98948
Chehalis	Chehalis	. . .	215	Western Washington Reservations 1620 Hewitt Ave. Everett 98201[2]
Hoh	Hoh	. . .	60	Same
Lower Elwha	Lower Elwha	. . .	290	Same
Lummi	Lummi	. . .	780	Same
Makah	Makah	. . .	570	Same
Muckleshoot	Muckleshoot	. . .	385	Same
Nisqually	Nisqually	. . .	202	Same
Port Gamble	Port Gamble	. . .	175	Same
Port Madison	Port Madison	. . .	190	Same
Puyallup	Puyallup	. . .	300	Same
Quileute	Quileute	. . .	310	Same
Quinault	Quinault	. . .	950	Same
Shoalwater	Shoalwater	. . .	30	Same
Skokomish	Skokomish	. . .	230	Same
Squaxin Isle	Squaxin Isle	. . .	135	Same
Swinomish	Swinomish	. . .	500	Same
Tulalip	Tulalip	. . .	600	Same
Spokane	Spokane	. . .	. . .	Wellpinit 99040
Salish	Kalispel	4,700	170	Agency Lapwai, Idaho 83540
		Wyoming		
Shoshone	Wind River	2,268,000	2,150	Fort Washakie 82514
Arapaho			3,000	

[2] The total acreage of the western Washington reservations is 651,547.

CAMPGROUNDS

Montana

Blackfeet Reservation (N.W. Mont., near Glacier Park)

    Chewing Backbone (4 mi. N. of St. Mary): 50 units, no water, toilets, no fee
    Duck Lake (U.S. 89 N. of St. Mary): 26 units, no water, toilets, no fee
    Two Medicine (State 49, 5 mi. N.W. of East Glacier): 15 units, water, toilets, fee
  Write: Blackfeet Agency, Browning, Mont. 59417

Crow Reservation (S.Cen. Mont.)[1]

    Crow Agency (Crow Agency): 5 units, water, toilets, no fee
    Spear Siding (I.90): 5 units, water, toilets, no fee
    Willow Creek (reservoir): 10 units, no water, toilets, no fee
  Write: Chairman, Crow Tribe, Crow Agency, Mont. 59022

Flathead Reservation (N.W. Mont.)[2]

    Blue Bay (16 mi. N.E. of Polson): 10 units, water, toilets, fee
    Kicking Horse Reservoir (4 mi. S. of Ronan): open campsites, no water, no toilets, fee
    Lower Crow Reservoir (8 mi. S.E. of Ronan): open sites, no water, no toilets, fee
    MacDonald Lake (11 mi. N.E. St. Ignatius): open sites, no water, toilets, fee
    Mission Creek (W. of St. Ignatius): open sites, no water, toilets, fee
    Nine Pipe Reservoir (5 mi. S. of Ronan): 10 units, water, toilets, fee
    Ravalli (across R.R. tracks): open sites, water, toilets, no fee
    St. Ignatius (N. of St. Ignatius): open sites, water, toilets, no fee
    St. Mary (11 mi. S.E. of St. Ignatius): open sites, no water, no toilets, fee
    Turtle Lake (5 mi. S.E. of Polson): open sites, no water, no toilets, fee
    Twin Lakes (13 mi. S.E. of St. Ignatius): open sites, no water, toilets, fee
    Upper Dry Fork (8 mi. N.W. of Hot Springs): open sites, no water, no toilets, fee
  Write: Confederated Tribes, Flathead Reservation, Dixon, Mont. 59831

Fort Belknap Reservation (50 mi. E. of Havre, Mont.)[3]

    Beaver Creek Park (Big Warm): 3 units, no water, toilets, no fee
    Big Warm Pool (Big Warm): 5 units, water, toilets, fee
    Little Chief Canyon (Lodge Pole): 15 units, water, toilets, no fee

---

[1] Good campgrounds are also available at Big Horn National Recreation Area.
[2] All persons 15 to 64 years old must have use permit.
[3] Also has 50 picnic sites.

Mission Canyon (Hays): 25 units, water, toilets, fee
Snake Butte (Harlem): 6 units, no water, toilets, no fee
Write: Fort Belknap Indian Community, Fort Belknap Agency, Harlem, Mont.   59526

Fort Peck Reservation (N.E. Mont.)

Brockton Park (S. of Brockton): 14 units, water, toilets, no fee
Lions Park (S.E. of Wolf Point): 150 units, water, toilets, no fee
Poplar Park (N.E. of Poplar): 150 units, water, toilets, no fee
Poplar Rest Stop (W. of Poplar): 14 units, no water, no toilets, no fee
Wolf Point Area (E. of Wolf Point): 6 units, no water, toilets, no fee

Rocky Boys Reservation (N.Cent. Mont.)[4]

Southeastern Township: open sites, water, toilets, fee
Write: Rocky Boys Reservation, Baldy Butte Inn, Box Elder, Mont.   59521

Oregon

Warm Springs Reservation (Cen. Oreg.)

Blue Lake (30 mi. N.W. of Warm Springs): 1 unit, no water, toilets, no fee
Dry Creek (4 mi. N.E. of Warm Springs): 25 units, no water, toilets, no fee
Indian Park (12 mi. S. of Warm Springs): 12 units, water, toilets, no fee
Kah-Nee-Ta (11 mi. N.E. of Warm Springs): 120 units, water, toilets, no fee
Trout Lake (30 mi. N.W. of Warm Springs): 20 units, no water, toilets, no fee
Write: Warm Springs Agency, Warm Springs, Oreg.   97761

Washington

Colville Reservation (N.W. Wash.)[5]

Bridge Creek (11 mi. N. of Keller): 2 units, no water, toilets, no fee
Buffalo Lake (5 mi. E. of Belvidere): 4 units, no water, toilets, no fee
Coyote Creek (9 mi. N.W. of Nespelem): 3 units, water, toilets, no fee
Gold Lake (18 mi. N. of Nespelem): 6 units, no water, toilets, fee
Lost Creek (9 mi. N. of Desautel): 3 units, no water, toilets, no fee
Nixon Twin Lakes (10 mi. W. of Inchelium): 12 units, water, toilets, fee
Owi Lake (10 mi. N.E. of Nespelem): 2 units, no water, toilets, no fee
Owi Lake (S.E. side, 10 mi. N.E. of Nespelem): 2 units, no water, toilets, no fee
Rainbow Beach (10 mi. W. of Inchelium): 35 units, water, toilets, fee
San Poil River (15 mi. S. of Republic): 12 units, no water, toilets, no fee
San Poil River (Rickards, 2 mi. N. of Keller): 2 units, no water, toilets, no fee
Scotch Creek (12 mi. N. of Desautel): 3 units, no water, toilets, no fee
Twin Lakes (Hidden Beach, 10 mi. W. of Inchelium): 3 units, no water, toilets, no fee
Twin Lakes (Rocky Point, 10 mi. W. of Inchelium): 7 units, no water, toilets, no fee
Write: Colville Agency, Coulee Dam, Wash.   99116

Makah Reservation (tip of N.W. Wash.)

Makah Bay Area (1 mi. S. of Neah Bay): 50 units, water, toilets, fee; also 20 trailer sites
Write: Western Washington Agency, 1620 Hewitt Ave., Everett, Wash.   98201

---

[4] Also has some trailer hookups, tipis sleeping four for rent. Group tours provided.
[5] All campgrounds charge a fishing fee.

Quieleute Reservation (W. Wash. on Pacific)

Tribal Park (La Push): 25 units, water, toilets, fee; also 25 trailer sites
Write: Western Washington Agency, 1620 Hewitt Ave., Everett, Wash.   98201

Quinault Reservation (40 mi. N. of Hoquiam)

Quinault Beach (Quinault): 150 units, no water, toilets, no fee
Tahola (1 mi. S. of Tahola): 15 units, water, toilets, fee; also 20 trailer sites
Write: Quinault Reservation, Tourism, 1620 Hewitt Ave., Everett, Wash.   98201

Spokane Reservation (N.E. Wash.)[6]

Benjamin Lake (3 mi. S. of agency): 10 units, no water, toilets, no fee
Big Chamokane (5 mi. S. of Ford): 25 units, water, toilets, no fee
Blue Creek (9 mi. N. of Wellpinit): 15 units, water, toilets, no fee
Ceremonial Grounds (Wellpinit): 100 units, water, toilets, fee
Little Falls (Little Falls Dam): 10 units, water, toilets, no fee
McCoy Lake (14 mi. N. of Old Fort): 20 units, no water, toilets, no fee
Turtle Lake (5 mi. N. of agency): 10 units, no water, toilets, no fee
Write: Programs Officer, Box 86, Wellpinit, Wash.   99040

Wyoming

Wind River Reservation (W. Cen. Wyo.)[7]

Little Wind River (1 mi. N. of Fort Washakie): open sites, water (pump), toilets (pit), no fee
Sacajawea (N. of Crowheart): open sites, water (pump), toilets (pit), no fee
Wind River (Wind River): open sites, water (pump), toilets (pit), no fee
Write: Fish and Game Department, Shoshone and Arapaho Tribes, Fort Washakie, Wyo.   82514

---

[6] Campgrounds at Ceremonial Grounds and Little Falls are open to the public; all others are closed to non-Indians. A boat-launching area is available at Little Falls.

[7] Picnicking permitted on all campgrounds.

CALENDAR OF INDIAN EVENTS

Date	Place	Event
	January	
1	White Swan, Wash.	Tribal New Year
Varies	Tulalip Reservation, Wash.	Treaty Day Feast
	February	
12–13	Kamiah, Idaho	Nez Percé War Dances
12	Pendleton, Oreg.	Umatilla Lincoln's Day
22	Toppenish, Wash.	George Washington Celebration
26–28	Lapwai, Idaho	Nez Percé Washington Day
	March	
Mid-month	Wapato, Wash.	Indian Fair
	April	
Early	Warm Springs, Oreg.	Spring Powwow
Mid-month	Warm Springs, Oreg.	Root Festival
Late	Umatilla, Oreg.	Umatilla Root Festival
	May	
1	Lapwai, Idaho	Nez Percé Festival
Mid-month	Tygh Valley, Warm Springs, Oreg.	Tygh Celebration
16–18	Spokane Reservation, Wash.	Smoo-ke-shin Powwow
Memorial Day	Swinomish Reservation, Wash.	Festival
Memorial Day	Taholah, Wash.	Quinault Days
30–31	Chehalis Reservation, Wash.	Tribal Day
	June	
1st weekend	Colville Reservation, Wash.	Horse Event
6–8	Yakima Reservation, Wash.	Games, Salmon Bake
19–21	Coeur d'Alene Reservation, Idaho	Waa-laa Days
22–23	Lummi Reservation, Wash.	Stomish Water Carnival
Late	Fort Washakie, Wyo.	Indian Days

Date	Place	Event
27–30	La Grande, Oreg.	Umatilla Festival
Last Friday	Craigmont, Idaho	Nez Percé Games
Late	Rocky Boys Agency, Mont.	Sun Dance

July

Early	Wolf Point, Mont.	Nez Percé Games
4	Craigmont, Idaho	Omaha Dances
3–4	Fort Kipp, Mont.	Indian Dances
4	Warm Springs, Oreg.	Parade, Dances
4	Yakima Reservation, Wash.	Indian Encampment
4	La Conner, Wash.	Swinomish Festival
4	Arlee, Mont.	Powwow
4–5	Colville Reservation, Wash.	Indian Celebration
4–5	Tahola, Wash.	Quinault Trout Derby
9–12	Blackfeet Reservation, Mont.	Indian Days
2d week	Worley, Idaho	Whaa-Laa Days
10–12	Crow Agency, Mont.	Re-enactment of Custer's Last Stand
2d week	Ethete, Wyo.	Arapaho Sun Dance
2d weekend	Browning, Mont.	Indian Days
Mid-month	Lame Deer, Mont.	Northern Cheyenne Powwow
3d week	Ethete, Wyo.	Arapaho Powwow
3d week	Poplar, Mont.	Iron Ring Celebration
Last week	Fort Washakie, Wyo.	Shoshone Sun Dance
Last week	Colville Reservation, Wash.	Suds 'n Sun Festival
Last week	Joseph, Oreg.	Chief Joseph Pageant
Late	Rocky Boys Agency, Mont.	Indian Days

August

Early	Kalispel Reservation, Wash.	Powwow
Early	Ashland, Mont.	Powwow
Early	Harlem, Mont.	Powwow
1st weekend	Sheridan, Wyo.	All American Indian Days
1st weekend	Suquamish, Wash.	Games and Clam Bake
5–8	Fort Hall, Idaho	Shoshone-Bannock Festival
Early	Usk, Wash.	Kalispel Powwow
Early	Frazer, Mont.	Red Bottom–Assiniboin
2d week	Warm Springs, Oreg.	Huckleberry Feast
2d week	Omak, Wash.	Omak Stampede
16–18	Colville Reservation, Wash.	Indian Fair
2d week	Wind River Reservation, Wyo.	Arapaho Powwow
Mid-month	Wind River Reservation, Wyo.	All-Indian Fair
Mid-month	Crow Agency, Mont.	Crow Fair
3d week	Craigmont, Idaho	Nez Percés Games, Feast
Last week	Lapwai, Idaho	Pi-Nee-Waus Days
Last week	Poplar, Mont.	Oil Celebration
Last week	Sheridan, Wyo.	All American Indian Days

Date	Place	Event
29–30	Makah Reservation, Wash.	Dances, Games
Late	Thermopolis, Wyo.	Water Pageant

September

Labor Day	Wind River, Wyo.	Arapaho Celebration
Labor Day weekend	Wellpinit, Wash.	Spokane Powwow
Labor Day	Warm Springs Reservation, Oreg.	Indian Ways
Labor Day	Ethete, Wyo.	Celebration
Labor Day	Lander, Wyo.	One Shot Antelope Hunt
16–19	Umatilla Reservation, Oreg.	Pendleton Roundup

November

9–11	Pendleton, Oreg.	Umatilla Veterans Day
11–13	Toppenish, Wash.	Indian Veterans Celebration
27–29	Lapwai, Idaho	Indian Thanksgiving
28	Umatilla Reservation, Oreg.	Thanksgiving Potluck

December

Christmas week	Umatilla Reservation, Oreg.	Indian Christmas
Christmas week	Fort Washakie, Wyo.	Holiday Dances
Christmas week	Ethete, Wyo.	Holiday Dances
Christmas week	Wind River Reservation, Wyo.	Holiday Dances

Miss Indian America Celebration, Sheridan, Wyoming.

The Eagle Dance, *Unto These Hills*, a drama of the Cherokee Indians, Cherokee, North Carolina.

THE SOUTHEAST

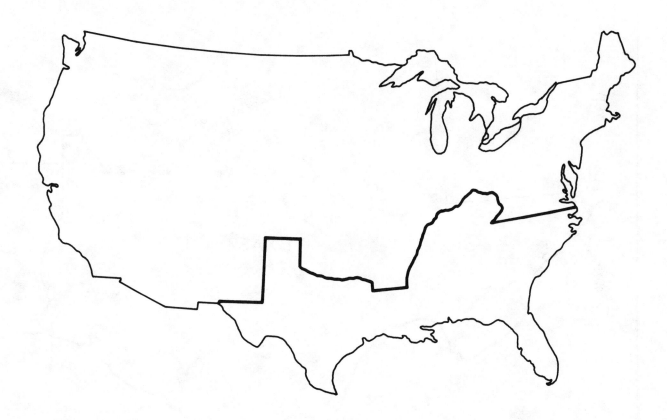

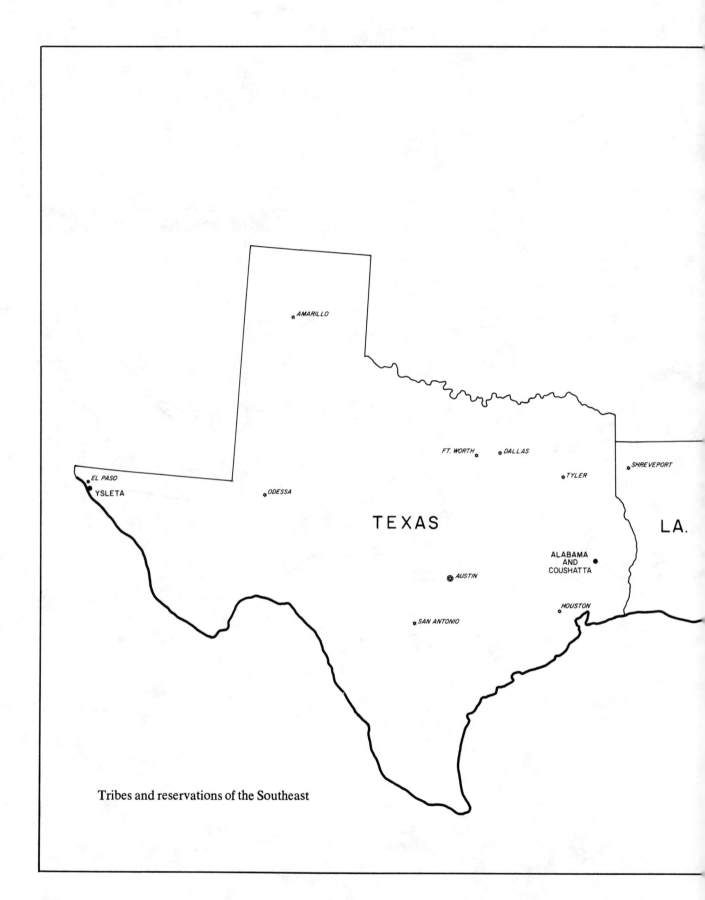

Tribes and reservations of the Southeast

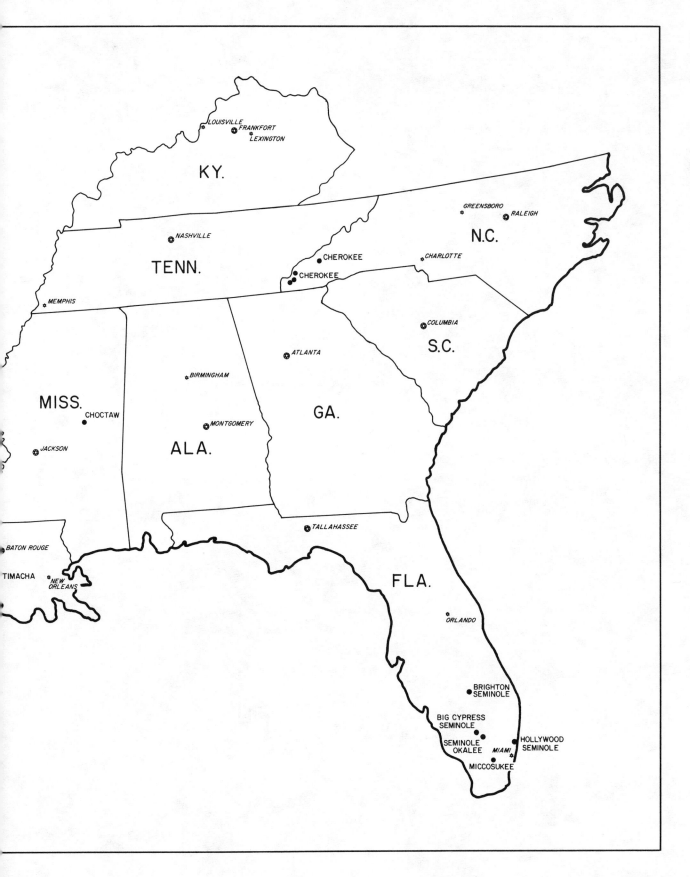

LOUISVILLE FRANKFORT
LEXINGTON

KY.

GREENSBORO RALEIGH

N.C.

NASHVILLE

TENN.

CHEROKEE

CHARLOTTE

CHEROKEE

MEMPHIS

COLUMBIA

S.C.

ATLANTA

BIRMINGHAM

MISS.

CHOCTAW

MONTGOMERY

GA.

ALA.

JACKSON

TALLAHASSEE

BATON ROUGE

TIMACHA NEW
ORLEANS

FLA.

ORLANDO

BRIGHTON
SEMINOLE

BIG CYPRESS
SEMINOLE

SEMINOLE
OKALEE

MIAMI

HOLLYWOOD
SEMINOLE

MICCOSUKEE

The Cherokees

Today the Cherokees are split into two major groups. The Western Cherokees live in Oklahoma. The Eastern Band of Cherokees are in North Carolina.

In the early 1700's the Cherokees occupied all of the southwest Allegheny mountain region of Virginia, the Carolinas, parts of Tennessee, northern Georgia, and northeastern Alabama. Today the Eastern Band of Cherokees live on the 56,000-acre Cherokee Indian Reservation in the Great Smoky Mountains, and the Western Cherokees live in Oklahoma. Those now called the Eastern Band refused to give up their lands and move to Oklahoma. They took refuge in the Great Smokies, and they are still there.

The Cherokees were for centuries hardy mountain men, self-reliant, industrious, and formidable. They were of the same stock as the Iroquois but were fiercely independent. Their blood brothers, the Mohawks, Oneidas, Senecas, Cayugas, and Onondagas, joined in the alliance called the Five Nations. Later the Tuscaroras joined, making it the Six Nations. But not the Cherokees. Indeed, they stood like a barrier on the southern flank of the Six Nations. The Iroquois never breeched their mountain stronghold. But white men did, and with them came trouble, disease, warfare, and dispossession.

The Cherokees were excellent farmers, expert hunters and fishers, and fine artists. They were intelligent and skillful traders and when necessary, fierce warriors.

American fur traders came through their mountain gaps, encroaching on their territory. On the

Cherokee woman potter.

south, the Spaniards and the French were making incursions. Soon the Spaniards held Florida; the French, Louisiana Territory.

The British needed allies. So did the Cherokees. They joined forces. But an unanticipated enemy almost destroyed the Cherokees—smallpox. It wiped out nearly half the tribe. Straightway on the heels of this disaster came open warfare with the Americans.

The fighting went on for more than forty years. The Cherokees lost much of their best lands. Bleeding and harried, the Cherokee leaders saw the futility of fighting. A new relationship with the whites was necessary. They turned to an accommodation of the white man's way. They adjusted to the white man's civilization. They accepted whites in their affairs. They intermarried. They developed industries. They prospered. They even adopted slavery and in time acquired more than a thousand black slaves.

In the meantime, one of their number gave them a dynamic gift. Sequoyah devised his famous syllabary, which made possible a written system of communication for the Cherokees. It had a profound influence on their lives. Sequoyah's mother was a Cherokee of mixed blood. His father was white. He was born in Tennessee about 1760 and grew up as a Cherokee in the wilderness. He could neither read nor write English, but after a hunting accident that lamed him, he turned to study. In the white missions he taught himself to read and write. Alone he laboriously worked out the Cherokee alphabet. It opened a new world of knowledge to the Cherokees. They acquired a printing press and started publication. They printed parts of the Bible and launched a Cherokee newspaper, the *Phoenix*.

At about the same time they established the

The Cherokee syllabary. *From Grace Steele Woodward*, The Cherokees, *Norman, University of Oklahoma Press, 1963.*

Even as John Ross was being sworn in, trouble was brewing. Gold was discovered in Georgia, some of it adjacent to the Cherokee territory. The governor of Georgia ruled that all Cherokee lands on which there were gold mines were the property of the state.

John Ross's former superior, Andrew Jackson, was now President. Under the Indian Removal Act of 1830, President Jackson established as national policy the removal of the Indians to the lands beyond the Mississippi. The Cherokees resisted and sought recourse in the courts. But the legal processes were slow, and bribery, treachery, and betrayal became rife. The slow piecemeal removal was on.

In 1835 there were about 16,500 Cherokees in Alabama, Georgia, North Carolina, and Tennessee. In a gathering at New Echota of some self-appointed Cherokees with officials of the United States government a document was signed in which the Cherokees agreed to removal beyond the Mississippi. In exchange for their lands in the South the Cherokees would get an extensive tract of land in Indian Territory and five million dollars. But since the "treaty" had not been negotiated with the Cherokee Nation and no official of the Cherokee Nation had signed it, the Cherokee Nation refused to honor it.

John Ross led the resistance against the "treaty." More than 15,600 Cherokees signed a petition against it. Ross took the petition to Washington, but government officials refused to see him, and he got nowhere. Instead, armed forces were sent to round up and remove the resisting Cherokees. About a thousand determined Cherokees took refuge in the Smoky Mountains of North Carolina. They thwarted every effort to capture and remove them.

But most of them could not escape. About fourteen thousand were removed and relocated in Indian Territory. Most of them made the eight-hundred-mile trek on foot. The ordeal, one of almost unparalleled suffering, lasted more than six months. About one-quarter of the Indians died. The Cherokees call it the Trail of Tears.

Those who made it into the mountains of North Carolina held fast. They knew the territory better

Cherokee National Council and founded a Cherokee capital at New Echota, Georgia, with a council of thirty-two elected members and an executive. That executive was John Ross, a remarkable leader. Although he was only one-eighth Cherokee, the Cherokees elected him principal chief of the Cherokee Nation.

At the time Ross was only thirty-eight years old. He was born in Rossville, Georgia, to a Scottish immigrant father and a quarter-blood Cherokee mother. He served as an adjutant under General Andrew Jackson, and married a Cherokee (she was to die in the terrible removal of the Cherokees to Indian Territory).

Eagle Dance, *Unto These Hills.*

Entrance of DeSoto, *Unto These Hills.*

than those sent to capture them. Frustrated in its efforts, the state of North Carolina stripped them of their rights. No Indian, it was ruled, could own land in the state.

Only the help of a friendly white trader, Colonel William Holland Thomas, saved them from losing everything. Under the law the Cherokees could not own land, but the colonel could. In his name he purchased land for them. He divided the territory into five districts: Bird Town, Paint Town, Wolf Town, Yellow Town, and Big Cone. The names remain today.

The Civil War brought more trouble. Most of the Cherokees, both those in North Carolina and those in Indian Territory, sided with the South. They even raised contingents to fight for the Confederacy. When the South lost, they lost. The Union government deposed John Ross, and after the war, as punishment, the government took away a good part of the reservation ceded to the Cherokees in Indian Territory. The United States Supreme Court ruled that the Cherokees in North Carolina, by refusing to move to Indian Territory after the signing of the New Echota "treaty," had

Entrance of DeSoto, *Unto These Hills.*

forfeited their rights to be part of the Cherokee Nation. Further, the court ruled, the North Carolina Cherokees could not be recognized as a separate nation.

Still, with both state and federal governments against them, the North Carolina Cherokees held on. At last, in 1876, they were granted formal title to the Qualla Reservation (45,000 acres, their largest land tract) and to the several smaller tracts scattered over five counties in North Carolina.

Meanwhile the Western Cherokees in Indian Territory had joined the Choctaws, Chickasaws, Creeks, and Seminoles in the federation of the Five Civilized Tribes. It was an interesting move, since the Cherokees had declined to join the Six Nations of the Iroquois, their own blood brothers, and yet joined in an alliance with four tribes of a different linguistic stock, the Muskhogeans.

Today the Cherokee Reservation in North Carolina is the largest reservation in the eastern United States. On or near it live nearly all the Cherokees of the Carolinas. A tribal government consisting of a principal chief and a tribal council of twelve runs its affairs. The tribe is engaged in a number of enterprises, the most important being tourism. About five million tourists pass through the reservation each year.

Cherokee arts and crafts are displayed and marketed at the Qualla Arts and Crafts Mutual. The main attraction of the season is the famous drama *Unto These Hills*, a portrayal of the story of the Cherokees, staged in a mountainside theater. It has been staged annually for many years.

Halfway across the continent, at Tsa-La-Gi, just south of Tahlequah, Oklahoma, the Western Cherokees stage their drama, *The Trail of Tears*, from late June through late August.

The Seminoles

It began as a dispute over slaves and turned into a wrangle over land. It escalated into two bloody wars and decades of resistance. When it was over, the Seminole Indians were dispossessed. Those who surrendered were resettled in Oklahoma. Those who refused to yield were fugitives in the Everglades.

Today the Florida Seminoles, about one thousand of them, are still there, living on four reservations. They maintain that they are the only Indians in the United States who never officially made peace with the government.

They were a fiercely independent, freedom-loving people. They held off the best the government could hurl against them—trained, well-equipped troops, overwhelming firepower, and such distinguished military officers as General Winfield Scott and General Andrew Jackson. The Seminoles who hid in the Everglades never yielded and never were conquered.

The Seminoles are mixed bloods. Basically they are Creeks, of the same Muskhogean stock as the Chickasaws and the Choctaws. Several centuries ago they intermarried with the Oconees, and later with the Yuchi, the Yamasee, and several other bands. In 1800 there were about two thousand of them.

Originally they lived in southern Georgia. When the whites moved into their country, they retreated into Florida. The Creeks called them Seminoles, their word for "runaways," or "separatists." In Florida they lived in villages of a hundred or more. Their palmetto-thatched huts, called "chickees," were built around an open square, somewhat similar to the plazas of the Pueblo Indians. A sedentary people, they tilled the soil. Each family had its own garden, and all worked in communal plots to grow food for the needy and for guests.

The Seminoles were expert builders of water craft to traverse the many waterways of their region. Those near the coasts built dugouts large enough for seafaring. They ventured great distances, exploring the Gulf of Mexico and even reaching Cuba and the Bahamas.

By the time the United States had become a nation, slavery had become an economic factor among the Seminoles. Florida belonged to Spain. The Seminoles owned black slaves, but their slavery system was not the same as that of the whites in Alabama and Georgia. Among the Seminoles the blacks had positions somewhat akin to

Florida Seminole children. *James Gaines, Florida News Bureau, Department of Commerce.*

A Florida Seminole Indian family, gathered in front of a *chickee* (a thatch-roofed hut). Several *chickees* make up a family (or camp) residence, each one serving as a room for eating-living, sleeping, and so on. *Seminole Tribe of Florida. Florida News Bureau, Tallahassee.*

A Seminole Indian patting out dough for frybread, to be cooked in a pan on logs. Note the stack of frybread on the upturned iron kettle and the four logs that make up the fire and hold the pan (they are pushed in as the fire burns). In the background are hollowed-out logs to hold the dried-corn kernels, which are ground with the pestle and then cooked into a drinkable, thin gruel called sofkee (which is being stirred by the girl). These are still mainstays in the diet of the Florida Seminoles. *Seminole Tribe of Florida. Florida News Bureau, Tallahassee.*

A Seminole Florida craftswoman. *Florida News Bureau, Department of Commerce.*

that of sharecroppers. Also the Seminoles intermarried with the blacks. Because life was better among the Seminoles, runaway slaves from Georgia and Alabama streamed into Florida. On their heels came the slaveowners. The Seminoles and Spaniards befriended the runaway slaves.

In the meantime the Creek Confederacy had agreed to return runaway slaves to their owners. The Seminoles wanted no part of this agreement. On this issue the Seminoles split from the Creeks.

In Washington the slavery question in Florida took on another aspect—land. The whites invading Florida ostensibly to recover runaway slaves took more than a passing interest in the country itself. They were after more than slaves. In the War of 1812 some of the Creeks sided with the British, some with the Americans. In 1814, Andrew Jackson's force invaded and defeated the "Red Sticks" (Creeks) supporting the British. The United States thereby acquired eight million acres. Three years later General Jackson, supposedly after runaway slaves, led a second invasion into Florida, still a possession of Spain. In 1819, Spain sold Florida to the U.S.

After that it was open season on runaway slaves in Florida. Slavecatchers poured in. They seized not only blacks but also half-blood and full-blood Seminoles and dragged them away to be sold in Georgia, Alabama, and slave markets wherever they could command a price. The Indians who managed to escape the raids hid in the swamps.

The Seminoles ceded about thirty-two million acres to the United States in return for a reservation of four million acres in central Florida. But even there they were not safe. More whites poured in. They increased the pressure on the Seminoles, even those living on their new reservation. Now there was talk of moving the Seminoles out of Florida altogether. The United States took the position that the Seminoles were Creeks and that they belonged on the Creek Reservation, by then established in Indian Territory.

After the Indian Removal Act of 1830 the government undertook to remove the Seminoles by force. They refused to budge. A brilliant young Seminole leader arose. His name was Osceola. He was not a chief, just a member of the tribe, but he fired the Seminoles to resistance. But at length some of the Seminoles agreed to move to Indian Territory. Then at the last moment they were told that only pure-blood Seminoles could go. All those with black blood would be sold into slavery. Intermarried for generations, the Seminoles refused to go. It would mean breaking up families, leaving behind free relatives to be sold into slavery.

A Seminole mother combs her daughter's hair. Note the mother's headpiece. Only a few of the older women now wear this hair style. *Seminole Tribe of Florida, Florida News Bureau, Tallahassee.*

A Seminole cattle ranch, Florida. *Florida News Bureau, Department of Commerce.*

Seminole Indians of Florida carving a dugout canoe. Such canoes were made in many sizes, some large enough to accommodate a whole family. Some crossed the Gulf of Mexico and ventured as far as the Bahamas. *Florida News Bureau, Department of Commerce.*

Violence flared. Indians attacked white settlements. General Wiley Thompson, the Indian agent, four of his officers, and a detachment of soldiers were ambushed and killed. The Second Seminole War was on.

Osceola, only in his early thirties, masterfully led the guerrilla warfare against the United States forces. Attempt after attempt was made to trap and capture him. All failed. He hid Seminole women, children, aged, and ailing deep in the Everglades, and with his men harassed and frustrated their pursuers.

In 1837 another general, Thomas S. Jesup, was sent to persuade Osceola to parley. After some negotiation, during which Osceola was guaranteed safe conduct, Osceola came to the meeting. He was seized, dragged off in chains, and imprisoned at Fort Moultrie, in South Carolina. There, three months later, broken in spirit, he died at the age of thirty-five.

The fighting went on. The Seminoles were enraged. They killed one of their own leaders, Charlie Amathla, who had been one of the signers of the removal treaty.

Many of the Seminoles who left Florida for relocation in Indian Territory never got there. They died on the trail, victims of sickness, improper food, bad weather, and inadequate transportation. Those who remained, the fugitive Seminoles, hid so far back in the swamps that they could not be found—much less subdued.

The Second Seminole War ended in 1842. There was one more Seminole outbreak in 1849. After that the will of the Seminoles was spent. They were decimated and pacified.

Today most of the Seminoles, about seventy-five hundred, live in Oklahoma or are dispersed among the general public. The descendants of those who never surrendered live on the Miccosukee and the three Seminole reservations in Florida. They are known for their colorful costumes and their arts and crafts.

The Seminole women are famed for the multicolored garments they sew from snippets of cloth. They tear cloth into strips, cut the strips into tiny pieces, and sew them together in intricate patterns. With this dextrous and fascinating patchwork, they make vivid shirts, blouses, skirts, aprons, and stoles.

They also make dolls, and they are skilled in carving, jewelry making and basket weaving. Seminole craftsmen may be seen at work in the Indian Village at Dania, between the Everglades and Fort Lauderdale. The Seminole Village Arts and Crafts Center is located on Stirling Road, in Hollywood, Florida.

Other Groups

In those regions where the white man first came in contact with the Indians along the Eastern Seaboard, few Indians remain today. Here the expression "no surviving groups" fittingly applies. In these areas most of the Indian tribes are described as "submerged" or "extinguished." The major organized groups of the Southeast, the Five Civilized Tribes, are long gone. Most of them live in Oklahoma. Those who remain are scattered among the southeastern and Gulf Coast states.

In Georgia, once the seat of the Cherokee Nation, still live a good many persons with Cherokee blood. One group is clustered in the area of Cal-

Ellen Gail Farmer, 1972 Choctaw Princess, Philadelphia, Mississippi.

A Choctaw craftswoman.

A Choctaw basketmaker.

Choctaw stickball sticks.

houn, not far from their early capital at New Echota. About six thousand of the Eastern Band of Cherokees live on the Cherokee Reservation in the Great Smokies of North Carolina. This is the largest federal reservation in the East.

Another forty thousand Indians, Lumbees, Machapungas, and mixed groups, are scattered over seven counties of North Carolina. Most of the Lumbees, the largest group, live in Perquimans County. Except for the Eastern band of Cherokees, the tribal life of the other surviving groups is gone, "extinguished."

About three thousand Indians live in Louisiana. Of these only about three hundred Chitimachas are under government supervision. The others, Houmas, Coushattas (Koasatis), Choctaws, and Tunicas, are scattered.

In South Carolina there are four separate surviving groups, the Catawbas, Croatans, Red Legs, and Brass Ankles. There are no reservations in the state.

In Alabama there are about six hundred Creeks, descendants of the Creeks who refused to go into exile in Oklahoma. Most of them now live in Escambia County.

Mississippi has a small Choctaw reservation. Possibly as many Indians are scattered through-

A Catlin drawing of a Choctaw stickball player. *Smithsonian Institution.*

216

out the state as live on the reservation.

A good many Indians of the Five Civilized Tribes passed through Arkansas on their way to resettlement in Oklahoma. About six hundred of their descendants live there today, most of them around Hot Springs or near the Oklahoma state line. There are no reservations in Arkansas.

Choctaw stickball players today.

A Choctaw drummer, Philadelphia, Mississippi.

Choctaw Social Dance, Philadelphia, Mississippi.

TRIBES AND RESERVATIONS

Tribe	Reservation or Location	Acres	Population	Address
		Florida[1]		
Creek	Miccosukee	333	130	Miccosukee Agency Homestead 33030
Seminole	Brighton	35,805	. . .	Seminole Agency Hollywood 33024
	Big Cypress	42,728	. . .	Same
	Seminole	480	275	Same
		Louisiana		
Chitimachas	Chitimachas	260	270	Choctaw Agency Philadelphia, Miss. 39350
		Mississippi		
Choctaw	Choctaw	17,200	3,800	Choctaw Agency Philadelphia, Miss. 39350
		North Carolina		
Eastern Cherokee	Cherokee	56,000	6,000	Cherokee Agency Cherokee 28719
		Texas		
Note: There are no reservations in Texas.				
Alabama-Coushatta	Alabama-Coushatta Tribal Enterprise, Livingston	4,350	500	Livingston 77351
Tiwa Pueblo	Ysleta	Village	160	El Paso 79917

[1] The total population of the four reservations in Florida is estimated at 2,600.

Seminole Indians. On the right is Sam Huff, in a patchwork "longshirt." On the left is Billy Bowlegs III. Bowlegs was a farmer and hunter. He was a patriarch who told his people of the need for education. He lived on the Brighton Reservation. *Florida News Bureau, Tallahassee.*

CAMPGROUNDS

There are no campgrounds in the Southeast.

CALENDAR OF INDIAN EVENTS

Date	Place	Event
		February
20–22	Seminole Reservation, Hollywood, Fla.	Seminole Powwow
		May
16–Labor Day	Cherokee, N.C.	Living Indian Village
		June
Late June–Labor Day	Cherokee, N.C.	*Unto These Hills*—Cherokee drama
		July
14–18	Ashville, N.C.	Indian Craftsman Fair
22–25	Philadelphia, Miss.	Choctaw Indian Fair
		October
8–11	Cherokee, N.C.	Fall Festival
19–24	Gatlinburg, N.C.	Indian Craft Fair
		Year Long
	Seminole Reservation Hollywood, Fla.	Seminole Okalee Village

Iroquois Dance of the False Face Society, from a painting by Arthur Jansson from masks in the American Museum of Natural History. *American Museum of Natural History*.

THE NORTHEAST

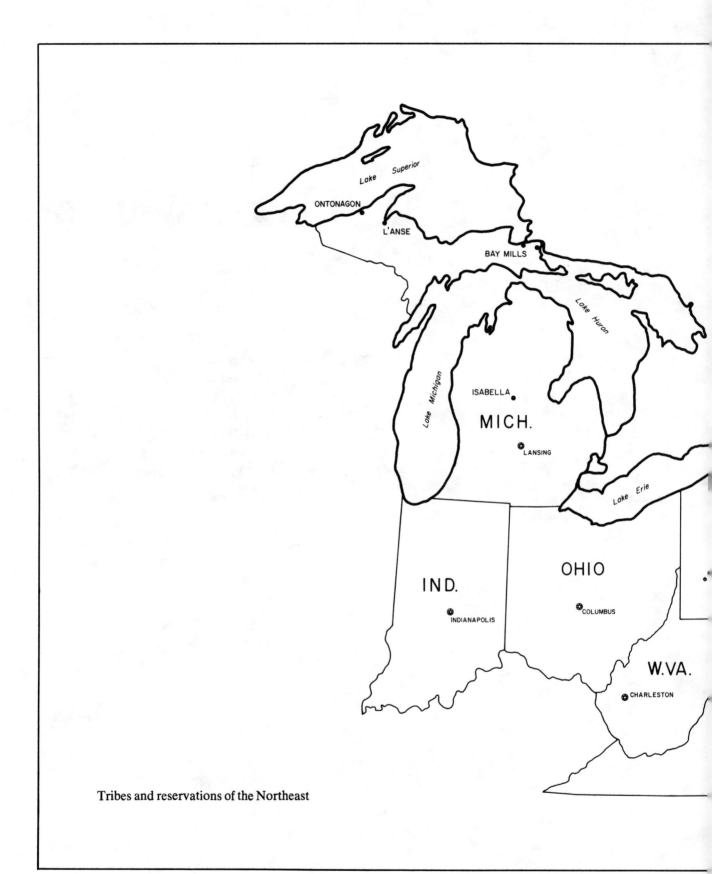

Tribes and reservations of the Northeast

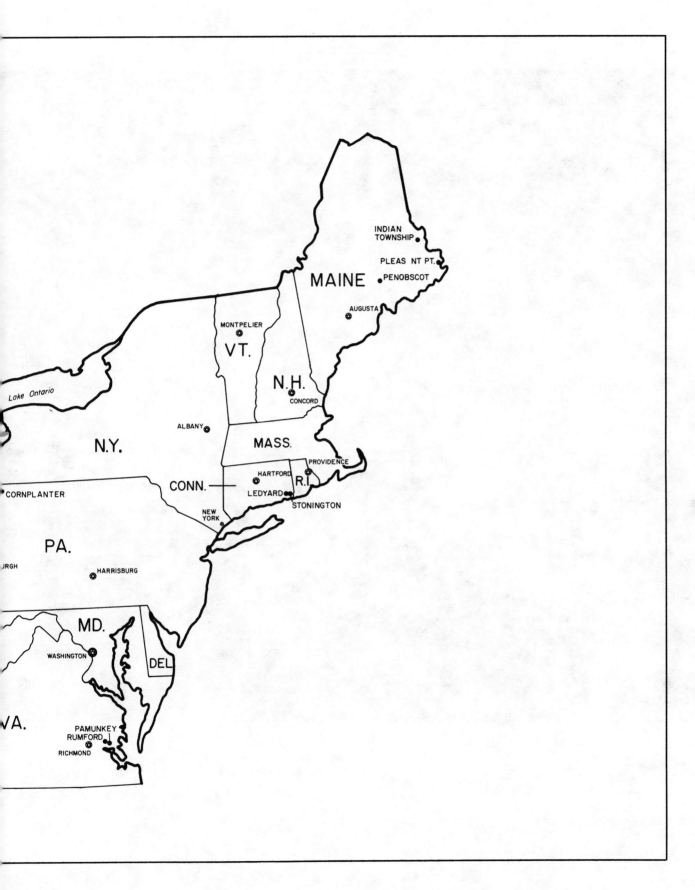

225

Tuscarora Indians, New York State. *Sheldon Toomer, New York State Department of Commerce.*

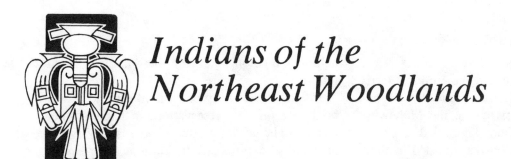

Indians of the Northeast Woodlands

1626—that was the year that Peter Minuit of the Dutch West India Company, bought from the Manhattan Indians Manhattan Island for twenty-four dollars' worth of trinkets and beads.

The Dutch were in New York, the English were in New England, the French were in Canada, the Spaniards were in Florida—and the Indians were in the middle.

When the curtain went up on this scene, the Iroquois and the Algonquians were engaged in a struggle to the death. The Algonquians were a great people, comprising more than one hundred tribes, among them the Delawares, Shawnees, Pequots, Narragansets, Wampanoags, Abnakis, the Penobscots, Mahicans and Mohegans. All of New England was once the domain of the Algonquians. Most of them lived in Connecticut, Rhode Island, and Massachusetts. They farmed, hunted, and took some food from the sea, but mainly they were woodland Indians. They protected their territory from intruding bands but continuously feuded among themselves. That was their fatal weakness.

When the first white men came, the Indians welcomed them. They even yielded their coastal areas with little reluctance and moved westward into the forests. But more and more whites came, expanding their coastal enclaves and pushing the Algonquians farther westward.

The time came when they could move no farther. They had reached the territory of their deadly enemies, the Iroquois. The Iroquois were powerful and hostile, almost unequaled in ferocity. They had pushed up from the south, overrunning all the country from the Carolinas to the St. Lawrence Valley. They controlled parts of Tennessee, Virginia, and Pennsylvania, and almost all of New York except the lower Hudson Valley, and their influence was felt north and west into the Huron, Erie and Ontario lakes region.

The confrontation between the Iroquois and the Algonquians was headlong. The white man's power plays caught them in the middle. The internecine warfare of the Algonquians made it impossible for them to unite to defend themselves against either the Iroquois or the English. The English made the most of this weakness, aggravating and promoting the feuds among the tribes.

The Iroquois for their part made friends with the English and with the Dutch. They cunningly contrived to use the whites for their own purposes against the Algonquians, against the French pushing southward from the St. Lawrence Valley, and against the threat of the American colonists. The Iroquois thus held the balance of power.

Weakened by their own division, the Algonquians were driven out. The English, with their policy of divide and conquer, crushed and defeated the Indians and the French.

The storm clouds were gathering for a showdown between the English and the colonists. When the American Revolution broke out, the Iroquois sided with the English. Chief Joseph Brant led the Mohawks against the Americans. Of the Six Iroquois Nations, only the Oneidas and the Tuscaroras sided with the colonists. As partisans both Algonquians and Iroquois faced the wrath of their white enemies. The deadliest weapons of the whites were disease, liquor, and prostitution. Against these weapons, regardless which side they fought on, the Indians lost.

Two years after the signing of the Declaration of Independence the fledgling American nation signed a treaty with the Delawares, one of the most important Algonquian tribes. A confederacy of Delawares controlled most of eastern Pennsylvania and southeastern New York. The next year, 1779, the Americans invaded the Iroquois territory the Iroquois had seized from the Algonquians. The four Iroquois tribes, the Mohawks, Senecas, Cayugas, and Onondagas, fled to Canada. Later all but the Mohawks returned to fight on the side of the colonists.

After the British were defeated, the Six Nations ceded most of their land to the United States. Both they and the Algonquians had lost the Northeast. Since then they have lived there only by the sufferance of the whites.

Today most of the Iroquois live on state reservations totaling eighty-seven thousand acres in New York State. The Mohawks live on Cornwall Island, near Canada; the Onondagas, near Nedrow; the Tonawanda Senecas, near Basom; the Tuscaroras, near Lewiston. A few Shinnecocks live on Long Island.

There are six state reservations in Maine, the two largest being Penobscot and Passamaquoddy. There is a scattering of Pennacook Indians in New Hampshire. Massachusetts has several settlements totaling about two thousand Indians.

Connecticut has a few Pequots, Mohegans, Niantics, and Scaticooks. There are two small groups of Narragansets in Rhode Island. In New Jersey there are possibly sixteen hundred residents with some Indian blood. About fifteen hundred Nanticokes live in Maryland, most of them in the Blue Ridge area. Several thousand Indians of Lumbee ancestry live in and around Baltimore.

In Pennsylvania, once the stronghold of the Delaware Confederacy, about two thousand Indians are scattered through the state. One of the points of interest is the Cornplanter Reservation, given by the Commonwealth of Pennsylvania to the Seneca chief Cornplanter in reward for his help to the colonists during the American Revolution.

In Virginia a group of Pamunkeys and Mattaponis live on state reservations in King William County. The largest group of Indians in Virginia, the Chickahominys, still function as an organized tribe with their own chief and tribal council. They live on both sides of the Chickahominy River in New Kent and Charles counties. There are also some Rappahannocks, Potomacs, Accohanocs, and Nansemonds and quite a number of mixed bloods in Virginia.

Today there is no federal reservation in the entire Northeast. The remaining Indians and those of Indian ancestry have been absorbed into the general population. Yet their presence is not extinguished. The many Indian names in the Northeast are reminders of the Indians who once roamed the shores and woodlands. Names of cities, towns, villages, rivers, bays, swamps, hills are mute reminders of what once was. The Indians are gone, but they have left their indelible mark.

The Algonquians are gone, dispersed across the continent. Many Iroquois still live in the Northeast. Some continue to engage in their clever and resourceful crafts. They make masks of wood, cornhusks, and horsehair. The maskmakers still have two secret cults, the Society of False Faces and the Bushyheads, and each year they join together to stage parades and celebrations. Some still gather materials to pursue their crafts, turtle shells, gourds, corn husks, wood, and stones. Some weave baskets, do beadwork, and make dolls. The Iroquois were the founders of the Iroquois League of Six Nations, perhaps the greatest confederacy of Indians. To this day some Iroquois are still working for an alliance of all Indians.

Passamaquoddy Indians, Peter Dana Point Reservation, Princeton, Maine. *Albert Dana, Princeton, Maine.*

An Iroquois Long House, Auburn, New York. *New York State Department of Commerce.*

TRIBES AND RESERVATIONS

Tribe	Reservation or Location	Acres	Population	Address
		Connecticut		
Pequot	Ledyard Town	. . .		Ledyard Sta., New London County 06339
			950	
Pequot	Stonington Town	. . .		Stonington New London County 06320
		Maine		
Passamaquoddy	Pleasant Point	100		Perry 04667
			1,000	
Passamaquoddy	Indian Township	18,000		Princeton 04668
Penobscot	Indian Island	4,400	600	Old Town 04468
		Michigan		
Chippewa	Bay Mills	2,189	250	Brimley 49715
Potawatomi	Hannahville	2,846	160	Escanaba 49829
Chippewa	Keweenaw	13,749	400	L'Anse 49946
Saginaw Chippewa	Isabella	1,223	345	Mt. Pleasant 44858
		New York		
Mohawk	St. Regis	14,640	2,300	Hogansburg 13655
Onondaga Oneida Cayuga	Onondaga	7,300	1,600	Nedrow 13120
Poospatuck	Poospatuck	60	85	Mastic, L.I. 11950
Seneca Cayuga	Cattaraugus	21,680	4,600	Irving 14081
Seneca Cayuga	Alleghany	30,469	1,200	Salamanca 14779
Shinnecock	Shinnecock	400	300	Southampton, L.I. 11968

Tribe	Reservation or Location	Acres	Population	Address
Tonawanda Seneca	Tonawanda	7,550	586	Basom 14013
Tuscarora	Tuscarora	5,700	650	Lewiston 14092
Seneca	Oil Spring	640	. . .	Cuba Lake 14727
		Pennsylvania		
Seneca	Cornplanter	. . .	2,200	Warren County 16365
		Virginia		
Mattaponi Pamunkey	State	125	2,200	King William County 23086

CAMPGROUNDS

There are no campgrounds in the Northeast.

CALENDAR OF INDIAN EVENTS

Date	Place	Event
	July	
1st–Labor Day	Hogansburg, N.Y.	Mohawk Indian Village
2d weekend	Lewiston, N.Y.	Powwow
Late	Pleasant Point Reservation, Maine	Indian Pageant
Late	Indian Township Reservation, Maine	Indian Pageant
Late	Indian Island Reservation, Maine	Indian Pageant
	August	
Varies	Onondaga Reservation, N.Y.	Green Corn Dance
Varies	St. Regis Mohawk Reservation, N.Y.	Green Corn Ceremony
Varies	Tonawanda Reservation, N.Y.	Indian Convention
Varies	Tuscarora Reservation, N.Y.	Community Fair
12–13	Barryville, N.Y.	Powwow
	September	
2–4	Southampton, L.I., N.Y.	Powwow

APPENDICES

Appendix A
Indian Museums

City or Location	Museum	Address
	ALABAMA	
Birmingham	Museum of Art	8th Ave. and 20th St. N. Birmingham 35203
	ARIZONA	
Camp Verde	Park Museum	Montezuma National Monument Camp Verde 86322
Coolidge	Park Museum	Casa Grande National Monument Coolidge 85228
Flagstaff	Northern Arizona Museum	Flagstaff 86001
Ganado	Hubbell Trading Post	National Historic Site Ganado 86505
Grand Canyon	Tusayan Museum	Grand Canyon National Park Grand Canyon 86023
Grand Canyon	Yavapai Museum	Grand Canyon National Park Grand Canyon 86023
Kingman	Mohave Museum	400 W. Beale Kingman 86401
Parker	Colorado River Tribe Museum	Rt. 1 Parker 85344
Phoenix	Heard Museum of Anthropology	22 E. Monte Vista Phoenix 85004
Phoenix	Pueblo Grande Museum	4619 E. Washington Phoenix 85034
Roosevelt	Tonto National Monument	Box 707 Roosevelt 85545
Tempe	State Museum	Tempe 85282
Tonalea	National Monument	Navajo National Monument Tonalea 86044
Tucson	State Museum	University of Arizona Tucson 85721
Window Rock	Navajo Tribal Museum	Window Rock 86515
	ARKANSAS	
Conway	State Museum	Conway 72032

City or Location	Museum	Address

CALIFORNIA

City or Location	Museum	Address
Banning	Malki Museum	11-895 Field Rd. Banning 92220
Berkeley	Robert H. Lowie Museum	University of California at Berkeley Berkeley 94720
China Lake	Maturango Museum	Indian Wells Valley China Lake 93555
Desert Hot Springs	Old Indian Pueblo	67-616 Desert View Desert Hot Springs 92240
Lakeport	Lake County Museum	175 3d St. Lakeport 95453
Los Angeles	County Museum	900 Exposition Blvd. Los Angeles 90007
Los Angeles	Southwest Museum	Highland Park Los Angeles 90036
Sacramento	State Indian Museum	2701 L St. Sacramento 95816
Sacramento	State Indian Museum	Fort Sutter Sacramento 95816
San Diego	Museum of Man	San Diego 92115

COLORADO

City or Location	Museum	Address
La Junta	Koshare Kiva	18th and Santa Fe La Junta 81050
Denver	Art Museum	100 W. 14th Ave. Parkway Denver 80207
Denver	Natural History Museum	City Park Denver
Denver	State Museum	E. 14th Ave. and Sherman Denver 80203
Mesa Verde	Park Museum	Mesa Verde 81330
Montrose	Ute Indian Museum	Ouray State Park 81427

CONNECTICUT

City or Location	Museum	Address
New Milford	Historical Society Museum	55 Main St. New Milford 06776
Uncasville	Tantaquidgeon Museum	New London Turnpike Uncasville 06382

DELAWARE

City or Location	Museum	Address
Dover	State Museum	316 S. Governors Ave. Dover 19901

FLORIDA

City or Location	Museum	Address
Gainesville	State Museum	University of Florida Gainesville 32601

City or Location	Museum	Address
Marathon	Southeast Museum	Marathon 33050
West Hollywood	Seminole Museum	Okolee Village U.S. 441 West Hollywood 33023

GEORGIA

City or Location	Museum	Address
Blakely	Kalomoki Mounds	Museum Route Blakely 31723
Calhoun	Preservation Project	New Echota Capital Calhoun 30701
Cartersville	Etowah Mounds	Rt. 1 Cartersville 30120
Indian Springs	Chief McIntosh Home	Rt. 23 Indian Springs 30231
Indian Springs	Creek Museum	State Park Indian Springs 30231
Spring Place	Chief Vann House	Spring Place 30705

IDAHO

City or Location	Museum	Address
Kooskia	Nee Mee Poo Museum	Star Route Kooskia 83539

ILLINOIS

City or Location	Museum	Address
Chicago	Natural History Museum	Lake Shore Dr. and Roosevelt Rd. Chicago 60605
Chicago	Newberry Library Center	60 W. Walton Chicago 60610
Morris	Old Time Village	Morris 60450

INDIANA

City or Location	Museum	Address
Bloomington	State Museum	University of Indiana Bloomington 47401
Indianapolis	Indian Heritage Museum	6040 Delong Rd. Indianapolis 46254

IOWA

City or Location	Museum	Address
McGregor	Effigy Mounds	McGregor 52157

KANSAS

City or Location	Museum	Address
Kansas City	Wyandotte Historical Society	7th St. and Barnett Ave. Kansas City 66101
Larned	Historical Society Museum	Larned 67550
Oberlin	Last Indian Raid Museum	Oberlin 67749
Scott City	El Quartelejo Museum	W. 5th St. Scott City 67871

City or Location	Museum	Address
Topeka	Kansas State Museum	120 W. 10th Topeka 66612

KENTUCKY

Lexington	Anthropology Museum	University of Kentucky Lexington 40506

LOUISIANA

Marksville	Prehistoric Museum	Overton St. Marksville 71351

MAINE

Castine	Wilson Museum	Castine 04421

MASSACHUSETTS

Bourne	Aptucxet Trading Post	Cape Cod Canal Bourne 02532
Cambridge	Peabody Museum	11 Divinity Ave. Cambridge 02138
Deerfield	Indian House Museum	Main St. Deerfield 01342
Grafton	Longhouse Museum	Hassabanisco Reservation Grafton 01519

MICHIGAN

Ann Arbor	Anthropology Museum	University of Michigan Ann Arbor 48104
Detroit	Anthropology Museum	Wayne State University Detroit 48202
Gross Village	Great Lakes Museum	Gross Village 48138
Harbor Springs	Chief Blackbird Museum	Harbor Springs 49740

MINNESOTA

Pipestone	National Monument	Box 727 Pipestone 56164
St. Paul	Historical Society Museum	Cedar St. and Central Ave. St. Paul 55110

MISSOURI

Columbia	Anthropology Museum	University of Missouri Columbia 65201
Miami	Lyman Museum	Rt. 2 Miami 65344
St. Louis	Cherokee Museum	3300 S. Broadway St. Louis 63147

City or Location	Museum	Address

MONTANA

Browning	Plains Indians Museum	Browning 59417

NEBRASKA

Chadron	Fur Trade Museum	Rt. 2 Chadron 69337
Murray	Turtle Mound Museum	Murray 68409

NEVADA

Reno	Historical Society Museum	1650 N. Virginia St. Reno 89503

NEW MEXICO

Albuquerque	Albuquerque Museum	Yale Blvd. Albuquerque 87106
Albuquerque	Maxwell Museum	Roma and University Blvd. Albuquerque 87106
Aztec	National Monument	Rt. 1 Aztec 87410
Bernalillo	Coronado Monument	Box 95 Bernalillo 87004
Gallup	Indian Arts Museum	103 W. 66th Ave. Gallup 87301
Penasco	Picurís Pueblo	Penasco 87553
Portales	Black Water Draw Museum	State 70 Portales 88130
Portales	Paleo-Indian Museum	Eastern New Mexico University Portales 88130
Roswell	Art Center	Roswell 88201
Santa Fe	American Research Museum	Santa Fe 87501
Santa Fe	Ethnology Museum	Santa Fe 87501
Santa Fe	Fine Arts Museum	Santa Fe 87501
Santa Fe	Hall of the Modern Indian	Santa Fe 87501
Santa Fe	Institute of Indian Arts	Cerillos Rd. Santa Fe 87501
Santa Fe	Navajo Ceremonial Arts Museum	704 Camino Lejo Santa Fe 87501
Santa Fe	Palace of Governors	Santa Fe 87501
Taos	Millicent Rogers Museum	Churchill Rd. Taos 87571

NEW YORK

Basom	Tonawanda-Seneca Museum	Tonawanda-Seneca Reservation Basom 14013
Brooklyn	Brooklyn Museum	E. Parkway at Washington Ave. Brooklyn 11238

City or Location	Museum	Address
Canandaigua	Historical Society Museum	55 N. Main St. Canandaigua 11424
Castile	Historical Society Museum	17 E. Park Rd. Castile 11427
Cooperstown	Indian Museum	1 Pioneer St. Cooperstown 13326
Fonda	Caughnawaga Museum	Fonda 12068
Fort Plain	Fort Plain Museum	Ft. Plain 13339
New York City	Museum of the American Indian	Broadway and 155th St. New York 10032
New York City	Primitive Art Museum	15 W. 54 St. New York 10019
New York City	Natural History Museum	Central Park and 79th St. New York 10026
Onchiota	Six Nations Museum	Onchiota 12968
Rochester	Arts and Sciences Museum	657 East Ave. Rochester 14607

NORTH CAROLINA

Boone	American Indian Museum	Boone 28607
Cherokee	Cherokee Indian Museum	Cherokee 28719

NORTH DAKOTA

Fort Berthold	Four Bears Park	Fort Berthold 58718
New Town	Affiliated Tribes Museum	Four Bears Park New Town 58763

OHIO

Columbus	State Museum	Ohio State University Columbus 43210

OKLAHOMA

Anadarko	Indian Hall of Fame	Anadarko 73005
Anadarko	Southern Plains Indian Museum	Anadarko 73005
Bacone	Museum	Bacone Junior College Bacone 74420
Bartlesville	Woolaroc Museum	State 123 Bartlesville 74003
Broken Bow	Memorial Museum	2d and Allen St. Broken Bow 74728
Lawton	Great Plains Museum	Lawton 73501
Miami	Ottawa County Museum	Miami 74354
Muskogee	College Museum	U.S. 62 and State 16 Muskogee 74401
Muskogee	Five Civilized Tribes Museum	Honor Heights Dr. Muskogee 74401

City or Location	Museum	Address
Norman	Stovall Museum	University of Oklahoma Norman 73069
Oklahoma City	Historical Society Museum	Wiley Post Blvd. Oklahoma City 73102
Okmulgee	Creek Indian Museum	Okmulgee 74447
Pawhuska	Osage Tribal Museum	Pawhuska 74056
Pawnee	Pawnee Bill Museum	U.S. 64 Pawnee 74058
Ponca City	Indian Museum	408 S. 7th St. Ponca City 74601
Sallisaw	Sequoyah's Home	State 101 Sallisaw 74955
Tahlequah	Cherokee Center	U.S. 62 Tahlequah 74464
Tahlequah	Cherokee History Museum	Murrell Mansion Tahlequah 74464
Tonkawa	Yellow Bull Museum	Tonkawa 74653
Tulsa	Gilcrease Museum	2500 W. Newton St. Tulsa 74127
Tulsa	Philbrook Museum	2727 S. Rockford Rd. Tulsa 74414

OREGON

Portland	Art Museum	S.W. Park and Madison Portland 97205

PENNSYLVANIA

Philadelphia	University Museum	University of Pennsylvania Philadelphia 19104

RHODE ISLAND

Ashaway	Tomaquag Memorial Museum	Burdickville Rd. Ashaway 02804
Exeter	Narragansett Museum	Exeter 02822

SOUTH DAKOTA

Gordon	Standing Soldier Museum	Gordon 57001
Martin	Indian Arts Museum	Martin 57551
Mobridge	Land of the Sioux Museum	Mobridge 57601
Pine Ridge Reservation	Mari Sandoz Museum	Pine Ridge Reservation 57770
Rapid City	Sioux Indian Museum	1002 St. Joseph St. Rapid City 57701
Vermillion	University of South Dakota Museum	University of South Dakota Vermillion 57069

City or Location	Museum	Address

TEXAS

Austin	Memorial Museum	Austin 78712
Harwood	Indian Museum	Harwood 78632

UTAH

Salt Lake City	Anthropology Museum	University of Utah Salt Lake City 84112

WASHINGTON, D.C.

Washington, D.C.	Indian Crafts Board	Department of the Interior Washington, D.C. 20240
Washington, D.C.	Smithsonian Institution	Washington, D.C. 20560

WASHINGTON STATE

Bridgeport	Fort Okanogan Museum	Bridgeport 98113
Seattle	Washington State Museum	University of Washington Seattle 98105

WEST VIRGINIA

Moundsville	Mound Museum	Moundsville 26041

WISCONSIN

Beloit	Logan Museum	Beloit College Beloit 53511
Hayward	Ojibwa Nation Museum	Hayward 54843
Milwaukee	City Museum	800 W. Wells Milwaukee 53233
Wisconsin Dells	Winnebago Indian Museum	Wisconsin Dells 53965

WYOMING

Casper	Fort Casper Museum	Casper 82601
Cheyenne	State Museum	23d and Central Ave. Cheyenne 82001
Cody	Plains Indians Museum	Cody 82414
Fort Bridger	Fort Bridger Museum	Ft. Bridger 82933
Fort Laramie	National Historic Site	Ft. Laramie 82212

Appendix B
Indian Organizations

[1] Includes organizations interested in Indians.

ARIZONA

American Indian Association, 120 W. 29th St., Tucson 85713

Arizona Commission for Indian Affairs, 1623 W. Adams, Phoenix 85007

Arizona Indian Association, 4311 N. 9th Ave., Phoenix 85014

Central Plains Indian Club, 5705 W. Sells Circle, Phoenix 85013

Indian Center, 2721 N. Central Ave., Phoenix 85004

Indian Center, 376 N. 1st Ave., Phoenix 85003

Indian Center, 120 W. 29th St., Tucson 85713

Indian Center, 529 W. 2d St., Winslow 86047

Indian Education Center, Arizona State University, Tempe 85281

National Indian Arts Council, Scottsdale 85252

United Indian Mission, 2920 N. 3d St., Flagstaff 86001

CALIFORNIA

American Indian Center, 3060 16th St., San Francisco 94118

American Indian Council, 1111 Washington St., Santa Clara 95050

American Indian Historical Society, 1451 Masonic Ave., San Francisco 94117

American Indian Historical Society, 206 Miguel St., San Francisco 94131

American Indian Lore Association, 12151 Firebrand St., Garden Grove 92640

Antelope Valley Indian League, 816 East Ave., Palmdale 93550

Committee for Indian Land, Life, Box 74151, Los Angeles 90004

Drum and Feather Club, 237 N. Coronado St., Los Angeles 90026

Federated Indians, 2727 Santa Clara Way, Sacramento 95817

Federated Indian Tribes, 9831 E. Arkansas, Bell Flower 90706

Fresno Indian Council, 2968 E. McKinley, Fresno 93703

Indian Advisory Commission, 1107 9th St., Sacramento 95814

Indian Association, 1314 Clay St., Oakland 94612

Indian Center, 600 S. New Hampshire, Los Angeles 90005

Indian Center, 2700 Meadowview Rd., Sacramento 95832

Indian Center, 225 Valencia, San Francisco 94103

Indian Center, 24 E. San Fernando St., San Jose 95113

Indian Center, 7950 Central Ave., Stanton 90680

Indian Coordination Council, 807 N. Madison, Stockton 95200

Indian Culture Center, University of California at Los Angeles, Campbell Hall, Los Angeles 90024

Inter-Tribal Council, 2991 Fulton Ave., Sacramento 96821

Intertribal Friendship House, 523 E. 14th St., Oakland 94601

Intertribal Friendship House, 15105 Thaits St., San Leandro 94577

League for American Indians, Box 389, Sacramento 95802

Little Big Horn Association, 6155 Burwood Ave., Los Angeles 90042

Many Trails Indian Club, 367 W. Spazier Ave., Burbank 91501

Mission Indian Federation, Temecula 92390

Native Women's Action Council, 4339 California St., San Francisco 94118

Shooting Star Foundation, 4040 W. 16th St., Lawndale 90260

Sierra Indian Center, 3958 E. Shepherd Ave., Clovis 93612

United American Indians, 448 N. San Pedro St., San Jose 95110

United Bay Indian Council, 51 9th St., San Francisco 99512

United California Indians, 2290 Elgin St., Oroville 95965

United Native Americans, Box 39925, Los Angeles 90039

United Native Americans, 2150 Taylor St., San Francisco 94108

Urban Indian Development Association, 1541 Wilshire Blvd., Los Angeles 90017

COLORADO

American Indian Development, Inc., 500 Zook Bldg., 431 Colfax Ave., Denver 80204

Call of the Council Drums, 1450 Pennsylvania St., Denver 80203

Crusade for Justice, 1567 Downing St., Denver 80218

DeSmet Indian Center, 1645 Williams St., Denver 80203

National Indian Youth Council, 3175 Colfax Sta., Denver 80200

Native American United, 2210 E. 16th Ave., Denver 80206

Wahkonta Club, 919 W. 39th St., Denver 80211

White Buffalo Council, Box 4131, Denver 80204

CONNECTICUT

American Indian Club, Box 251, Willimantic 05226

Save the Children Foundation, Boston Post Rd., Norwalk 06850

IDAHO

Indian Advisory Committee, Boise 83702

ILLINOIS

Adapt Program, 1630 W. Wilson, Chicago 60640

American Indian Center, 738 W. Sheridan Rd., Chicago 60613

American Indian Foundation, 205 W. Wacker Dr., Chicago 60606

Chicago Indian Village, 1354 W. Wilson, Chicago 60640

Drums, 2239 N. Kimball, Chicago 60647

Indian Council Fire, 1263 W. Pratt Blvd., Chicago 60626

Indians for Indians, Inc., 4606 Kenmore N., Chicago 60640

Indian Village, 5101 St. Charles, Bellwood 60104

Native American Committee, 1362 W. Wilson, Chicago 60640

Native American Program, University of Illinois, Chicago 60680

St. Augustine's Center, 4710 Sheridan Rd., Chicago 60640

IOWA

American Indian Center, 1114 W. 6th St., Sioux City 51103

KANSAS

Indian Center, 1001 N. Kansas Ave., Topeka 66608

Mid-America Indian Center, Box 1638, Wichita 67201

LOUISIANA

Indian Angels, 2541 Adams Ave., Baton Rouge 70805

MAINE

Aroostock Indians Association, Ricker College, Houlton 04730

Department of Indian Affairs, 108 Grove St., Augusta 04330

MARYLAND

Indian Studies Center, 1817 E. Baltimore St., Baltimore 21231

MASSACHUSETTS

Boston Indian Council, 150 Tremont St., Boston 02111

MICHIGAN

American Indians, Unlimited, 515 E. Jefferson, Ann Arbor 48104

American Indian Services, 60 E. McNichols, Highland Park 48203

Associated Indians, 3901 Cass Ave., Detroit 48201

Commission for Indian Affairs, State Capitol Bldg., Lansing 48900

Indian Association, 6405 Turner Rd., Flushing 48433

Indian Foundation, 26265 W. River Rd., Grosse Ile 48138

Indians of North America, 23745 E. LeBost Dr., Novi 48050

North American Indian Association, 2230 Witherell St., Detroit 48201

North American Indian Club, 8760 Troy Rd., Oak Park 48237

MINNESOTA

American Indian Center, 475 Cedar St., St. Paul 55102

American Indian Movement, 1315 E. Franklin St., Minneapolis 55404

American Indian Movement, 261 E. 8th St., St. Paul 55109

Committee for Indian Youth, 2639 University Ave., St. Paul 55114

Department of Indian Work, 3045 Park Ave., Minneapolis 55407

Department of Indian Work, 1671 Summit Ave., St. Paul 55105

Indian Advancement Association, Box 416, Minneapolis 55401

Indian AFDC League, 3103 18th Ave., S., Minneapolis 55407

Indian Anti-Poverty Commission, 2803 Bryant Ave., N., Minneapolis 55411

Indian Center, 727 Hennepin, Minneapolis 55440

Indian Center, 5633 Regent Ave., N., Minneapolis 55440

Indian Club, 94 N. St. Albans, St. Paul 55104

Indian Dance Club, 817 E. Franklin Ave., Minneapolis 55401

Indian Guidance Center, 1718 3d St., N., Minneapolis 55404

Indian Inter-Tribal Association, 451 Mendota, St. Paul 55114

Indian Inter-Tribal Association, 175 Charles Ave., St. Paul 55114

Indian Neighborhood Club, 1401 E. 24th St., Minneapolis 55406

Indian Student Association, University of Minnesota, Minneapolis 55455

Inter-Tribal Council, 432 Sherburne, St. Paul 55103

Ira Hayes Friendship House, 1671 Summit Ave., St. Paul 55105

Mayor's Task Force, 1927 2d Ave., South Minneapolis 55411

Midwest Indian Center, 2533 Nicollet Ave., Minneapolis 55404

Twin Cities Chippewa Council, 2215 Park Ave., Minneapolis 55440

Twin Cities Chippewa Council, 1592 Hoyt Ave., E., St. Paul 55105

Twin Cities Sioux Council, 2215 Park Ave., Minneapolis 55440

Urban American Indian Comm., 2215 Park Ave., Minneapolis 55440

Urban Indian Federation, 2509 W. 54th St., Minneapolis 55410

Urban Sisseton-Wahpeton Sioux, 1128 5th St., N.E., Minneapolis 55418

MONTANA

Department of Indian Affairs, Mitchell Bldg., Helena 59601

NEBRASKA

American Indian Enterprises, Box 19226, Eppley Airbase, Omaha 68119

Indian Community Center, 2957 Farnum, Omaha 68131

Neighborhood House, 1001 N. 19th St., Omaha 68108

NEVADA

Indian Affairs Commission, Carson City 89701

Indian Youth Council, Box 118, Schurz 89427

Inter-Tribal Council, 1995 E. 2d St., Reno 89502

NEW MEXICO

Central Clearing House, 107 Cienega St., Santa Fe 87501

Commission on Indian Affairs, 330 E. Palace Ave., Santa Fe 87501

Indian Advisory Commission, Box 1667, Albuquerque 87107

Indian Community Center, 200 W. Maxwell, Gallup 87017

Indian Youth Council, 3202 Central, S.E., Albuquerque 87106

Indian Youth Council, Box 892, Gallup 87301

Southwest Association, Indian Affairs, Box 1964, Santa Fe 87501

NEW YORK

Association on Indian Affairs, 432 Park Ave., New York City 10016

Commission on Indian Affairs, 1450 Western Ave., Albany 12203

Council of Jewish Federations, 729 7th Ave., New York City 10019

Fellowship of Indian Workers, 475 Riverside Dr., New York City 10027

Indian Community House, 40 E. 35th St., New York City 10016

Indian Cultural Workshop, 1165 Broadway, New York City 10001

Indian Women's League, 495 West End Ave., New York City 10024

National Council of the Churches of Christ, 475 Riverside Dr., New York City 10027

National Council of the Episcopal Church, 815 2d Ave., New York City 10017

Pine Tree Culture Center, 695 Elmwood Ave., Buffalo 14222

United Presbyterian Board, 475 Riverside Dr., New York City 10027

NORTH CAROLINA

Cherokee Boys Club, Box 507, Cherokee 28719

Indian College Foundation, 1419 Elizabeth Ave., Charlotte 28204

NORTH DAKOTA

Indian Affairs Commission, 2021 3d St., N., Bismarck 58501

Indian Affairs Commission, Rolla 58367

Indian Club, Box 816, Bismarck 58501

OHIO

Indian Center, 2600 Church St., Cleveland 44113

OKLAHOMA

American Indian Center, 1608 N.W. 35th, Oklahoma City 73117

Association of American Indian Physicians, 721 N.E. 14th St., Oklahoma City 73190

Cherokee Community Organization, 605 E. Downing, Tahlequah 74464

Indian Center, 603 W. 11th St., Tulsa 74127

American Indian Law Review, University of Oklahoma College of Law, 630 Parrington Oval, Norman 73069

Indian Opportunity Center, 555 Constitution Ave., Norman 73069

Indian Opportunity Center, 1433 N.W. 5th, Oklahoma City 73106

OIO Referral Center, 1410 E. 46th St., N., Tulsa 74103

OIO Urban Center, 5050 N. Peoria, Tulsa 74126

OREGON

Indian Arts and Crafts Center, 734 Burnside, Portland 97214

Indian Arts Festival, Box 193, La Grande 97850

State Advisory Commission, Salem 97301

United Indian Center, 435 N.W. 22d Ave., Portland 97210

PENNSYLVANIA

American Friends Service, 160 N. 15th St., Philadelphia 19107

Indian League of Nations, 1139 Lehman Pl., Johnstown 15902

Indian Rights Association, 1505 Race St., Philadelphia 19102

SOUTH DAKOTA

All Indian Association, Eagle Butte 57570

Black Hills Council, 25 St. Francis St., Rapid City 57701

Catholic Social Service, 303 N. Summit, Sioux Falls 57104

Community Service Center, Rapid City 57701

Council of Seven Fires, 1304 N. Main, Sioux Falls 57104

Han-pa-o-ye, Box 624, Northern State College, Aberdeen 57401

Indian Center, Box 288, Yankton 57078

Indian Leadership Council, Rt. 3, Box 9, Rapid City 57701

Institute Indian Studies, University of South Dakota, Box 122, Vermillion 57069

Lakota Aomiciye, Black Hills State College, Spearfish 57783

Minnehaha Indian Club, 1413 Thompson Dr., Sioux Falls 57105

Mother Butler Indian Center, Box 788, Rapid City 57701

South Dakota Commission on Indian Affairs, Pierre 57501

United Presbyterian Church, Huron College, Huron 57350

Wap'ha, University of South Dakota, Vermillion 57069

TEXAS

Commission for Indian Affairs, State Capitol Bldg., Austin 78700

Indian Center, 722 N. Beacon, Dallas 75214

Inter-Tribal Association, Box 1842, Dallas 75221

Southwest Indian Organization, 334 N. Rider, Pampa 79065

UTAH

Church of the Latter Day Saints, 18 E. North Temple, Salt Lake City 84111

Governor's Commission for Indian Affairs, State Capitol Bldg., Salt Lake City 84100

WASHINGTON, D.C.

American Indian Center, 519 5th St., S.E. 20003

American Indian Cultural Foundation, 918 18th St., N.W. 20000

Americans for Indian Opportunity, 1820 Jefferson, N.W. 20036

Arrow, Inc., 1000 Connecticut Ave., N.W. 20036

Bureau of Catholic Indian Missions, 2021 H St., N.W. 20006

Commission of Indian Affairs, C Street, N.W. 20240

Friends Committee, 245 2d St., N.E. 20002

Futures for Children, 5612 Parkston Rd. 20016

National Council of American Indians, 1346 Connecticut Ave., N.W. 20036

Winnetour Foundation, 1346 Connecticut Ave., N.W. 20036

WASHINGTON STATE

Indian Center, 1900 Boren Ave., Seattle 98101

Indian Community Center, S. 2308 Balfour Blvd., Spokane 99206

Indian Community Center, N. 1007 Columbus, Spokane 99202

Kinatchiptapi Indian Council, 3004 S. Alaska St., Seattle 98108

Northwest Indian Center, Gonzaga University, Spokane 99202

Seattle Indian Center, 3419 Densmore N., Seattle 98103

United Indians of All Tribes, 1407 7th Ave., Seattle 98101

WISCONSIN

American Indian Movement, 3328 W. Lisbon Ave., Milwaukee 53208

Coalition of Native Tribes, 132 N. Charter St., Madison 53706

Consolidated Tribes, Box 3318, Milwaukee 53208

Hay-Lush-Ka Society, Box 4934, Milwaukee 53200

Human Rights Commission, 1 W. Wilson St., Madison 53702

Indian Information and Action, 1414 N. 27th St., Milwaukee 53208

Appendix C
Tribal and Indian-Interest Publications

ARIZONA

Apache Drumbeat, Bylas   85530

Awathm Awahan, Salt River Tribal Office, Rt. 1, Box 120, Scottsdale   85251

Contemporary Indian Affairs, Navajo Community College Press, Many Farms   86503

DNA in Action, Window Rock   86515

Dine' Baa-Hani', Box 527, Ft. Defiance   86504

Fort Apache Scout, Box 86, White River   85941

Fort Yuma Newsletter, Box 890, Yuma   85364

Gila River News, Box 97, Sacaton   85247

Gum-U (How are You?), Supai   86425

Hopi Action News: The Winslow Mail, Winslow   86047

Hopi Crier, Hopi Day School, Oraibi   86039

ICAP Newsletter, Arizona State University, Tempe   85281

Indian Highways, Christian School, 708 S. Lindon Lane, Tempe   85281

Indian Mailman, 4402 N. 1st Ave., Phoenix   88013

Indian Programs, University of Arizona, Tucson   85721

Journal of American Indian Education, Arizona State University, Tempe   85281

Navajo Education Newsletter, Navajo Area BIA, Window Rock   86515

Navajo Times, Window Rock   86515

Newsletter, Navajo Community College, Many Farms   86053

The Padre's Trail, St. Michaels   86511

Papago Bulletin, Box 364, Sells   85364

Quechan News, Box 1169, Yuma   85364

River Tribes Review, Colorado River Agency, Parker   85344

Rough Rock News, Demonstration School, Chinle   86503

Sandpainter, Box 791, Chinle   86503

Smoke Signals, Rt. 1, Box 23-B, Parker   85344

Yaqui Bulletin, 4730 W. Calle Tetakusin, Tucson   85710

Yoida Nava, Arizona Western College, Yuma   85364

CALIFORNIA

The American Indian, 3053 16th St., San Francisco   94103

CA League for AM Indians, Box 389, Sacramento   95802

Chemehuevi Newsletter, 2804 W. Ave. 31, Los Angeles   90065

Cherokee Examiner, Box 687, South Pasadena   91030

Coyote, Rt. 1, Box 2170, Davis   95616

Early American, 708 Mills Ave., Modesto   95350

Five Feathers News, Box W, Lompoc   93436

Indian Archives, Antelope Indian Circle, Box 790, Susanville   96130

Indian Historian, 1451 Masonic Ave., San Francisco   94117

Indian Newsletter, Box 106, Pala   92059

Indians All Tribes, 4339 California St., San Francisco   94118

Indians Illustrated, 3028 W. Beverly, Los Angeles   90057

Indian Voice, Box 2033, Santa Clara   95051

Lassen-Modoc Newsletter, Box 266, Susanville   96130

Namequa Speaks, 4339 California St., San Francisco   94118

News, American Indian Culture Center, University of California at Los Angeles, 405 Hilgard Ave., Los Angeles   90024

Newsletter, Concern for Indians, Box 5167, San Francisco   94101

Smoke Signal, 2727 Santa Clara Way, Sacramento 95817

Smoke Signals, Box 2477, Santa Clara 95051

Speaking Leaves, Box 2000, Vacaville 95688

Talking Leaf, Indian Center, 600 S. New Hampshire, Los Angeles 90005

Teepee Talk, Box 501, Porterville 93258

Tehipite Topics, Box 5396, Fresno 93755

Tribal Spokesman, 2991 Fulton Ave., Sacramento 96821

Tsen-Akamak, Rt. 1, Box 2170, Davis 95616

Uida Reporter, 1541 Wilshire, Los Angeles 90017

Warpath, Box 26149, San Francisco 94126

Wassaja, 1451 Masonic Ave., San Francisco 94117

COLORADO

Denver Native Americans United, 2210 E. 16th Ave., Denver 80206

Indian Times, Box 4131, Denver 80204

Native American Rights, 1506 Broadway, Boulder 80302

Southern Ute Drum, Ignacio 81137

USS News, Box 18285, Denver 80218

FLORIDA

Alligator Times, 6073 Sterling Rd., Hollywood 33024

IDAHO

NAS-NW Newsletter, University of Idaho, Moscow 83843

Native Gem, Boise 83702

Nee-Me-Poo Tum Tyne, Lapwai 83540

New Breed News, Box 7309, Boise 83707

Sho-Ban News, Fort Hall 83203

ILLINOIS

Amerindian, 1263 W. Pratt Blvd., Chicago 60626

Cross & Calumet, 4710 N. Sheridan Rd., Chicago 60640

Indian Voices, 1126 E. 59 St., Chicago 60637

Native American Committee, 1362 W. Wilson Ave., Chicago 60640

News, American Indian Center, 411 N. LaSalle St., Chicago 60605

Warrior, American Indian Center, 1630 W. Wilson Ave., Chicago 60640

INDIANA

Indian Progress, 1095 Division St., Noblesville 46060

Tosan, 318 N. Tacoma St., Indianapolis 46201

IOWA

City Smoke Signals, 1114 W. 6th St., Sioux City 51103

KANSAS

Indian Leader, Haskell Junior College, Lawrence 66044

News, Indian Center of Topeka, 407 W. Lyman Rd., Topeka 66608

MAINE

Indian School Bulletin, T.R.I.B.E., Inc., Bar Harbor 04609

Maine Newsletter, 42 Liberty St., Gardiner 04345

Maine Indian Newsletter, Pine Street, Freeport 04032

MARYLAND

Evening Sun, Calvert and Center St., Baltimore 21200

MASSACHUSETTS

Newsletter, Indian Council, 150 Tremont St., Boston 02111

MICHIGAN

Great Lakes Voice, Box 305, St. Ignace 49781

Michigan Indian, 300 S. Capitol Ave., Lansing 48926

Nishnawbe News, 214 Kaye Hall, Marquette 49855

Tribal Trails, 911 Franklin St., Petoskey 49770

MINNESOTA

A.I.M. News, 1337 E. Franklin Ave., Minneapolis 55404

Focus Newsletter, Capitol Square Bldg., St. Paul 55101

ICAP Newsletter, Bemidji State College, Bemidji 56601

Mille Lac News, Omania 56359

Moccasin Telegraph, Grand Portage 55605

Nett Lake News, Nett Lake 55772

Red Lake Newsletter, Red Lake 56671

Seventh Fire, 261 E. 8th St., St. Paul 55101

Smoke Signals, 475 Cedar, St. Paul   55102

Tri-State ICAP Newsletter, Box 26, Cass Lake 56601

White Earth Reservation, Box 274   White Earth

Wig-I-Wam, 3045 Park Ave., Minneapolis 55407

MISSISSIPPI

Choctaw Community News, Rt. 7, Box 21, Philadelphia   39350

MISSOURI

Indian Center, 3220 Independence Ave., Kansas City   64124

MONTANA

Absaraka, Crow Indian Agency, Crow Agency 59022

Arrow, St. Labre's Indian School, Ashland 59003

Birney Arrow, Box 552, Busby   59016

Blackfeet Cap News, Browning   59801

Browning Sentinel, Box 340, Browning   59417

Buffalo Grass Newsletter, 508 Toole, Missoula 59801

Camp Crier, Ft. Belknap Agency, Harlem 59526

Char-Koostah, Confederation of Salish and Kootenai Tribes, Dixon   59831

Eyapi Oaye, Assiniboin and Sioux, Poplar 59255

Glacier Reporter, Browning   59417

Hi-Line Herald, 426 1st St., Havre   59501

Ho Tanka, Brockton High School, Brockton 59213

Hunter, North American Indian League, Box 7, Deer Lodge   59772

Indian Signs, Blackfeet Tribal Business Council, Browning   59417

Morning Star News, Lame Deer   59043

Northern Cheyenne News, Lame Deer   59043

Official Rumors, Lame Deer   59043

Rocky Boy News, Rocky Boy Rt., Box Elder 59521

Wotanin, Box 11, Poplar   59255

NEBRASKA

Indian Progress, 1403 21st St., Central City 68826

Native American, 2224 Leavenworth St., Omaha 68102

Nebraska Trails, 902 "O" St., Lincoln   68508

NEVADA

Many Smokes, Box 5895, Reno   89503

Native Nevadan, 1995 E. 2d St., Reno   89502

Newsletter, Pyramid Lake Indian Reservation, Nixon   89424

Valley-Round-Up, Sho-Pai Business Council, Owyhee   89832

Warpath, Stewart Indian School, Stewart   89437

WRPT Newsletter, Walker River Indian Reservation, Schurz   89427

NEW JERSEY

Pow Wow Trails, Box 258, S. Plainfield   07080

NEW MEXICO

Aborigine, Box 892, Gallup   87301

American Indian Law Newsletter, 1915 Roma Ave., N.E., Albuquerque   87106

American Indian Law Students Association, 1117 Stanford, N.E., Albuquerque   87106

Americans Before Columbus, National Indian Youth Council, 3102 Central, S.E., Albuquerque   87106

Apache Scout, Mescalero   88340

Broncos Monthly News, Sanostee Rural Station, Shiprock   87420

Capital News, Santo Domingo   87052

Concerned Indian, Box 482, Albuquerque 87103

Drumbeat, Institute of American Indian Arts, Cerrillos Road, Santa Fe   87501

Eight Northern Pueblos News, Rt. 1, Box 71, Santa Fe   87528

Indian Extension News, New Mexico State University, Las Cruces   88001

Jicarilla Chieftain, Dulce   87528

Keresan, Box 3151, Laguna   87026

KTDB Radio, Box 18, Ramah   87321

Native American Scholar, 123 4th St., S.W., Albuquerque   87101

Navajo Assistance, Box 96, Gallup   87301

Southern Pueblos Bulletin, 1000 Indian School Rd., N.W., Albuquerque   87103

Southwestern Association on Indian Affairs, Box 1964, Santa Fe   87501

Thunderbird, Albuquerque Indian School, 1000 Indian School Rd., N.W., Albuquerque 87103

Zuñi Tribal Newsletter, Zuñi   87327

NEW YORK

Akwesasne Notes, Rooseveltown   13683

American Indian Horizons, Box 18 Church St. Sta., New York   10008

American Indian News, 5 Tudor City Pl., New York   10017

American Indian Women Newsletter, 20-53 19th St., Astoria, Queens   11102

Ethnohistory, American Society for Ethnohistory, Amherst   14226

Indian Affairs, 432 Park Ave. S., New York 10016

Kinzua Planning Newsletter, Seneca Nation of Indians, Box 231, Salamanca   14779

O He Yoh Noh, Alleghany Indian Reservation, Salamanca   14779

Si Wong Geh, Cattaraugus Indian Reservation, Box 97, Versailles   14168

Tonawanda Indian News, Bloomingdale Road, Akron   14001

War Drums Newsletter, American Indian Cultural Workshop, 144-09 161 St., Jamaica   11434

NORTH CAROLINA

Cherokee Boys Newsletter, Box 507, Cherokee 28719

Cherokee One Feather, Cherokee   28719

Cherokee Times, Cherokee   28719

Qualla Reservation News, Cherokee Agency, Cherokee   28719

NORTH DAKOTA

Action News, Box 605, New Town   58763

Arrow News, Mandaree High School, Mandaree 58737

Bells of Saint Ann, St. Ann's Indian Mission, Belcourt   58316

Northern Light, St. Michael   58370

Sentinel, White Shield School, Roseglen   58775

Three Tribes Herald, Parshall   58770

Turtle Mountain Echoes, Box 1B, Belcourt 58316

Weekly Bulletin, Wahpeton School, Wahpeton 58075

OHIO

Cleveland Crier, 2600 Church Ave., N.W., Cleveland   44113

OKLAHOMA

American Baptist Voice, Okmulgee   74447

American Indian Crafts and Culture, Box 3538, Tulsa   74152

Buckskin, Eufaula   74432

Cavo Transporter, Box 34, Concho   73022

Cherokee Nation News, Box 119, Tahlequah 74464

Cherokee Report, Tahlequah   74464

Chey-Arap Bulletin, 108 E. Cavanaugh, El Reno 73036

Drumbeat Magazine, Box 3504, Tulsa   74152

Indian Journal, Eufaula   74432

Indian School Journal, Chilocco Indian School, Chilocco   74635

Oio Newsletter, 555 Constitution, Norman 73069

Smoke Dreams, Riverside High School, Anadarko 73005

Talking Leaves, Skiatook   74070

OREGON

Chemawa American, Chemawa   97822

Rainbow People, Box 164, John Day   97845

Tomahawk, Warm Springs   99761

PENNSYLVANIA

Indian Truth, 1505 Race St., Philadelphia 19102

Pan-American Newsletter, 1139 Lehman Pl., Johnstown   15902

SOUTH DAKOTA

Blue Cloud Quarterly, Blue Cloud Abbey, Marvin 57251

Flandreau Spirit, Flandreau Indian School, Flandreau   57028

Great Plains Observer, 218 S. Egan, Madison 57042

Keyapi, Ft. Thompson   57339

Letan Wankatakiya, University of South Dakota, Vermillion 57069

Luchip Spearhead, 600 W. 12th St., Sioux Falls 57104

News, United Sioux Tribes, Star Rt. 3, Pierre 57501

News Bulletin, Cheyenne River Agency, Eagle Butte 57625

Newsletter, American Indian Research Center, Marvin 57251

Oglala Nation News, Pine Ridge 57770

Paha Sapa Wahosi, South Dakota State College, Spearfish 57783

Pierre Chieftain, Pierre Indian School, Pierre 57501

Red Cloud Country, Red Cloud Indian School, Pine Ridge 57770

Rosebud Sioux Herald, Rosebud 57570

Scout, Episcopal Church, Lower Brulé 57548

Shannon County News, Pine Ridge 57770

Sioux Journal, Eagle Butte 57625

Sioux San Sun, Public Health Service Indian Hospital, Rapid City 57701

Sisseton Agency News, Sisseton Agency, Sisseton 57262

Standing Rock Star, Box 202, Bullhead 57621

Wopeedah, Immaculate Conception Mission, Stephan 57346

Woyakapi, St. Francis Mission, St. Francis 57572

TENNESSEE

Chahta Anumpa: The Choctaw Times, Box 12392, Nashville 37212

TEXAS

The Raven Speaks, Box 35733, Dallas 75235

Talking Leaves, American Indian Center, 722 N. Beacon St., Dallas 75223

UTAH

Eagle's Eye, Brigham Young University, Provo 84601

Eagle Views, Intermountain Indian School, Brigham City 84302

Indian Affairs, Brigham Young University, Provo 84601

Indian Liahona, 115 E. S. Temple St., Salt Lake City 84111

Newsletter, St. Christopher's Mission, Bluff 84512

Outlook, Box 1249, University of Utah, Logan 84321

Ute Bulletin, Ute Indian Tribe, Ft. Duchesne 84026

WASHINGTON, D.C.

AIO Legislative Alert, 1822 Jefferson Pl., N.W. 20036

Indian Record, Bureau of Indian Affairs, 1951 Constitution Ave., N.W. 20242

Legislative Review, Indian Legal Information Service, 1785 Massachusetts Ave., N.W. 20036

NCAI Sentinel, 1346 Connecticut Ave., N.W. 20036

NCIO News, 726 Jackson Pl., N.W. 20036

WASHINGTON STATE

Alaska Native Brotherhood, 1521 16th Ave. E. Seattle 98102

Anica News, 1306 2d Ave., Seattle 98101

Independent American, Star Rt., Coulee Dam 99116

Indian Center News, 1900 Boren Ave., Seattle 98101

Indian Notes, Box 66, Wellpinit 99040

Indian Voice Stoww, 33324 Pacific Hwy., Federal Way 98002

Kee-Yoka, Community Action Program, LaConner 98257

Makah Newsletter, Makah Tribal Council, Neah Bay 98357

Northwest Indian News, 1900 Boren Ave., Seattle 98101

Northwest Indian Times, Gonzaga University, Spokane 99202

Nugguam, Box 1118, Taholah 98587

Our Heritage, Box 451, Nespelem 99155

Quileute Newsletter, Quileute Tribal Council, LaPush 98350

Rawhide Press, Wellpinit 99040

Renegade, Box 719, Tacoma 98401

Renegade, Franks Landing, Nisqually 98501

See Yahtsub, Marysville 98270

Squol-Quol News, Marietta 98268

Tribal Tribune, Colville Tribe, Nespelem 99155

Yakima Nation Review, Box 151, Toppenish 98948

Yakima Reservation News, Yakima County Extension Service, Yakima 98901

WISCONSIN

Great Lakes Agency News, Great Lakes Indian Agency, Ashland 54806

Menominee County and Town News, Keshena 54135

Menominee News, Neopit 54150

Menominee Prints, Keshena 54135

Voice, Laona 54541

We-Sa-Mi-Dong, Rt. 2, Hayward 54843

Native American Council, 204 Hagestad Student Center, River Falls 54022

WYOMING

American Indian News, Box 217, Ft. Washakie 82514

Smoke Signals: All American Indian Days, Box 451, Sheridan 82801

BIBLIOGRAPHY

PART ONE   *America's Indians*

WHO ARE THE INDIANS?

Brandon, William. *The American Heritage Book of Indians*. New York, American Heritage Publishing Company, 1961.

Collier, John. *Indians of the Americas*. New York, W. W. Norton & Company, Inc., 1947.

Driver, Harold E. *Indians of North America*. Chicago, University of Chicago Press, 1961.

Josephy, Alvin M., Jr. *The Indian Heritage of America*. New York, Alfred A. Knopf, Inc., 1968.

La Farge, Oliver. *A Pictorial History of the American Indian*. New York, Crown Publishers, Inc., 1956.

Underhill, Ruth M. *Red Man's America*. Chicago, University of Chicago Press, 1953.

THE MANY TRIBES

Boyd, William C. *The Blood Groups and Types*. Ann Arbor, Viking Fund, 1951.

Cooke, David C., and William Moyers. *Famous Indian Tribes*. New York, Random House, Inc., 1954.

Sterling, Mathew. *Indians of the Americas*. Washington, D.C., National Geographic Society, 1957.

Wormington, H. M. *Ancient Man in North America*. Denver, Denver Museum of Natural History, 1957.

THE MANY TONGUES

Boas, Frank. *Handbook of American Indian Languages*. Washington, D.C., U.S. Government Printing Office, 1911.

Sapir, Edward. *Central and North American Indian Languages*. Berkeley, University of California Press, 1949.

Terrell, John Upton. *American Indian Almanac*. New York, World Publishing Company, 1971.

Wissler, Clark. *Indians of the United States*. Garden City, N.Y., Doubleday & Company, Inc., 1966.

THE INDIANS, AMERICA'S DISPLACED PERSONS

Foreman, Grant. *Indian Removal: The Emigration of the Five Civilized Tribes of Indians*. Norman, University of Oklahoma Press, 1932.

———. *Last Trek of the Indians*. Chicago, University of Chicago Press, 1946.

Hagan, William T. *American Indians*. Chicago, University of Chicago Press, 1961.

THE BASKETMAKERS

Amsden, Charles. *The Ancient Basketmakers*. Los Angeles, Southwest Museum, n.d.

Barrett, S. M. *Pomo Indian Basketry*. Berkeley, University of California Press, 1908.

Cain, H. Titomas. *Pima Indian Basketry*. Phoenix, Heard Museum of Anthropology, 1962.

Dixon, Roland B. *Basketry: Designs of Indians of Northern California*. New York, American Museum of Natural History, 1902.

Evans, Glen T., and T. N. Campbell. *Indian Baskets*. Austin, Texas Memorial Museum, n.d.

Robinson, A. E. *Basket Weavers of Arizona*. Albuquerque, University of New Mexico Press, 1954.

Speck, Frank. *Decorative Art and Basketry of the Cherokee*. Milwaukee, Milwaukee Public Museum, 1920.

THE POTTERY MAKERS

Bunzell, Ruth. *The Pueblo Potter*. New York, Columbia University Press, 1929.

Fontana, Bernard. *Papago Indian Pottery*. Seattle, University of Washington Press, 1963.

Goodard, Pliny E. *Pottery of the Southwest Indians*. New York, American Museum of Natural History, 1945.

Marriott, Alice. *María: The Potter of San Ildefonso*. Norman, University of Oklahoma Press, 1948.

THE GIFTS OF THE INDIANS

Castetter, E. F., and W. H. Bell. *Pima and Papago*

Indian Agriculture. Albuquerque, University of New Mexico Press, 1942.

Solomon, Julian H. *Book of Indian Crafts and Indian Lore.* New York, Harper & Brothers, 1928.

Verrill, Alphous. *Foods America Gave the World.* Boston, L. C. Page & Company, 1937.

Weatherwax, George. *Indian Corn in Old America.* New York, Macmillan Company, Inc., 1954.

SYMBOLS

Kroeber, A. L. *Arapaho: Decorative Art and Symbolism.* New York, American Museum of Natural History, 1902.

Newcomb, Franc, and M. C. Wheelwright. *A Study of Navajo Symbolism.* Cambridge, Mass., Harvard University Press, 1956.

Wissler, Clark. *The American Indian.* New York, Oxford University Press, 1922.

Wyman, Leland. *Navajo Indian Painting.* Boston, Boston University Press, 1959.

PIPES

Brooks, Jerome E. *The Mighty Leaf.* Boston, Little, Brown & Company, 1952.

Brown, Joseph Epes, ed. *The Sacred Pipe: Black Elk's Account of the Seven Rites of the Oglala Sioux.* Norman, University of Oklahoma Press, 1953.

Field Museum of Natural History. *The Use of Tobacco Among the North American Indians.* Chicago, Linton Anthropology Leaflet 15, 1924.

Robert, Joseph C. *The Story of Tobacco in America.* New York, Alfred A. Knopf, Inc., 1952.

BEADWORK

Coleman, Sister Bernard. *Decorative Designs of the Ojibwa.* Washington, D.C., Catholic University of America, 1947.

Lyford, Carrie A. *Quill and Beadwork of the Western Sioux.* Lawrence, Kans., U.S. Indian Service, 1940.

Orchard, W. C. *Beads and Beadwork of the American Indian.* New York, Museum of the American Indian, 1929.

Wissler, Clark. *Indian Beadwork.* New York, American Museum of Natural History, 1927.

JEWELRY

Adair, John. *The Navajo and Pueblo Silversmiths.* Norman, University of Oklahoma Press, 1944.

Hegemann, Elizabeth Compton. *Navaho Silver.* Los Angeles, Southwest Museum, 1962.

Hunt, W. Ben. *Indian Silversmithing.* Milwaukee, Bruce Publishing Company, 1960.

Mera, Harry P. *Indian Silverwork in the Southwest.* Globe, Ariz., King Publishing Company, 1959.

PAWN

Egan, Fred. *The American Indian.* Chicago, Aldine Press, 1966.

Hegemann, Elizabeth Compton. *Navaho Silver.* Los Angeles, Southwest Museum, 1962.

Levine, Stuart, and Nancy O. Lurie. *The American Indian Today.* De Land, Fla., Everett-Edwards, Inc., n.d.

McNitt, Frank. *The Indian Traders.* Norman, University of Oklahoma Press, 1962.

INDIAN RELICS IN EUROPE

Hotz, Gottfried. *Indian Skin Paintings from the American Southwest.* Tr. by Johannes Malthaner. Norman, University of Oklahoma Press, 1970.

Hunter, John E. *Inventory of Ethnological Collections.* Milwaukee, Milwaukee Public Museum, 1967.

Underhill, Ruth. *Pueblo Crafts.* Phoenix, Phoenix Indian School, 1945.

TRIBAL GOVERNMENT

Brophy, William A., and Sophie D. Aberle. *The Indian: America's Unfinished Business.* Norman, University of Oklahoma Press, 1966.

Shepardson, Mary. "Navajo Ways in Government," *American Anthropologist*, Vol. 63 (1963).

U.S. Bureau of Indian Affairs. *Where to Learn More About Indians.* Washington, D.C., U.S. Government Printing Office, 1970.

POLICE AND JUDICIAL PROCEDURES ON THE RESERVATIONS

Arrow, Inc. *The American Indian Court System.* New York, Arrow, Inc., 1968.

Office of Indian Law. *Improving Tribal Justice.* Tempe, Arizona State University, 1970.

U.S. Commission on Civil Rights. *Justice.* Washington, D.C., U.S. Government Printing Office, 1961.

U.S. Department of the Interior. *Federal Indian Law.* Washington, D.C., U.S. Government Printing Office, 1958.

FEDERAL ASSISTANCE TO THE INDIANS

U.S. Bureau of Indian Affairs. Booklets, pamphlets, and papers. Washington, D.C., U.S. Government Printing Office.

THE PAN-INDIAN MOVEMENT

Cahn, Edgar S. *Our Brother's Keeper.* New York, World Publishing Company, 1969.

Hertzberg, Hazel. *The Search for an American Indian Identity.* Syracuse, N.Y., University of Syracuse Press, 1971.

Josephy, Alvin M., Jr. *The Patriot Chiefs.* New York, Viking Press, Inc., 1961.

Lurie, Nancy O. *The Contemporary American Scene.* New York, Random House, Inc., 1971.

Thomas, Robert K., and Shirley Hill Witt. *The American Indian Today.* De Land, Fla., Everett-Edwards, Inc., 1968.

Wax, Murray. *Indian Americans: Unity and Diversity.* New York, Prentice-Hall, Inc., 1971.

URBAN INDIANS

Bahr, Howard M., Bruce A. Chadwick, and Robert C. Day. *Native Americans Today.* New York, Harper & Row, 1972.

Deloria, Vine, Jr. *Custer Died for Your Sins.* New York, Macmillan Company, Inc., 1969.

Nichols, Roger L., and George R. Adams. *The American Indian: Past and Present.* New York, Xerox College Publishing, 1971.

Steiner, Stan. *The New Indians.* New York, Harper & Row, 1968.

Waddell, Jack O., and O. Michael Wilson. *The American Indian in Urban Society.* Boston, Little, Brown & Company, 1972.

INDIAN JOURNALISM

See Appendix C.

PART TWO   *Visiting Indian Country*

CEREMONIALS

Aberle, D. F., and O. C. Stewart. *Navajo and Ute Peyotism.* Boulder, University of Colorado Press, 1957.

Coolidge, M. R. *The Rainmakers: Indians of Arizona and New Mexico.* Boston, Houghton Mifflin Company, 1939.

Hassrick, Royal. *The Sioux: Life and Customs of a Warrior Society.* Norman, University of Oklahoma Press, 1964.

Roediger, Virginia. *Ceremonial Costumes of the Pueblo Indians.* Berkeley, University of California Press, 1941.

Tyler, Hamilton. *Pueblo Gods and Myths.* Norman, University of Oklahoma Press, 1964.

Underhill, Ruth. *Papago Indian Religion.* New York, Columbia University Press, 1946.

Waters, Frank. *Masked Gods: Navajo and Pueblo Ceremonialism.* Albuquerque, University of New Mexico Press, 1950.

WHEN INDIANS DANCE

Evans, Bessie, and May G. Evans. *American Indian Dance Steps.* New York, A. S. Barnes & Company, 1931.

Fergusson, Erna. *Dancing Gods.* New York, Alfred A. Knopf, Inc., 1931.

Mason, Bernard. *Dances and Stories of the American Indian.* New York, A. S. Barnes & Company, 1944.

Squires, John L., and Robert E. McLean. *American Indian Dances.* New York, Ronald Press Company, 1963.

BUYING ARTS AND CRAFTS

Dockstader, Frederick. *Indian Art in America.* Greenwich, New York Graphic Society, 1962.

Douglas, F., and Rene d'Harnoncourt. *Indian Art of the United States.* New York, Museum of Modern Art, 1941.

Hunt, W. Bernard. *The Golden Book of Indian Crafts and Lore.* New York, Simon & Schuster, Inc., 1960.

Mason, Bernard S. *The Book of Indian Crafts and Costumes.* New York, A. S. Barnes Publishing Company, 1946.

PART THREE   *Guide to Indian Country*

The Southwest

EXPLORING THE PUEBLO COUNTRY

Dale, Edward Everett. *Indians of the Southwest.* Norman, University of Oklahoma Press, 1950.

Hewett, Edgar Lee. *The Pueblo Indian World.* Albuquerque, University of New Mexico Press, 1945.

Parsons, Elsie. *Pueblo Indian Religion.* Chicago, University of Chicago Press, 1939.

Tyler, Hamilton A. *Pueblo Gods and Myths.* Norman, University of Oklahoma Press, 1964.

Waters, Frank. *The Man Who Killed the Deer.* New York, Farrar and Rinehart, Inc., 1942.

THE KIVA, THE SECRET PLACE OF THE MOST HIGH

Parsons, Elsie W. *Pueblo Indian Religion.* Chicago, University of Chicago Press, 1939.

THE MYSTERY OF THE INDIAN RUINS

Bandelier, Adolph F. *The Delight Makers.* New York, Dodd, Mead & Company, 1918.

Butcher, Devereau. *Exploring Our Prehistoric Indian Ruins.* Washington, D.C., National Parks Association, n.d.

Wormington, H. W. *Prehistoric Indians of the Southwest.* Denver, Denver Museum of Natural History, 1947.

THE NAVAJOS

Correll, J. Lee, and Edith L. Watson. *Welcome to the Land of the Navajos.* Window Rock, Ariz., Navajo Tribal Museum, 1969.

Kluckhohn, Clyde, and Dorothea Leighton. *The Navaho.* Garden City, N.Y., American Museum of Natural History and Doubleday & Company, 1962.

Newcomb, Franc Johnson. *Hosteen Klah: Navajo Medicine Man and Sand Painter.* Norman, University of Oklahoma Press, 1964.

Underhill, Ruth. *The Navajos.* Norman, University of Oklahoma Press, 1956.

TURQUOISE

Underhill, Ruth. *Pueblo Crafts*. Phoenix, Phoenix Indian School, 1945.

NAVAJO RUGS

Amsden, Charles. *Navajo Weaving*. Albuquerque, University of New Mexico Press, 1949.

Kahlenberg, Mary H., and Anthony Berlant. *The Navajo Blanket*. New York, Praeger Publishing Company, Inc., 1972.

Kent, Kate P. *The Story of Navajo Weaving*. Phoenix, Heard Museum of Anthropology, 1961.

Reichard, Gladys A. *Navajo Shepherd and Weaver*. New York, J. J. Augustine, 1936.

THE HOPIS

Museum of Northern Arizona. *Hopi Indian Arts and Crafts*. Flagstaff, Northern Arizona Society of Science, 1951.

O'Kane, Walter Collins. *The Hopis: Portrait of a Desert People*. Norman, University of Oklahoma Press, 1953.

Thompson, Laura, and Alice Joseph. *The Hopi Way*. Chicago, University of Chicago Press, 1944.

Waters, Frank. *Book of the Hopi*. New York, Viking Press, Inc., 1963.

THE ZUÑIS

Dutton, Bertha P. *The Friendly People*. Santa Fe, Museum of New Mexico Press, 1963.

Stevenson, M. C. *The Zuñi Indians*. Washington, D.C., U.S. Bureau of Ethnology, n.d.

THE SACRED KACHINAS

Colton, Harold S. *Hopi Kachina Dolls*. Albuquerque, University of New Mexico Press, 1959.

Fewkes, Jesse W. *Hopi Kachinas Drawn by Native Artists*. Glorieta, N.Mex., Rio Grande Press, Inc., 1967.

Wright, Barton, and Evelyn Roat. *This Is a Hopi Kachina*. Flagstaff, Museum of Northern Arizona, 1962.

THE PIMAS AND THE PAPAGOS

Joseph, Alice, Rosamond Spicer, and Jane Chesky. *The Desert People*. Chicago, University of Chicago Press, 1949.

Shaw, Ann Moore. *Pima Indian Legends*. Tempe, Arizona State University, 1963.

Underhill, Ruth. *The Papago Indians of Arizona*. Lawrence, Kans., Haskell Institute Press, 1955.

Webb, George E. *A Pima Remembers*. Tucson, University of Arizona Press, 1959.

THE APACHES

Hayes, Jess G. *Apache Vengeance*. Albuquerque, University of New Mexico Press, 1954.

Opler, Morris E. *An Apache Way of Life*. Chicago, University of Chicago Press, 1941.

Sonnichsen, C. L. *The Mescalero Apaches*. Norman, University of Oklahoma Press, 1958.

The Central Region

THE SIOUX

Hyde, George. *A Sioux Chronicle*. Norman, University of Oklahoma Press, 1956.

Lowie, Robert D. *Indians of the Plains*. Garden City, N.Y., Museum of Natural History Press, 1963.

McLaughlin, Marie. *Myths and Legends of the Sioux*. Bismarck, N.Dak., Bismarck Tribune Company, 1916.

Vestal, Stanley (pseud. Walter S. Campbell). *Sitting Bull, Champion of the Sioux: A Biography*. Norman, University of Oklahoma Press, 1957.

THE CHIPPEWAS

Blair, Emma. *Indian Tribes of the Upper Mississippi Valley*. Cleveland, 1911.

Coleman, Sister Bernard. *Ojibwa Myths and Legends*. Minneapolis, Ross and Haines, n.d.

Quimby, George I. *Indian Life in the Upper Great Lakes*. Chicago, University of Chicago Press, 1960.

Swanton, John R. *Indian Tribes of North America*. Washington, D.C., U.S. Bureau of American Ethnology, 1952.

THE INDIANS OF OKLAHOMA

McReynolds, Edwin C. *Oklahoma: A History of the Sooner State*. Norman, University of Oklahoma Press, 1954.

————, Alice Marriott, and Estelle Faulconer. *Oklahoma: The Story of Its Past and Present*. Norman, University of Oklahoma Press, 1961.

Wright, Muriel. *A Guide to the Indian Tribes of Oklahoma*. Norman, University of Oklahoma Press, 1951.

The Northwest

THE INDIANS OF THE PACIFIC NORTHWEST

Davis, Robert T. *Native Arts of the Pacific Northwest*. Palo Alto, Calif., Stanford University Press, 1949.

Drucker, Philip. *Indians of the Northwest Coast*. New York, McGraw-Hill Book Company, Inc., 1955.

Garfield, V., and Linn Forest. *The Wolf and the Raven*. Seattle, University of Washington Press, 1948.

Stern, Theodore. *The Klamath Tribe*. Seattle, University of Washington Press, 1965.

THE BLACKFEET

Ewers, John C. *The Blackfeet: Raiders on the Northwestern Plains*. Norman, University of Oklahoma Press, 1958.

———. *The Story of the Blackfeet*. Lawrence, Kans., Haskell Institute Press, 1944.

Grinnell, George Bird. *Pawnee, Blackfoot, and Cheyenne*. New York, Charles Scribner's Sons, 1961.

Schultz, James W. (Apikuni). *Blackfeet and Buffalo: Memories of Life Among the Indians*. Ed. by Keith C. Seele. Norman, University of Oklahoma Press, 1962.

THE CROWS

Lowie, Robert H. *The Crow Indians*. New York, Rinehart & Company, Inc., 1956.

Wildscheet, W., and John Ewers. *Crow Indian Beadwork*. New York, Museum of the American Indian, 1959.

THE NEZ PERCÉS

Davis, Russell, and Brent Ashabranner. *Chief Joseph: War Chief of the Nez Percé*. New York, McGraw-Hill Book Company, Inc., 1962.

Haines, Francis. *The Nez Percés: Tribesmen of the Columbia Plateau*. Norman, University of Oklahoma Press, 1955.

THE SHOSHONES

Hebard, Grace R. *Washakie*. Cleveland, Arthur H. Clark Company, 1930.

Trenholm, Virginia Cole, and Maurine Carley. *The Shoshonis: Sentinels of the Rockies*. Norman, University of Oklahoma Press, 1964.

The Southeast

THE CHEROKEES

Foreman, Grant. *The Five Civilized Tribes*. Norman, University of Oklahoma Press, 1934.

Malone, H. T. *Cherokees of the Old South*. Athens, University of Georgia Press, 1956.

Rights, Douglas L. *The American Indian in North Carolina*. Winston-Salem, N.C., John F. Blair, 1957.

Woodward, Grace Steele. *The Cherokees*. Norman, University of Oklahoma Press, 1963.

THE SEMINOLES

Boyd, Mark F. *Florida Aflame: The Seminole War*. Tallahassee, Florida Board of Parks and Historical Memorials, 1951.

Capron, Louis. "Florida's Wild Indians, the Seminole," *National Geographic*, December, 1956.

Emerson, William Canfield. *The Seminoles*. New York, Exposition Press, 1954.

McReynolds, Edwin C. *The Seminoles*. Norman, University of Oklahoma Press, 1957.

OTHER GROUPS

Fundaburk, Emma, and M. Foreman. *Sun Circles and Human Hands*. Luverne, Ala., 1957.

Newcomb, William W. *The Indians of Texas*. Austin, University of Texas Press, 1961.

Swanton, John R. *Indians of the Southeastern United States*. Washington, D.C., U.S. Bureau of American Ethnology Bulletin 137, 1946.

The Northeast

INDIANS OF THE NORTHEAST WOODLANDS

Hunt, George T. *The Wars of the Iroquois*. Madison, University of Wisconsin Press, 1940.

Leach, Douglas E. *Flintlock and Tomahawk*. New York, Macmillan Company, 1958.

Sylvester, Herbert M. *Indian Wars of New England*. Boston, W. B. Clarke Company, 1910.

Wilson, Edmund. *Apologies to the Iroquois*. New York, Farrar, Straus & Cudahy, 1960.

INDEX

264

266